Banister Fletcher

A History of Architecture for the Student, Craftsman and Amateur

being a comparative view of the historical styles from the earliest period

Banister Fletcher

A History of Architecture for the Student, Craftsman and Amateur
being a comparative view of the historical styles from the earliest period

ISBN/EAN: 9783337369583

Printed in Europe, USA, Canada, Australia, Japan

Cover: Foto ©Andreas Hilbeck / pixelio.de

More available books at **www.hansebooks.com**

Some Standard Books on Architecture & Building, Professional Practice, Ornament, etc.

Published by B. T. BATSFORD,

94, High Holborn, London.

LONDON CHURCHES OF THE XVIIth AND XVIIIth CENTURIES.

A selection of the most remarkable Ecclesiastical Buildings, including St. Paul's Cathedral, erected within and around the ancient City Walls between the years 1630 and 1730, from the designs of Inigo Jones, Sir Christopher Wren, Hawksmoor and Gibbs. Illustrated in a series of 64 plates reproduced in collotype from exceptionally fine photographs specially taken for the work, and 130 illustrations in the text. With Historical and Descriptive Accounts by George H. Birch, F.S.A. Price £4 4s. net, half bound morocco.

[Just published.

ARCHITECTURE OF THE RENAISSANCE IN ENGLAND.

Illustrated by a Series of Views and Details from Buildings erected between the years 1560 and 1635, with Historical and Critical Text. By J. Alfred Gotch, F.S.A., F.R.I.B.A. Two volumes containing 145 folio plates, 118 being reproduced from photographs taken expressly for the work, and 180 illustrations in the text. Price £7 7s. net, in cloth portfolio ; or £8 8s. net, half bound morocco.

ITALIAN RENAISSANCE DETAIL AND ORNAMENT.

Drawn by Geo. J. Oakeshott, A.R.I.B.A. 40 lithographic plates, folio, buckram. Price £1 12s.

"We have nothing but praise for this work, which is throughout carefully and conscientiously carried out. The author deserves commendation for his choice of subjects, no less than for his illustration of them. —*The British Architect.*

STREETS AND CANALS IN VENICE.

100 beautiful plates, reproduced in heliogravure, illustrating the most Remarkable Buildings and the most Picturesque Views in Venice. With Descriptive and Historical Notices of the subjects, edited by FERDINAND ONGANIA. Price £5 5s. net, in handsome binding, morocco back and cloth sides, gilt and gilt top.

AN ANALYSIS OF ANCIENT DOMESTIC ARCHITECTURE IN GREAT BRITAIN.

By F. T. DOLLMAN, Architect, and J. R. JOBBINS. Containing 161 lithographic plates, with Descriptive Text. Two volumes. 4to, half bound, roxburghe style. First published at £5 5s. ; price £2 2s. net.

This beautiful and comprehensive work is unrivalled for its faithful illustrations of some of the finest examples of our Mediæval Domestic Architecture.

DETAILS OF GOTHIC ARCHITECTURE.

Measured and Drawn from Existing Examples of the XIIth, XIIIth, XIVth and XVth Centuries. By J. K. COLLING, Architect. 190 lithographed plates, forming two handsome volumes. 4to, cloth gilt. First published at £5 5s. ; price £2 2s. net.

A most complete and practical work ; the drawings for which were made on the spot by the author, from his own measurements, and their correctness and beauty are well known.

ORDERS OF ARCHITECTURE.

GREEK, ROMAN and ITALIAN. Edited, with Notes, by R. PHENÉ SPIERS, F.S.A., F.R.I.B A. Second Edition, with four new plates, including one of Greek Mouldings, by R. W. SCHULTZ, 24 plates. Imp. 4to, cloth. Price 10s. 6d.

"Should be considered as an indispensable possession by all students of architecture."—*The Architect.*

WREN'S TOWERS AND STEEPLES.

A Descriptive, Historical and Critical Essay. By A. T. TAYLOR, A.R.I.B.A. With upwards of 50 illustrations. Demy 8vo, fancy boards. Price 4s. 6d.

THREE PERIODS OF ENGLISH ARCHITECTURE.

I. AT WORK. II. ASLEEP. III. AWAKING. With illustrations. By THOMAS HARRIS, F.R.I.B.A. Large 8vo, buckram. Price 7s. 6d.

"Whether discussing the ground plans of Tudor houses, or the legitimate use of iron and aluminium among the building materials of the near future, Mr. Harris interests you, and by a pleasant non-combative argument sets in motion many trains of thought. . . . It is freely illustrated and well printed, so that to loiter over its pages is a genuine pleasure."— *The Studio.*

BUNGALOWS AND COUNTRY RESIDENCES.

A Series of Designs and Examples of Recently Executed Works. By R. A. BRIGGS, F.R.I.B.A. Third and Enlarged Edition, containing 39 plates, with descriptions. 4to, cloth. Price 12s. 6d.

"The views given embrace such a variety of style, and such charm of treatment, both internal and external, that he would be hard to please who could not find among them a design of a cottage or bungalow to suit both his pocket and his æsthetic tastes."—*St. James's Budget.*

FARM BUILDINGS.

Their Construction and Arrangement. By A. DUDLEY CLARKE, F.S.I. With numerous plans and other illustrations. Crown 8vo, cloth. Price 6s. net.

*** This work has been adopted as the text-book by the Surveyors' Institution.

"A pre-eminently practical book. . . The plans are excellent."—*The Builder.*
"Mr. Clarke's handbook is the best of its kind."—*Surveyor.*

PROFESSOR BANISTER FLETCHER'S VALUABLE TEXT BOOKS FOR ARCHITECTS AND SURVEYORS.

Arranged in Tabulated Form and fully indexed for Ready Reference.

QUANTITIES.

THE MOST COMPLETE, CONCISE, AND HANDY WORK ON THE SUBJECT. Sixth Edition, thoroughly revised and enlarged, to which is added an example of the complete Taking-off, Abstracting, and Billing in all Trades of an Entrance Lodge. With 16 Lithographic Plates, giving Plans, Elevations, and Sections, and numerous Illustrations in the text. Crown 8vo, cloth. Price 7s. 6d.

"It is no d ubt the best work on the subject extant."—*The Builder.*
"A safe, comprehensive, and concise text-book on an important technical subject. We imagine few surveyors' or architects' shelves will be without it."—*British Architect.*

DILAPIDATIONS.

Fourth Edition, revised and enlarged, with all the most recent Legal Cases and Acts. Crown 8vo, cloth. Price 6s. 6d.

"An excellent compendium on the Law and Practice of the subject o f which it treats."—*The Builder.*

THE LONDON BUILDING ACT, 1894.

Comprising the Act, printed in extenso, together with a full Abstract giving all the Sections of the Act which relate to building, set out in Tabular Form for easy reference, and an Introduction showing the leading alterations made by the Act, together with the various Sections of Acts unrepealed, and the Bye-Laws and Regulations remaining in force. Second Edition, revised, with Appendices of Cases and Forms and a full Index. Illustrated with 19 Coloured Plates, showing the thickness of walls, plans of chimneys, &c. Crown 8vo, cloth. Price 6s. 6d.

"It is the Law of Building for London in one volume."—*Architect*.
"The Abstract of the portion of the Act relating to building is very useful as a finger-post to the Sections in which the detailed regulations in regard to various operations of building are to be looked for—an assistance the more desirable from the fact that the Act is by no means well or systematically arranged."—*The Builder*.

LIGHT AND AIR.

With Methods of Estimating Injuries, Reports of most recent Cases, &c. Third Edition, revised and enlarged, with 26 Coloured Diagrams. Crown 8vo, cloth. Price 6s. 6d.

"By far the most complete and practical text-book we have seen. In it will be found the cream of all the legal definitions and decisions."—*Building News*.

VALUATIONS AND COMPENSATIONS.

With Appendix, giving Forms of Precedents, and Valuation Tables, being a New Edition of "Compensations," to which are added Chapters on Valuations. Crown 8vo, cloth. Price 6s. 6d.

"This text-book should prove very useful to students preparing for the examinations of the Surveyors' Institution."—*The Surveyor*.

ARBITRATIONS.

Second Edition, revised in accordance with the New Arbitration Act and giving the Act in full, with an Appendix of Forms. Crown 8vo, cloth. Price 5s. 6d.

"Will be found especially useful to young surveyors as a compendium of the knowledge which professional experience gives in more concrete form, and with infinite variety of detail."—*The Surveyor*.

THE PLUMBER AND SANITARY HOUSES.

A PRACTICAL TREATISE ON THE PRINCIPLES OF INTERNAL PLUMBING WORK. By S. STEVENS HELLYER. Fifth Edition, revised and enlarged. With 27 Plates, and 262 Woodcut Illustrations. Thick royal 8vo, cloth. Price 12s. 6d.

"The Fifth Edition is an exhaustive treatise on the subject of House Sanitation, comprising all that relates to Drainage, Ventilation, and Water Supply within and appertaining to the house, not only pointing

out what are the best methods and apparatus, but also showing what
appliances should be avoided, and the reasons for and against."—
Journal R.I.B.A.
". . . As a Technological Handbook for Students, Architects, and
Sanitary Experts, Mr. Hellyer's treatise is *unsurpassed.*"—*Building
News.*
"The best Treatise existing on Practical Plumbing."—*The Builder.*

BUILDING CONSTRUCTION AND DRAWING.

FIRST STAGE OR ELEMENTARY COURSE. Specially adapted
for the use of Students in Science and Technical Schools.
By C. F. MITCHELL, Lecturer on Building Construction,
Polytechnic Institute. Third Edition, revised and enlarged,
with 600 Illustrations, fully dimensioned. Crown 8vo, cloth.
Price 3*s.*

"An excellent and trustworthy little treatise, prepared and illustrated
in a very thorough and practical spirit."—*The Builder.*
"The illustrations are accurate and clear, every part having the
dimensions figured."—*Building News.*

BUILDING CONSTRUCTION.

ADVANCED AND HONOURS COURSES. By C. F. MITCHELL,
Compiled for Students preparing for the Examinations of the
Science and Art Department, the R. I. B. A., Surveyors'
Institution, the City Guilds, &c. Containing 504 pp. of
text, and over 220 Illustrations. Crown 8vo, cloth. Price
5*s.* 6*d.*

"It is a most admirable work for students and young men engaged in
building. . . . Very complete and accurate."—Mr. J. T. HURST.
"A valuable addition to the text-books suited for architectural students.
. . . We find it up-to-date and concisely arranged. . . . The illustrations
are well drawn and numerous."—*Building News.*
"Within the limits of the size adopted it is difficult to imagine a more
judicious selection of valuable information and instruction in building
construction than this work presents. . . . Mr. Mitchell's two books
should be in the hands of every architect's pupil, and will be found
excellent value for the small price."—*The Builder.*

ESTIMATING.

A METHOD OF PRICING BUILDERS' QUANTITIES FOR COM-
PETITIVE WORK. By GEORGE STEVENSON. Second Edition, the prices carefully revised. Crown 8vo, cloth. Price
6*s.* 6*d.*

"A very useful help to those who wish to price an estimate without
having to resort to a price book."—*Building News.*

REPAIRS.

HOW TO MEASURE AND VALUE THEM. A Handbook for
the use of Builders, Decorators, etc. By the Author of
"Estimating." Crown 8vo, cloth. Price 3*s.* 6*d.*

"We recommend all young men in the Building Trades who are likely
to be called upon to do any estimating, to obtain this little book and
make it their pocket *vade-mecum.*"—*Illustrated Carpenter and Builder*

HOUSE DRAINAGE.

A Handbook for Architects and Building Inspectors. By G. A. T. MIDDLETON, A.R.I.B.A. Illustrated by 19 plates and diagrams. Second Edition, revised. Crown 8vo, cloth. Price 3s. 6d.

"In this little book Mr. Middleton enunciates the accepted principles of house drainage. . . . The diagrams are drawn to a good scale."—*Building News.*

STRESSES AND THRUSTS.

Being a Revised and Enlarged Edition of "STRAINS IN STRUCTURES." By G. A. T. MIDDLETON, A.R.I.B.A. With 89 Illustrations. Crown 8vo, cloth. Price 5s.

"The most simple and exhaustive treatise that has yet appeared upon the determination of stresses in quiescent structures, and it should prove of great use to architects, students, and all connected with the building trade. Its utility in preparing for examinations will be very great."—*Illustrated Carpenter and Builder.*

SHORING AND UNDERPINNING.

A TREATISE ON. By C. A. STOCK, ARCHT. With numerous illustrations on 10 lithographic plates. Second Edition, revised by F. R. Farrow, F.R.I.B.A. 8vo, cloth. Price 4s. 6d.

"A valuable addition to the practical library of the architect and builder. . . . Very comprehensive. We heartily recommend it to all readers."—*Building News.*

DANGEROUS STRUCTURES.

A Handbook for Practical Men. By G. H. BLAGROVE. With illustrations. 8vo, cloth. Price 3s.

"A handy little manual for practical men, suggesting ready means for getting over difficulties which frequently occur in practice."—*Engineering.*

"We recommend this book to all architects and students of building." *Building News.*

A HANDBOOK OF ORNAMENT.

With 300 plates, containing about 3,000 illustrations of the Elements and Application of Decoration to Objects. By F. S. MEYER, Professor at the School of Applied Art, Karlsruhe. Second English Edition, revised by Hugh Stannus, F.R.I.B.A., Lecturer on Applied Art, National Art Schools, South Kensington. Thick 8vo, cloth gilt, gilt top. Price 12s. 6d.

"An encyclopædia of all that is best in every application of decorative work."—*Science and Art.*

"A library, a museum, an encyclopædia, and an art school in one. To rival it as a book of reference one must fill a bookcase."—*The Studio.*

"The author's acquaintance with ornament amazes, and his three thousand subjects are gleaned from the finest examples the world affords." *The Architect.*

A HISTORY OF ARCHITECTURE

UPON

THE COMPARATIVE METHOD.

"The spirit of antiquity, enshrined
In sumptuous buildings, vocal in sweet song,
In picture speaking with heroic tongue,
And with devout solemnities entwined—
Strikes to the seat of grace within the mind :
Hence forms that glide with swan-like ease along
Hence motions, even amid the vulgar throng,
To an harmonious decency confined,
As if the streets were consecrated ground,
The city one vast temple,— dedicate
To mutual respect in thought and deed."
WORDSWORTH.

A

HISTORY OF ARCHITECTURE

FOR THE

STUDENT, CRAFTSMAN, AND AMATEUR

BEING

A COMPARATIVE VIEW

OF

THE HISTORICAL STYLES

FROM THE EARLIEST PERIOD

BY

BANISTER FLETCHER, F.R.I.B.A.

Professor of Architecture in King's College, London
Fellow of King's College, London

AND

BANISTER F. FLETCHER, A.R.I.B.A.

Instructor in the Architectural Studio, King's Coll., London
Godwin Bursar R.I.B.A., 1893. R.I.B.A. Essay Medallist, 1896

WITH 115 PLATES, MOSTLY COLLOTYPES, AND OTHER
ILLUSTRATIONS IN THE TEXT

LONDON
B. T. BATSFORD, 94, HIGH HOLBORN
1896

DIAGRAM TABLE

OF THE

SYSTEM OF CLASSIFICATION

FOR EACH STYLE.

1. **Influences.**

    I.   GEOGRAPHICAL.
    II. GEOLOGICAL.
    III. CLIMATE.
    IV. RELIGION.
    V.   SOCIAL AND POLITICAL.
    VI. HISTORICAL.

2. **Architectural Character.**

3. **Examples.**

4. **Comparative Table.**

5. **Reference Books.**

GERMAN, BELGIAN, AND SPANISH RENAISSANCE.

ENGLISH RENAISSANCE.

CONTENTS.

LIST OF ILLUSTRATIONS.

GREEK ARCHITECTURE—*continued.*

ROMAN ARCHITECTURE.

EARLY CHRISTIAN ARCHITECTURE.

BYZANTINE ARCHITECTURE.

ROMANESQUE ARCHITECTURE IN ITALY, FRANCE, GERMANY, AND SPAIN.

ROMANESQUE ARCHITECTURE, Etc.—*continued.*

ENGLISH ARCHITECTURE, ROMANESQUE (NORMAN) AND GOTHIC.

GOTHIC ARCHITECTURE IN FRANCE, BELGIUM, HOLLAND, GERMANY, ITALY, ETC.

ABBREVIATIONS.

B.M.— British Museum.

S.K.M.—South Kensington Museum.

L.F.D.—Lewis F. Day.

development of their different styles. The natural productions of a country, we shall find, whether wood, brick, or stone, determine to a large extent its style of art.

In Egypt under this heading we should notice the abundance of limestone that existed in the north, of sandstone

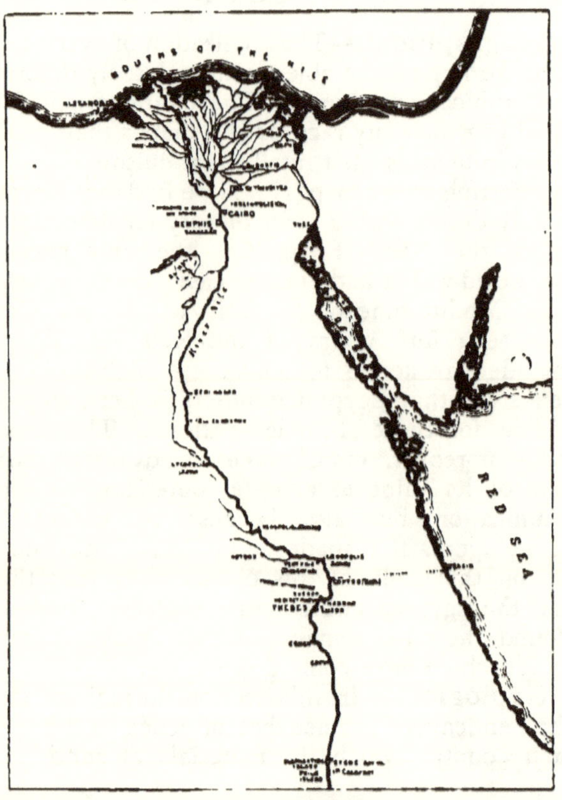

1. MAP OF EGYPT.

in the central region, and of granite in the south. The latter is principally found near Assouan (Syene), and is called Syenite. This hard and lasting building material influenced largely the architecture of the country, and to its durable qualities is due the fact that we have so many remains. Bricks were also employed, but were generally

PREFACE.

THE Authors' aim in writing this book has been, not only to give in clear and brief form the characteristic features of the architecture of each people and country, but also to consider those influences which have contributed to the formation of each special style.

They are of opinion that in published works upon the subject, Architecture has often been too much isolated from its surroundings, and that the main points of the physical geography, social progress, and historical development of each country require to be understood by those who would study and comprehend its particular style.

In order to bring out the effects of these influences, and also the qualities of the styles themselves, a *comparative* and *analytical* method has been adopted, so that by the contrast of qualities the differences may be more easily grasped. For instance, the special character of Gothic architecture becomes manifest when put in comparison with the Classic and Renaissance styles; and, furthermore, the shades of difference in the local or national phases of each, can also be equally drawn out by a similar comparative treatment.

The styles themselves are then analyzed and the parts contrasted; the analysis being carried out on the basis of the essential parts which every building possesses. As this system pervades the whole book, either the influences, character, examples, or comparative features of each style, can be contrasted with those in any other style. This then is the scheme of the book, which has been divided into five sections in each period, as follows:

1. INFLUENCES.
    i. Geographical.
    ii. Geological.
    iii. Climate.
    iv. Religion.
    v. Social and Political.
    vi. Historical.
2. ARCHITECTURAL CHARACTER.
3. EXAMPLES OF BUILDINGS.
4. COMPARATIVE.
    A. Plan, or general distribution of the building.
    B. Walls, their construction and treatment.
    C. Openings, their character and shape.
    D. Roofs, their treatment and development.
    E. Columns, their position, structure and decoration.
    F. Mouldings, their form and decoration.
    G. Decoration, as applied in general to any building.
5. REFERENCE BOOKS.

SECTION 1 is divided into the six leading influences that may be expected to shape the architecture of any country or people, the first three being structural, the next two the civilizing forces, and the last containing those external historical events which may alter or vary the foregoing.

SECTION 2 describes the character of the architecture, that is, its special quality, and the general effect produced by the buildings as a whole.

SECTION 3 contains the examples, *i.e.* the chief buildings in each style, briefly named and described, being the *corpus*, which the preceding influences affect and from which the subsequent comparative analysis is deduced.

SECTION 4 is this comparative analysis, in which every style of architecture is regarded as the solution of certain fundamental problems, *i.e.* each building must have all or most of the parts A to G, and consequently there is both interest and instruction to be gained in learning and comparing how each style has solved these points of the problem.

SECTION 5 gives authorities and more especially directs the reader who wishes to pursue the study of any style in further detail.

In treating of the buildings themselves under section 3 the authors have endeavoured to avoid long descriptions, which are necessarily technical and intolerably dry, and difficult to follow, even by those who have had the technical training, and have either the building or complete drawings of it before them. They have therefore provided the largest possible number of illustrations, and have confined the text to brief, but it is hoped vivid, notes of the special qualities and characteristics of the building referred to.

For the illustrations, photographs of large size have been reduced and printed in Collotype by the Direct Photo Engraving Company, Limited, who have also executed the blocks from the line drawings of special plans, maps, and features made by the authors.

It is hoped that the book will appeal not only to students who require an outline of architectural history as part of their artistic and professional education, but also to the increasing number of art workers who are interested in architecture in its relation to those accessory arts in which they are engaged. Lastly ; it is believed that a work in which architecture is treated as a result and record of civilization, will prove attractive to that increasing public which interests itself in artistic development.

29, NEW BRIDGE STREET,
   LUDGATE CIRCUS, E.C.
     New Year's Day, 1896.

NOTE.—The publication of the book has been delayed for many months in consequence of want of time necessary to read and correct the final proofs.

A
HISTORY OF ARCHITECTURE

ON THE

COMPARATIVE METHOD.

GENERAL INTRODUCTION.

*"Deal worthily with the History of Architecture and it is worthy to take its place with the History of Law and of Language."—*FREEMAN.

IN introducing this Comparative treatment of Historical Architecture, we propose to give a general outline sketch of the course which the art has taken up to the present time in Europe, also in those countries, such as Egypt and Assyria, which have influenced that development.

In Architecture we should be led to include every building or structure raised by human hands. Architecture is here defined as construction with an artistic motive : the more the latter is developed, the greater is the value of the result.

The first habitations of man were undoubtedly those that nature afforded, such as caves or grottoes, which demanded little labour on his part to convert into shelters against the fury of the elements, and attacks from his fellows or wild animals.

As soon as man rose above the state of rude nature, he naturally began to build more commodious habitations for himself, and some form of temple for his god.

To pass, however, at once into Historic times, we find that in Egypt a system of architecture prevailed which consisted of a massive construction of walls and columns, in which the column closely spaced, short, and massive, carried lintels, which in their turn supported the flat beamed roof. Assyrian architecture developed in general with the same constructive principle of a column supporting a beam,

although the arch was known and used, and the influence
of Egyptian and Assyrian architecture on the architecture
of Greece is apparent in many directions. Grecian architecture is considered by many to have had its origin in the
wooden hut or cabin formed of posts set in the earth, and
covered with transverse beams and rafters, and this was the
type which was developed in the early Mycenian period into
the *prodomus* of the Greek house. This timber architecture,
copied in marble or stone, was naturally at first very simple
and rude; the influence of the material, however, was soon
felt, when the permanence and value of stone aided in the
growth of the art. It should be noted, however, that many
writers hold that Greek architecture is developed from an
early stone type. As civilization and technical skill, moreover, advanced, the qualities of refinement in detail and
proportion were perceived, and the different orders of architecture—Doric, Ionic, and Corinthian—came into existence.
(By the word "order" we mean certain methods of pro-
portioning and decorating a column, and the part it supports,
i.e., the entablature.) These "orders" are the characteristic
features of Greek architecture, and the beauty and grace
with which they were treated, and the artistic and mathe-
matical skill with which they were constructed, illustrate
the keen artistic temperament of the Greeks.

Greece eventually succumbed to the conquering Romans
who, however, adopted their architecture, and in many
cases employed Greek artists in the erection of their buildings. While borrowing this trabeated architecture, they
added the use of the arch, which they had probably already
learnt to construct from the Etruscans, the ancient inhabitants of Central Italy.

This dualism is a very important fact to remember,
because, as we shall see, it eventually ended in the exclusion
of the beam altogether, and in the employment of the arch
alone, throughout the entire constructive system of the
building. The *column and arch* were then used conjointly
by the Romans for some time, good examples being the
Colosseum at Rome (No. 36), and the Triumphal Arches
(No. 38). In the numerous buildings which the Romans
erected, we at once notice that the column has, in the

generality of cases, become merely a decorative feature, the actual work of support being performed by the piers of the wall behind, connected together by semicircular arches.

As time went on, however, such practical people as the Romans could not but discard a feature which was no longer utilitarian, so the column even as a decorative feature disappeared, and the arcuated system it had masked was exposed.

Columns, when used, were now again constructive, as in many of the great basilicas, in which the semicircular arches spring directly from their capitals. As the Romans conquered the whole of the then known world, that is to say, most of what is now known as Europe, so this feature of the semicircular arch was introduced in every part, by its use in the settlements which they founded. Roman architecture was prevalent in Europe in a more or less debased form up to the tenth century of our era, and is the basis on which European architecture is founded. The gradual breaking up of the Roman Empire, the formation of separate European states, and other causes which we shall enumerate separately, led to many variations on this semicircular arched style, both in construction and decoration.

The transition commenced in the tenth, eleventh, and twelfth centuries, when the later Romanesque, so called as being derived from the Roman style, was in vogue. Constructive necessity, aided largely by inventive genius led, in the latter part of the twelfth century, to the introduction of the pointed arch.

The pointed arch is the keynote of what is known as the Gothic or pointed style, which prevailed throughout Europe during the thirteenth, fourteenth, and fifteenth centuries, when those glorious cathedrals and churches were erected, which form the most emphatic record of the religious feeling and character of the Middle Ages.

We may broadly summarize past styles of architecture as being divided into two great types, each depending on a great constructive principle, and we may place any style yet devised under one of these divisions, which are: (1) the *Classic*, or the architecture of the beam, and (2) the *Gothic*, or the architecture of the arch.

The early styles, including Greece, belong to the former. Roman architecture is a composite transition style, whose goal, if unchecked, would seem to have been the combination of the round arch and dome that we see in the great examples of the Byzantine style. It was left to the Gothic style to formulate a complete system of arcuated construction, the working out of which was marvellously alike in all countries. It was a style, moreover, in which a decorative system was closely welded to the constructive, both uniting to reflect a more intense expression of its age than had, perhaps, hitherto been achieved in previous architecture.

The revival of the arts and letters in the fifteenth century was a fresh factor in the history of architecture. The condition of Europe at that period was one of ripeness for a great change, the Gothic system, whether in architecture or in civilization regarded as a whole, may fairly be said to have culminated. Its latest works were tinged by the coming change, or showed signs of becoming stereotyped by the repetition of mechanical forms.

The new force was the belief that old Rome had been wiser and more experienced than the then existing period, and the result was the earnest study of every Classic fragment, whether of art or literature, that had been preserved or could be recovered. For some three centuries this belief held good, till by the opening up of Greece to travel, the tradition was modified by the admission of Grecian remains to an equal or supreme place, beside or above those of Rome.

This second phase had not, however, an equal success for divers reasons; a reaction was at hand in favour of mediæval ideals, whether in the church, art, or the State.

A conscious effort was then made—the most earnestly in England—to modify the current that had been flowing since the year 1500. Some of the results of this attempt may be traced by the student wise enough to follow up the clues indicated in our concluding pages. In acquainting himself with the buildings given in those lists, he may feel that few of the diverse elements of our perplexed civilization, at the end of the nineteenth century, have failed to find some architectural expression.

EGYPTIAN ARCHITECTURE.

"Those works where man has rivalled nature most,
Those Pyramids, that fear no more decay
Than waves inflict upon the rockiest coast,
Or winds on mountain steeps, and like endurance boast."

1. INFLUENCES.

i. Geographical.—The civilization of every country has been, as we hope to be able to show, largely determined by its geographical conditions. The characteristic features of the land in which any race dwells shapes their mode of life and thus influences their intellectual culture.

On referring to the map (No. 1) we find that Egypt consists of a sandy desert with a strip of very fertile country on the banks of the Nile. Egypt was the only nation of the ancient world which had at once easy access to the Northern Sea, or Mediterranean, as well as to the Eastern, or Arabian sea ; for by way of the Red Sea, Egypt always commanded an access to both these highways. The consequence was that Egypt had outlets for her own productions and inlets for those of foreign nations. The possession of the Nile, moreover, was of immense advantage, not only on account of its value as a trade route, and as a means of communication, but also because its waters were the fertilizing agents that made desert sands into fruitful fields. It was on the banks of this classic river that the ancient cities of the Egyptians were naturally placed; here, therefore, are found the chief remains of the Tombs, Temples, and Pyramids which have come down to us.

ii. Geological.—In this section throughout the volume we shall endeavour to trace that influence on the architecture of each country which the materials at hand had in the

faced with some harder material. We may also note the absence of wood of a kind suitable for building, for we find only small forests of palm and acacia existed.

iii. Climate.—The climate is equable and of even temperature, snow and frost are wholly unknown, while storm, fog, and even rain are rare, which accounts to a large extent for the good preservation of the temples. The climate was thus of importance in developing the qualities of the architecture, admitting of simplicity of construction, for though it demanded some protection against heat there was no necessity to provide against inclement weather. Egypt has been said to have but two seasons, spring and summer.

iv. Religion.—A close connection between religion and architecture is everywhere manifest at this epoch. The priesthood was powerful, possessed of almost unlimited authority, and equipped with all the learning of the age. The religious rites were traditional, unchangeable, and mysterious. A tinge of mystery is one of the great characteristics of the Egyptian architecture as well in its tombs as in its temples. The Egyptians attained to a very high degree of learning in astronomy, mathematics, and philosophy; the remains of their literature have been preserved to us in the papyri, or MSS. written on paper made from the pith of the papyrus. In theory the religion was monotheistic, but in practice it became polytheistic, a multiplicity of gods was created by personifying natural phenomena, such as the sun, moon, stars, etc., as well as the brute creation. The Egyptians were strong believers in a future state; hence their care in the preservation of their dead, and the erection of such everlasting monuments as the Pyramids. Herodotus informs us that the dwelling-house was looked upon by them as a mere temporary lodging, the tomb being the permanent abode.

> " What availed thee thy other buildings ?
> Of thy tomb alone thou art sure.
> On the earth thou hast nought beside ;
> Nought of thee else is remaining."

v. Social and Political.—Under this heading we find that a dense population was employed on public works, for which they probably received no other pay but their food ;

the state of cheap labour thus produced was eminently favourable to the execution of great public works. In addition there existed a centralized despotic government, which perhaps more than any other form favours the execution of monumental works. It is assumed by some that the spare time which occurs during the annual floods enabled the population to be employed on these state buildings. It is also possible that the transport of stone required for the Pyramids, etc., was effected by means of rafts floated down at this season. During the reign of Rameses II. the captives and foreigners, who had largely increased, were also put to enforced labour upon the public works, as in the first chapter of the book of Exodus we learn how the natives viewed with alarm the growing numbers and power of these strangers.

vi. **Historical.**—Egyptian civilization is the most ancient of any of which we have a clear knowledge; its history has come down to us from Holy Scripture and from Greek and Roman authors, but more particularly from the Egyptian buildings, by which it can be traced as far back as 4,000 years B.C. The Pyramids are thought to be a thousand years older than any building which has yet been discovered in Western Asia, the subject of our next division. The Kings or Pharaohs (from the title " Peraa " = " great house ") have been arranged in thirty dynasties, extending down to B.C. 340. These have been based on the list of Manetho, an Egyptian priest who lived B.C. 300, and compiled a history of Egypt in Greek. The nineteenth dynasty, founded by Rameses I. (B.C. 1400-1366), may be taken as the most brilliant epoch of Egyptian art. The evidence of his greatness, and that of his grandson, Rameses II. (B.C. 1333-1300), as builders, is to be seen among the Temples of Thebes and elsewhere. The twenty-sixth dynasty takes us to the time when the country was conquered by the Persians in B.C. 527, from whom it was wrested by the great Grecian general, Alexander the Great, in B.C. 332. On Alexander's death and the division of his empire Egypt passed to Ptolemy, one of Alexander's generals, who founded a dynasty that ruled from B.C. 323 to B.C. 31. After the wars which ended in the death of Cleopatra, Egypt passed, as did the whole of the then known world, into the hands of the conquering Romans, and became a Roman province. On the spread of Mahometanism, in A.D. 638, Egypt was conquered by the Arabs, who left important monuments. In A.D. 1517 it became a part of the Turkish dominions.

2. ARCHITECTURAL CHARACTER.

The principal remains of ancient Egyptian architecture are the Pyramids (or royal tombs of the kings) and the temples. Contrast in this respect Egypt with Assyria, where the palaces of the kings are the chief remains. The Egyptian wall-paintings and sculptures, jewellery, bronze implements and utensils, which have been unearthed from their temples or tombs, show that the race had attained to a high degree in art. As regards their architecture, the impression which forms itself in the mind of the spectator is that here was building for eternity; for all the remains have a character of immense solidity, and, as a general rule, of grand uniformity.

The Pyramids are the most extravagant of all ancient buildings in many ways. The relative return in impressiveness and the higher beauties of the art is comparatively small when compared with the amount of labour, expense, and material used in their erection. It must be borne in mind that the Pyramids were built for a special purpose. If the pyramid had been left at half its height, it would have remained a national observatory, but as it was closed over, its object was astrological. It was in the lifetime of the founder intended to furnish an accurate horoscope, and on his death to form a secure tomb.

The Architectural Character of the temples is striking and characteristic. The buildings decrease in height from front to back, and form a disconnected collection of various sized buildings, often built at different times, and thus form a direct contrast to the harmonious whole of a Greek temple, which is all comprised within one "order" of columns, and which is distinctly both in appearance and reality one building.

The character of the tombs consists in the planning of their mysterious chambers and corridors, which, covered with paintings and hieroglyphics, produce an effect of gloom and solemnity on the spectator.

3. EXAMPLES.

THE GREAT SPHINX

(No. 2), whose date is unknown, is situated near the great pyramids, and is a natural rock cut to resemble a Sphinx, with rough masonry added in parts. An Egyptian Sphinx had the head of a king, a hawk, a ram, or a woman, on the body of a lion. The dimensions of the Great Sphinx are as follows: it is 65 feet high, the face is 13 feet 6 inches wide, the mouth 8 feet 6 inches long, the body 188 feet long. The original builders are unknown; it was excavated in 1816 by Captain Cariglia, who found a temple between the paws.

THE GREAT PYRAMIDS

(or Royal Tombs) at Gizeh, near Cairo, were all erected during the fourth dynasty (B.C. 3766?-3566), and are the next earliest remains of Egyptian architecture.

The **first** or Great Pyramid (Nos. 2 and 3) was erected by **Cheops** (B.C. 3733-3700).

The **second** Pyramid was erected by **Cephron** (B.C. 3666-3633).

The **third** Pyramid by **Mycerinos** (B.C. 3633-3600).

They were built during their lifetime by these kings of the fourth dynasty as their tombs. The governing idea was to secure immortality for the king by the preservation of his mummy.

A large number of pyramids have been discovered, but the most remarkable are those at Gizeh, near Cairo. The principal one is that by Cheops, as mentioned above. Shortly, it is square on plan, 760 feet each way, its area being 13 acres, *i.e.*, twice the extent of St. Peter's, Rome, or equal to the size of Lincoln's Inn Fields, in London. Each

of the faces of the pyramid is an equilateral triangle laid
sloping, and meeting in a point. The height is 484 feet.
The angle which the sides make with the ground is 51
degrees 51 minutes. The entrance is on the north side,
and the sides face directly north, south, east, and west, as in
all the pyramids. The entrance (No. 3) is 47 feet 6 inches
above the base; it first slopes downwards, and afterwards

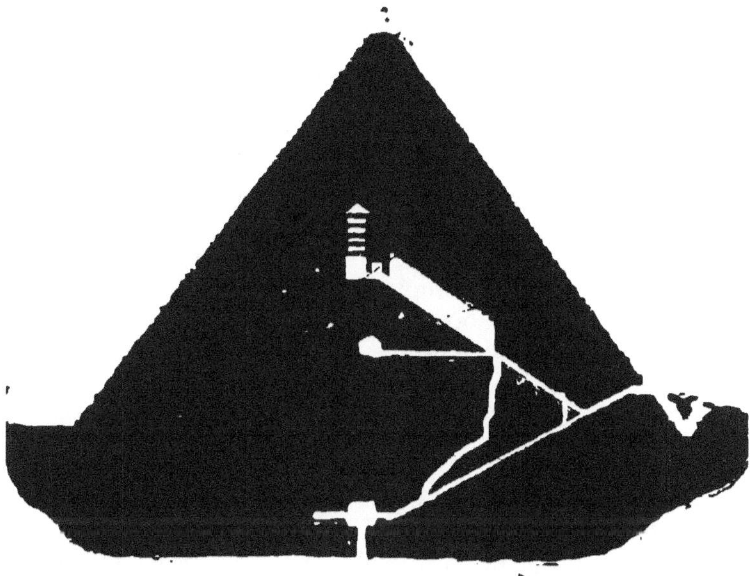

3. SECTION OF GREAT PYRAMID AT GIZEH, SHOWING KING'S
AND QUEEN'S CHAMBERS AND PASSAGES.

reascends towards the heart of the pyramid, where the
king's chamber is situated. The upper part is elaborately
constructed with stones one above the other, and the
entrance is protected by a massive stone acting as a port-
cullis, fitting into a rebate or recess, and weighing from 50
to 60 tons. In this chamber was placed the sarcophagus of
the king, containing his embalmed body, and two air
channels led to the outer face of the pyramid for ventilation.
There were two other chambers in the Great Pyramid, one

from a passage leading off that to the king's chamber, and one below the ground.

The face of the Pyramid is now stepped in tiers of 4 feet built in limestone, but originally these were cased in to a sloping face with granite from Syene.

TOMBS.

Beyond these royal tombs are others for private individuals, which take the form of

a. *Truncated pyramids of the earlier period.*
b. *The rock-cut tombs* in later times (eighteenth and nineteenth dynasties).

In the latter there was one entrance unconcealed, the body being hidden in a well of great depth, which had a concealed entrance in the thickness of the wall.

Note.—The value of these from an historical point of view is very important, because they are decorated with representations of the person as he lived, executed in stucco and coloured. Inscriptions enable us to fix the exact dates.

The **Tomb of Beni Hassan** (No. 4) in Central Egypt is a well-known example of the rock-cut tombs. It was erected during the twelfth dynasty (B.C. 2466-2233), a period which was particularly remarkable for the progress of the arts of peace.

The great entrance with columns is generally considered to be from a wooden origin, and to be a prototype of the Greek Doric column.

The columns are slightly fluted and have an entasis, while the projecting roof has false stone beams, carved to imitate wooden ones.

The **Tomb of Manepthah** at Thebes (B.C. 1300-1266) is one of the most important, consisting of chambers and corridors splendidly decorated, descending in a sloping direction into the mountain, and ending in a circular pit which leads to the mummy chamber.

TEMPLES.

The purposes for which they were used and their component parts are important.

They are not like our churches, which are places of worship for the people, nor yet like Greek temples, although in this latter case the worshippers stood outside; but they were sanctuaries where only the king and priests penetrated.

Mysteries and processions formed a great part of the religious services.

The student is here referred to Mr. Lockyer's theories as to the orientation of temples with regard to the particular stars.

The earliest temples consisted of one small chamber with statue and altar (ex. at Elephantine), approached by a flight of steps, and in this form are generally considered to be the prototypes of the Greek temples. These smaller temples were afterwards enlarged by adding chambers for the priests, and courts, colonnades, and halls, all within a garden or court surrounded by a high wall.

In order that the student may understand the general distribution of the parts of an Egyptian temple, a plan is here given of the small south temple of Karnac (No. 5), on the eastern bank of the Nile, which may be taken as a fair example of the plan of an Egyptian temple.

The entrance to the temple was between "pylons," or massive sloping towers, on each side of the gateway (No. 7). In front of the entrance were sometimes placed obelisks, and again in front of these an avenue of sphinxes, forming a splendid approach to the temple. This entrance gave access to the large outer courtyard, which being open to the sky in the centre, and therefore called hypæthral (from two Greek words, meaning "under the air"), was surrounded by a double

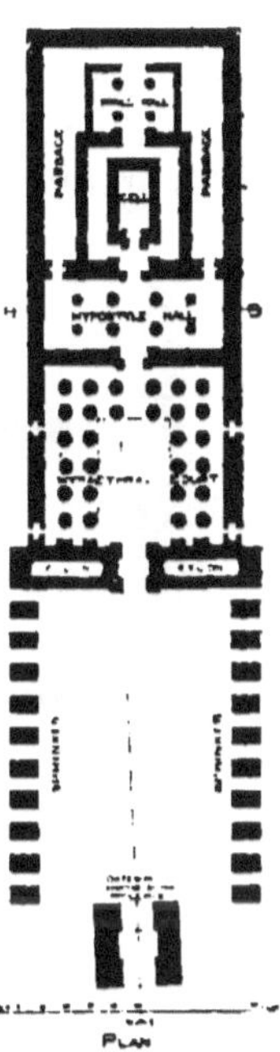

5. Small South Temple of Karnac.

colonnade on three sides, and led up to the hypostyle
hall, in which the light was admitted by means of a
clerestory above, formed by the different height of the
columns (section BB, No. 6). "The mass of the central
piers, illumined by a flood of light from the clerestory,
and the smaller pillars of the wings gradually fading into
obscurity, are so arranged and lighted as to give an idea
of infinite space. Moreover, the beauty and massiveness
of the forms, and the brilliancy of their coloured decorations, all combine to stamp such halls as the greatest of
man's architectural works" (Fergusson). In later times the

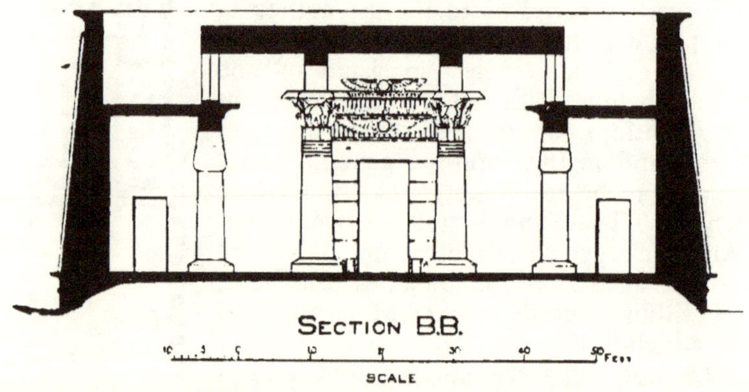

6. SMALL SOUTH TEMPLE OF KARNAC.

hall was lighted (No. 8) over low screen walls placed between
the columns. Beyond this is the cell, surrounded by a passage, and at the rear is a smaller hall. These last chambers
must have all been dark or imperfectly lighted.

The whole collection of buildings forming the temple was
surrounded by a tall blank wall, as high as the buildings
themselves.

The gateway in this example, at the commencement of the
avenue of sphinxes, was erected by the Ptolemys, and, like
many Egyptian buildings, differs in axis of plan from the
direction of the main building.

(a.) At **Thebes**, the capital of Egypt during the
eighteenth and nineteenth dynasties (B.C. 1700-1200),

are some of the most important remains, occupying an area 2¼ miles north to south, and 3½ miles east to west.

Among these are :

On the Eastern bank, the Temples at **Karnac** and **Luxor**.

On the Western bank, the Temple of **Medinet-Habou** and the **Rhamession** (B.C. 1500).

The Temple at **Karnac** is the grandest, extending over an area 1200 feet in length by 360 feet in width, and is connected with the Temple at Luxor by an avenue of sphinxes.

The general disposition of plan follows what has already been described, but we should note in particular the grand hypostyle hall of 130 columns, and which covers the same area as Notre Dame at Paris. The central avenue is 85 feet high, as compared to 147 feet at Amiens, and the columns are 12 feet in diameter. The smaller columns on either side are 42 feet in height and 9 feet in diameter.

Note this clerestory over the central columns, an early form of lighting more fully developed in the Gothic period.

The central columns have lotus capitals in blossom to admit the light more easily ; the side columns have lotus-bulb capitals, on which the light would fall (No. 11).

(*b.*) During the Greek and Roman period many temples were erected. Of these the temple at Edfou (B.C. 180-160) (No. 8) is one of the most important.

OBELISKS

are monumental pillars, employed as an appendix to a temple. . All were monoliths, *i.e.*, in one stone, square on plan, and tapering gently, with a pyramidal summit. The height was usually about nine to ten diameters, the four faces were slightly rounded, and cut with hieroglyphics. The capping was of metal, for the groove into which it was fitted is visible in some cases.

In Egypt obelisks were placed in pairs in front of the façade of the temple. The quarrying and transport of such a mass of stone without the power of a steam-engine was an engineering feat of considerable skill.

Many obelisks were removed to Rome by the emperors, and at least twelve are in that city. That in the centre of the Piazza of St. John Lateran is the largest in existence, and is of red granite from Syene. (It is 104 feet high, or with the pedestal 153 feet, weighs about 600 tons, is 9 feet square at the base, and 6 feet 2 inches square at the top.)

Example in England : the obelisk on the Thames Embankment (No. 9), 68 feet 6 inches high, 8 feet square at the base, and weighs 180 tons.

DWELLINGS.

All these have disappeared, being only built of sun-dried bricks. Houses are shown on paintings and sculptures which have come down to us, from which they appear to have had one, two, or three storeys.

In the absence of any authentic remains, an illustration of the Egyptian House is given (No. 10), conjecturally restored, and erected at the Paris Exhibition, 1889, by M. Charles Garnier. The design was founded on an ancient painting, and had a garden in front, laid out in a formal style, with fish-ponds. The house was divided by a corridor in the centre, giving access to the rooms. The staircase at the back led to a verandah, and also to a flat roof, extending the whole length of the building. The upper part of the house was painted a bright yellow, and the long external wooden columns blue ; in effect the whole building was full of colour.

4. COMPARATIVE.

A. **Plans** of the temples have already been slightly compared with the Greek examples (page 13), and we have noticed that they were especially planned for inside effect. The hypostyle hall crowded with pillars, seemingly unlimited in size, and mysteriously illuminated from above, realized the grandest conceptions of Egyptian planning (No. 5). Externally we have the massive pylons to form their chief façade, contrasted by the slender obelisks which usually stood in front of them, while the approach was through an impressive avenue of innumerable sphinxes.

The erection of these temples was progressing during many centuries by means of continual additions; in this respect they resemble our own English cathedrals; as also in their disregard for symmetry, in the planning of one part in relation to another, as may be seen in many of the later temples erected under the Ptolemys, the little temple on the island of Philæ being a special instance. The walls, the pylons, and other features are placed on different axes, free from any pretence of regularity. The freedom and picturesqueness of grouping thus obtained is remarkable.

B. **Walls** were immensely thick; in the more important buildings they were of granite, in the less important of brick faced with granite.

The face of the temple walls slopes inward towards the top, which gives it a massive appearance. Viollet-le-Duc traces this batter to the employment of mud for the walls of early buildings (No. 7). No columns, the especial feature of Greek work, appear on the outside; there is merely a massive blank wall crowned with a characteristic cornice, consisting of a large hollow and roll moulding. For the purposes of decoration, the walls, even when of granite, were generally covered with a fine plaster, in which were executed low reliefs, treated with bright colour (No. 7). Simplicity, solidity, and grandeur, qualities obtained by broad masses of unbroken walling, are the chief characteristics of the style.

C. **Openings** were all square-headed and covered with massive lintels. It is essentially a trabeated style, and the arch does not appear to have been used. Window openings are seldom found in temples, light being admitted by the clerestories in the earlier examples at Thebes, or over the low dwarf walls between the columns, as at Luxor or Philæ (Nos. 6 and 8).

D. **Roofs** are flat, and composed entirely of massive

blocks of stone laid on to the columns. In the rock-cut temples the ceilings are sometimes slightly arched in form, and at the tomb of Beni-Hassan the roofing is also made to represent timber construction.

E. **Columns.** The papyrus, a tall, smooth reed, and the lotus, a large white water-lily of exquisite beauty, offered many suggestions; the stalks were made to represent the column, and at intervals to appear to be tied by bands (No. 11). The capitals, which are derived from the lotus plant, are as follows :

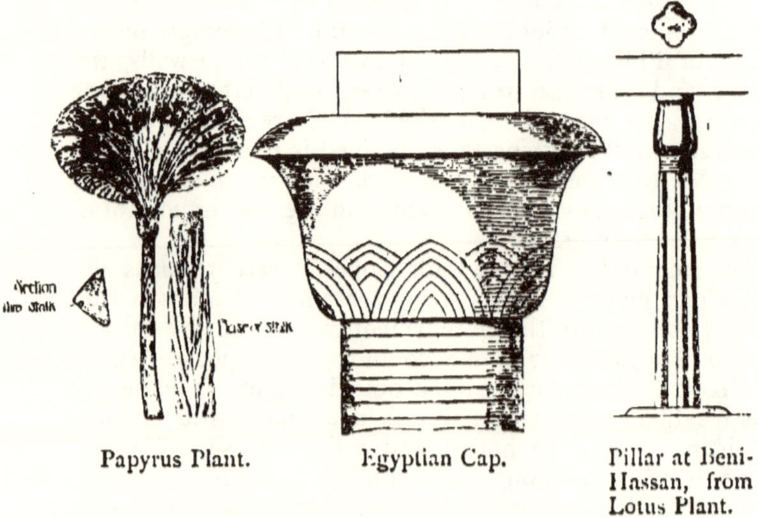

Papyrus Plant.   Egyptian Cap.   Pillar at Beni-Hassan, from Lotus Plant.

11. DIAGRAM SHOWING ORIGIN OF EGYPTIAN COLUMN, FROM LOTUS AND PAPYRUS PLANTS.

(*a.*) The lotus bud (conventionalized), and tied round by stalks (No. 11).

(*b.*) The fully-grown lotus flower, which formed a bell-shaped capital, and was ornamented with colour decoration or sculptured (No. 11).

(*c.*) The " palm " capital, the main outline of the palms being painted. (No. 8.)

(*d.*) The Isis capital, as at Denderah, where the capitals were made up of the heads of the goddess Isis on which rested a model of a pylon.

F. **Mouldings** are few in number, viz., the hollow and bead generally used in conjunction, but the bead is also used by itself. The two together invariably crowned the upper part of the pylons. (Nos. 7 and 10.)

G. **Decoration** is an important feature in the style. The Egyptians were masters in the use of colour, chiefly using the primaries—blue, red, and yellow. The preparation of the surface for colour was as follows: The wall was chiselled smooth and covered with a thin layer of plaster or cement; after which a coloured wash was put over the whole. The figures or hieroglyphics were then drawn on with a red line by an artist, being corrected with a black line by the chief artist; the sculptor next incised the outline, rounding slightly the inclosed form towards its boundaries. The whole was then ready for the painter, who executed his work in the strong hues of the primary colours. (See the Egyptian Court at the Crystal Palace.) The hieroglyphics were often, however, incised direct on the granite and then coloured, as may be seen on the sculptures at the British Museum. These hieroglyphics were instructive as well as decorative, and it is from them that we learn most of what we know of Egyptian history.

We may note in passing the great power the Egyptians possessed of conventionalizing, *i.e.*, when natural objects, such as the lotus plant, the palm, and others, were copied or used as the *motif* for a design, they were treated by the artists in a way suitable to the material in which they were working. The distinguishing, or essential, features of the natural object, or its class, thus passed by a process of idealizing into forms adapted for ornamentation.

5. REFERENCE BOOKS.

Numerous works of the Egyptian Exploration Fund.
Perrot and Chipiez, " History of Art in Egypt."
"Ten Years Digging in Egypt," by Prof. Flinders Petrie.
" Egyptian Decorative Art," by Prof. Flinders Petrie.
"Ancient Egypt," by Prof. George Rawlinson, M.A., is a very interesting account of the Egyptians.
Prof. Maspero, " Dawn of Civilization."

"An Egyptian Princess," by Georg Ebers.   (Historical Novel.)

Visit the Egyptian Court at the Crystal Palace ; also at the British Museum study the various kinds of capitals. The Museum should be visited thoroughly, as it contains a most complete collection of Egyptian antiquities, which will give the student a more thorough knowledge of the style than the reading of many books, and in an infinitely shorter space of time.

WESTERN ASIATIC ARCHITECTURE.

1. INFLUENCES.

i. **Geographical.**—On referring to the map (No. 12) it will be seen that the buildings, which we propose to discuss very shortly under this head, are situated in the valley of the Tigris and Euphrates, a country which may be styled the cradle and tomb of nations and empires. The plain of Mesopotamia, once the seat of a high civilization was irrigated from the Euphrates and Tigris, by innumerable canals, and was highly cultivated, supporting a huge population round Nineveh and Babylon. Now it has vegetation solely in the wet season.

The earliest period of which we have knowledge, commences at the mouth of the great rivers draining the country. In this respect we can contrast with the history of Egypt, the Pyramids and earlier work being at Cairo, towards the mouth of the Nile, and the later work at Philæ, far inland. In Western Asiatic architecture the march of civilization spreads northwards from Babylon (the Gate of God) to Nineveh, while in Egyptian architecture it spread southward towards Edfou and Philæ, but in both cases it develops from the sea inland.

ii. **Geological.**—The whole district of Chaldæa or Lower Mesopotamia is alluvial, being formed of the thick mud or clay deposited by the two rivers, the Tigris and the Euphrates.

This soil, containing no stone nor bearing any trees, can be made into bricks, which thus became the building material. In consequence of expense, kiln-dried bricks were only used

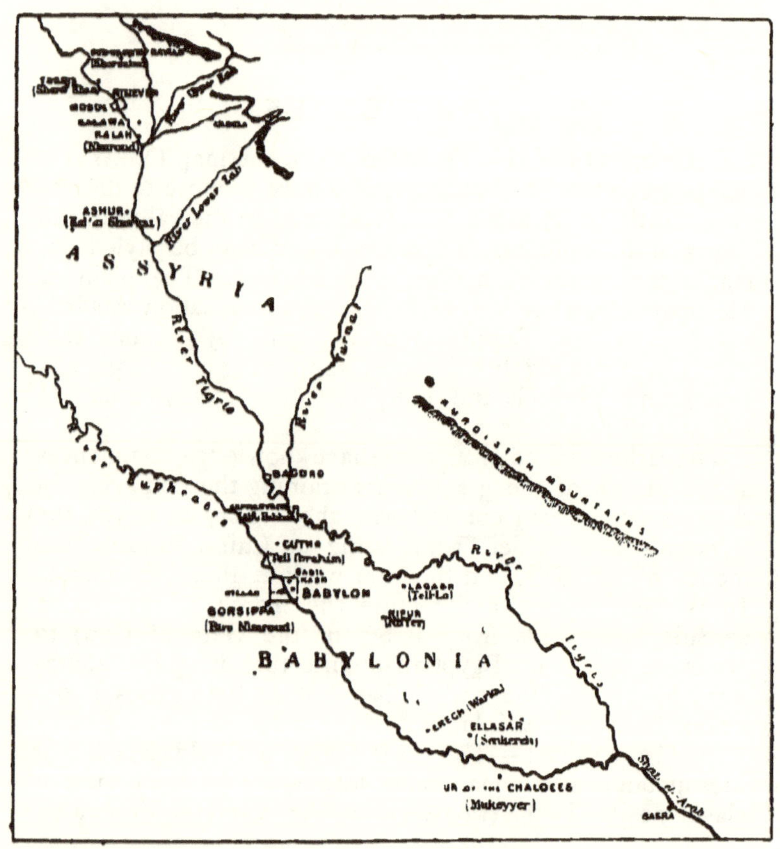

12. MAP OF BABYLONIAN AND ASSYRIAN EMPIRES.

for the facing, the general body of the walls being constructed of the ordinary sun-dried bricks.

However, bricks seem to have been glazed or vitrified, and used in different colours as a facing. As a cementing material, bitumen or pitch, seems to have been used, applied in a heated state. It was obtained from bitumen springs found in the district, as at Is, on the Euphrates. Mortar, made of calcareous earth, was used in the latest times.

In Assyria, where stone was not scarce, the walls were also faced, on the inside and out, with alabaster or limestone slabs, on which were engraved the bas-reliefs or inscriptions, which are so important from an historical point of view.

iii. **Climate.**—The unhealthy exhalations from the vast swamps in Chaldæa, and the swarms of aggressive and venomous insects which infest the entire region during the long summer, rendered elevated positions for the towns and palaces not only desirable, but almost essential. Moreover, during the rainy season torrents fall for weeks at a time.

iv. **Religion.**—The people were worshippers of the heavenly bodies, and of the powers of nature, such as the wind, thunder, the sun and the moon, etc. The number of omen tablets which have survived bear witness to their extreme superstition.

Religion was not favourable to constructive art among the Persians. They worshipped Ormuzd as god of light and good, under the symbol of fire, as opposed to Ahriman, the god of darkness, and promoter of evil. They had consequently no images, and they had also no temples, because sacrifices were conducted in the open air. The essential element was therefore wanting for the rise and development of constructive art. In later times, Egypt and the Greek colonies of Asia Minor being subject to the Persians, Egyptian and Grecian artists were employed by the Persian kings.

v. **Social and Political.**—From what we know of their history, we judge that the Assyrians were a sturdy, warlike, and cruel people.

In their battles, the conquering monarchs took thousands of prisoners, and these were employed in raising the enormous mounds mentioned hereafter. It has been calculated by Rawlinson, that the great mound of Koyunjik—which represents the palaces of Nineveh itself—would require the united exertions of 10,000 men for twelve years to raise the mound only, after which the palace would have to be built. Their sculptures in alabaster exhibit considerable technical skill and refinement, while the repoussé pattern work on bronze bowls, shields, and gate fittings is also noticeable.

The cuneiform inscriptions consist of groups of strokes in the form of wedges, placed upright and horizontally, hence the name. These characters were impressed on clay tablets or cylinders, while still moist, with a triangular ended instrument of wood, bone, or metal. Libraries of these strange MSS.' were formed on a large scale, and by their translation our knowledge has been acquired.

vi. Historical.—From the study of Assyrian history we can glean certain facts which considerably assist us in forming our divisions of the periods. The earliest Babylonian king mentioned in the cuneiform, or arrow-headed, inscriptions was Eannadu, who reigned B.C. 4500. The empire thus founded gradually extended its dominion to the north, following the course of the great river Tigris. In B.C. 1700 Assyria, the northern part of the early Babylonian empire, asserted her independence and became the great power of Western Asia.

Of the Assyrian kings, among the more celebrated was Sargon (B.C. 722-705), who erected the great palace at Khorsabad. This Sargon was the first Assyrian king who came in contact with the Egyptian army, then in alliance with the Philistines, a combination which, however, he defeated. The Assyrians conquered and occupied Egypt in B.C. 672, sacking the ancient city of Thebes in B.C. 666. Egypt, however, finally shook herself free from the Assyrian yoke. The destruction of Nineveh took place in B.C. 609, and the great Assyrian kingdom was divided among its conquerors, Assyria being handed over to the Medes. Babylon then took the leading place until it was finally conquered by the Persian general Cyrus in B.C. 539, from which date it remained under the rule of the Persians until the time of Alexander the Great about B.C. 300, when it became a possession of the Greeks. About a thousand years after Alexander's invasion and short-lived conquest, the Arabs overran the country and settled there—Bagdad forming a new capital of great magnificence. A few hundred years after, the Turks, a barbarous people pouring in from the east, settled in the country, which is at the present moment in a desolate state owing to Turkish misrule.

2. ARCHITECTURAL CHARACTER.

The appearance of the monuments must be entirely left to the imagination : one can only guess at the effect of the towering masses of the palaces, planted on the great mounds, and approached from the plains by broad stairways. The colossal winged bulls of the portal led to an audience-chamber paved with carved slabs of alabaster. Here a dado, twelve feet high, of sculptured slabs, of a soft grey colour, was surmounted by a wall lining of glazed and brightly coloured brickwork, wrought in friezes of men and animals ; over all was probably a beamed roof of cedar, through which small openings gave a sufficient illumination.

3. EXAMPLES.

WESTERN ASIATIC ARCHITECTURE

can be divided into three tolerably distinct periods. Of these the first is the **Babylonian period** or Chaldæan period (B.C. 2234-1520), which is essentially a **temple-building** epoch.

THE FIRST OR BABYLONIAN PERIOD.

Principal **remains** :
Temple of Birs Nimroud near Babylon.
Temple at Khorsabad.
According to Colonel Rawlinson's investigations the temple of Birs-Nimroud was dedicated to the seven heavenly spheres.
In Chaldæa every city had its temple, and attached was the "ziggurat" (meaning holy mountain), which was a temple observatory, with the temple on the top platform, from which observations could be made.

These temples appear to have been constructed in receding terraces, several storeys in height, and each of a different coloured brick; access to these storeys was obtained by stairs. The angles of these temples were orientated, in contrast to the Egyptian pyramids, whose faces were so placed. A walled inclosure surrounded the whole structure.

Our readers will remember the attempts of the Babylonians to build a tower which should "reach to heaven" (Gen. xi. 4), and it is a fact worth noting that both here and in the pyramids of Egypt, countries both remarkable for their dulness and sameness of aspect, man should have attempted his highest flights of audacity in the way of artificial elevations.

THE SECOND OR THE ASSYRIAN PERIOD

(B.C. 1290 to the destruction of Babylon by Cyrus in B.C. 538) comprised the second period. This period is essentially a **palace-building** epoch.

Principal **remains** :

At Nimroud.

At Nineveh (or Koyunjik).

At Khorsabad.

We find that the same principle of raising the buildings on terraces, from 20 to 50 feet high, is followed in the designing of these palaces as we found in the case of the previous temples. Each terrace gradually decreased in area from the one below it, and was probably faced with glazed tiles of different colours.

The excavations at Nineveh (or Koyunjik) tell us practically all we know of this period. Many of the sculptures which lined the walls are at the British Museum, and should be visited.

The remains at **Nimroud** and **Khorsabad**, near the ancient city of Nineveh, were raised on a mound or terrace made of bricks, from 30 to 50 feet high, on which platform was placed the structure. The palaces were faced externally and internally with stone. In the interior, above a sculptured dado of alabaster about 8 feet high, which seems to have been sometimes treated with colour, the walls were faced with hard-baked bricks of some size, painted and glazed in the fire, and forming a continuous frieze. Many conjectural restorations have been made by various writers.

The great entrance portals to the palace were flanked by great human-headed bulls, 19 feet in height. Examples of these are now preserved in the British Museum. These man-bulls have a mystical meaning; they were reproductions of the supposed creatures that guarded the sun-gates of the East and West, to which they were dedicated.

From the bas-reliefs we are able to say that the chambers, which were narrow in proportion to their length, were lighted by windows, probably high up in the walls. The roof was probably constructed on solid wooden beams, though others have supposed barrel vaults to have been in use.

The Palace of Gudæa (B.C. 2800), explored by one of the French expeditions, is typical. Its plan is simple, the entrance being by a broad gateway leading into a central quadrangle, the gateway being flanked by curious guard-rooms, penetrating far into the wall, and evidently intended as shelters from the hot weather. Round this quadrangle were grouped the principal buildings, on one side offices and store-rooms, on the other the royal apartments, divided into two portions, the public rooms, and the women's quarters. This type of plan obtains in all oriental palaces up to the present day.

THE THIRD OR PERSIAN PERIOD

commences with Cyrus, B.C. 538, and ends with Alexander, B.C. 333.

> **Remains:**
> At Susa, Persepolis, and Passagardæ, consisting of palaces, tombs, and temples.

The Persians were a hardy race from the mountainous district north of the Persian Gulf. Having conquered the Assyrians under Cyrus, B.C. 538, and having no architecture of their own, they proceeded to copy and adopt that of the conquered Assyrians, as the Romans in after times assimilated that of the Greeks.

In the neighbourhood of Susa and Persepolis, the new

cities which they built, good stone was, however, to be found, and, as a consequence, many details, which are wanting in the earlier periods, have come down to us. For instance, in Assyria the walls remain, but the columns, being of wood, have disappeared.

In Persia the columns and doorways, which were of marble, remain, but the walls are in many cases destroyed, being of thinner construction, and the naked brick exposed.

At **Persepolis** the customary platform, already mentioned as a part of the palaces, is cut out of the solid rock, and not built up of bricks, as in the earlier Assyrian examples. This platform is approached by a staircase of black marble, each step rising about four inches.

The principal **remains** of this vast palace are :

The Propylæa by Xerxes.

The columns of the Great Hall, 67 feet high, by Xerxes, and other portions (No. 13).

The rock-cut Tomb of Darius is an imperishable copy of the façade of this palace (see Texier's great work), in which are found the "double-bull" capitals supporting the cornice cut out of the solid rock. The evidence of these columns goes to show that they were copied from wooden forms of the earlier Assyrian capitals, the wooden beam supporting the roof resting on the back of the bulls. The smaller columns have voluted capitals, fluted shafts, and moulded bases (No. 13).

At **Susa** some splendid decorations in coloured brick, were lately excavated, and are now in the Louvre at Paris.

4. COMPARATIVE.

A. **Plan.**—It should be noticed that the temples of the early period and the palaces of the later period are all raised on a terrace some 30 feet to 50 feet in height, and that the buildings on this terrace are grouped round a quadrangle. In the planning of the temples we should note that, whereas the sides of the Egyptian temples face the cardinal points, the angles of the Assyrian temples face these points. The Egyptian temples were designed for

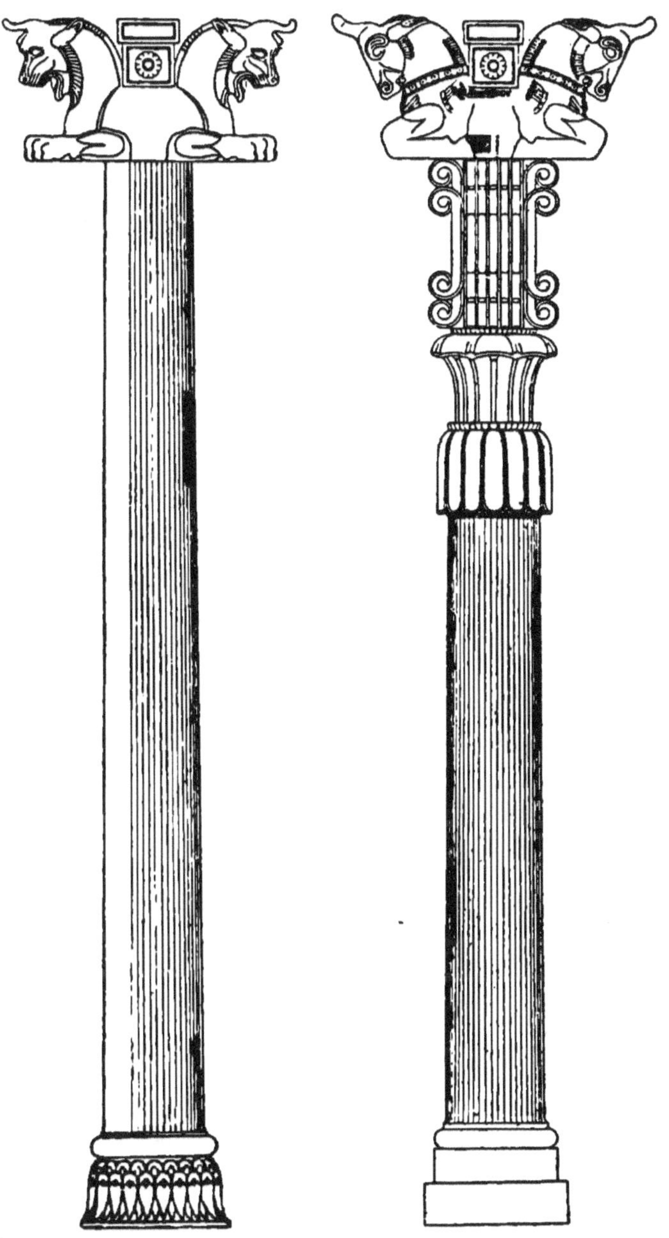

13. COLUMNS FROM GREAT HALL OF XERXES, PERSEPOLIS.

internal effect, while the Assyrian palaces were designed so as to be effective internally and externally, being raised on the platforms mentioned above.

B. **Walls.**—The Assyrians in the early period only used stone as a facing to their brick walls, contrasting with the solid marble work of the Greeks, and with the constructive use of stone and granite by the Egyptians.

Most of what we know of the life of the Assyrians is obtained from the facing slabs of alabaster with which they clothed their brick walls.

C. **Openings.**—The lighting to the temples is conjectural, but it appears, very probably, to have been effected by means of a "clerestory," somewhat similar to that in use in the Egyptian temples.

The use of the arch, both circular and pointed, was practised by the Assyrians, as is proved by the discoveries of Sir Henry Layard at Nimroud, and at Khorsabad, in the city gateways, discovered by M. Place. We find semi-circular arches springing from the backs of winged bulls with human heads, which kept watch in pairs at each of the portals.

D. **Roofs.**—The roofing appears to have been probably effected by means of timber beams thrown from one column to the next, and resting on the backs of the "double-bull" capitals. Some restorers show the halls of the palaces as vaulted with brick tunnel vaults.

E. **Columns.**—It is assumed by Mr. Fergusson that their columns were primarily of wood, stone columns being introduced in the later period, by the Persians, in the buildings at Persepolis, which they erected after their return from Egypt.

These columns had characteristic "double-bull" capitals (No. 13), and the Ionic scroll is noticeable in some examples. The columns therefore did not need to be so massive as in Egyptian architecture, where stone roofs had to be supported. The stone columns of the later period were probably founded on the timber posts of the earlier period.

F. **Mouldings.**—As in the case of Egypt, in West Asia the use of mouldings does not appear to have been advanced to any great extent. In the Assyrian palaces the sculptured

slabs and coloured surfaces took their place. At Persepolis
the bead and hollow may be noticed in the columns, while
the volutes of the capital are treated with plain sinkings.

G. **Decoration.**—It is from the decorative treatment of
Assyrian architecture that we can trace much of the peculiar
and characteristic detail used by the Greeks. On the
sculptured slabs already mentioned at Koyunjik (Nineveh),
two miles of which were uncovered, are represented buildings with columns and capitals of Ionic and Corinthian form
in embryo.

Further, we may say with some certainty that Greece
took from Assyria the idea of the sculptured friezes, the
coloured decorations, and the honeysuckle and guilloche
ornaments; the latter may be seen in a pavement slab from
the palace at Koyunjik, now in the British Museum.

The Corinthian column, as mentioned, seems probably to
have been derived from Egypt and Assyria. From Asia
Minor Greece took the Ionic column—a prototype being
also seen at Persepolis—perfecting it with that consummate
skill and grace with which she transformed her borrowings.
From Egypt, it is considered by some, that Greece took the
Doric order, as exemplified in the Tomb of Beni-Hassan,
and in the Temple of Deir-el-Bahari, on the Nile!

5. REFERENCE BOOKS.

Perrot and Chipiez, " History of Art in Chaldæa and
Assyria."

Charles Texier, " Description de l'Arménie, la Perse,
et la Mésopotamie."

A. H. Layard, " Nineveh and its Palaces."

" Chaldea," by Z. A. Ragozin.   (A most interesting
account of the people and their history.)

M. Victor Place, " Assyrie."

Flandin and Coste's " Voyage en Perse."

" Sarchedon," by Whyte Melville.   (Historical Novel.)

A visit to the Assyrian Galleries and basement of the
British Museum will afford much interest and information
to the student. Such a visit will impress him with the
dignity and importance of the style.

GREEK ARCHITECTURE.

" Fair Greece ! sad relic of departed worth !
Immortal, though no more ; though fallen, great !"—BYRON.

I. INFLUENCES.

i. **Geographical.**—A reference to the map of Greece (No. 14) shows a country surrounded on three sides by the sea, possessed of many natural harbours, convenient for the development of trade. By means of these havens the Phœnician merchants in early times carried on commerce with the country. The influence of the sea in fostering national activity should not be forgotten—an influence, by the way, which has done much for the English race. Again, the mountainous character of the country, with scarcely a road until Roman times, was calculated to isolate the inhabitants into small groups, and was instrumental in producing a hardy and adventurous people, such as we might expect to make good colonists, which the Greeks undoubtedly were.

ii. **Geological.**—In regard to the geological formation of Greece, the principal mineral production was marble, the most monumental building material in existence ; and one which favours purity of line and refinement in detail. This material is found in great abundance in the limestone mountains of Pentelicus, six miles from Athens, and in the island of Paros. The country was also rich in silver, copper, and iron.

iii. **Climate.**—The climate of Greece is noticeable for the hot sun and the heavy rains, factors which were probably to a large extent answerable for the porticoes which were the feature of their temples.

iv. **Religion.**—The Greek religion was a worship of the natural phenomena, of which the gods were personifications. The priests had to perform certain rites, but they were not an exclusive class, and often only served for a period, retiring afterwards into private life. Both men and women officiated, and a small bright cella takes the place of the mysterious halls of the priest-ridden Egyptians.

The characters of democratic Athens and conservative

14. MAP OF GREECE.

Egypt are reflected in the difference between the Acropolis and Karnac.

v. **Social and Political.**—The origin of the early inhabitants seems doubtful, but they were known to the ancients under the name of Pelasgi, and appear to have migrated from Asia. Their eastern origin is deducible from their religion, Herodotus informing us that the names of the Greek gods had been transplanted from Egypt. The early or Pelasgic period may be taken as extending to the time of the Grecian war against Troy, which we note here as proving the early connection of the inhabitants of Greece with Asia. It was 500 years, however, after the fall of Troy, that the new Hellenic civilization is evinced in the construction of the Temple of Corinth, the earliest Doric temple that we know, it being erected in the seventh century B.C.

In regard to the people themselves, it is clear how the national games and religious festivals united them in reverence for their religion, and gave them that love for music, the drama, and the fine arts, and that great emulation in manly sports and contests, which distinguished the race.

We must remember that the people led what we should call an open-air life ; the public ceremonies and the administration of justice were carried on in the open air.

Again, the Greeks, as indicated above, were great colonists, and emigration, especially to the coast of Asia Minor and the Mediterranean, was a government measure dating from about B.C. 700, undertaken not only to establish trade, but also to reduce the superfluous population.

For this reason we shall be prepared to find that many of the important buildings of Greek architecture, especially in the Ionic style, are in their colonies of Asia Minor, and that this connection with the East must have had some influence upon their architecture.

vi. Historical.—The poems of Homer give us a picture of the earliest days of Greece. Whether or no the war with Troy be an actual fact, what is related has a substratum of truth, and the tale probably arose out of the early settlements of the Greeks in north-west Asia. From the time of the Persian wars in the fifth century B.C. we have the history of Herodotus, at which period the cities of Greece had settled down in their several forms of government—tyrannic, aristocratic, or democratic—and most of their colonies had been founded. The Persians under Cyrus having conquered Babylon, also seized the kingdom of Lydia, where they came in contact with Greek colonies in that district and disputes arose, the result being the Persian wars. At the battle of Marathon, B.C. 490, the first Persian invasion of Greece was unsuccessful, and in B.C. 480 the naval victory of Salamis decided the fate of the second under

Xerxes. The growth of Athens then excited the jealousy of Sparta, and the Peloponnesian War which followed, lasted from B.C. 431 to 402. The rule of Pericles (B.C. 444-429) marks the climax of Athenian prosperity.

Sparta became the chief power in Greece, until the rise of Thebes and Macedonia took place ; the latter had not hitherto been considered as a Greek state, but, by the ability of Philip and his son Alexander the Great, it succeeded to the leadership of all Greece. In B.C. 334 Alexander set out on his great expedition, and in six years he subdued the Persian empire, besieged and took Tyre, and received the submission of Egypt, where he founded and gave his name to the famous city of Alexandria. His conquests extended to northern India. He died at Babylon in B.C. 323. The effects of his conquest were most important in introducing Hellenic civilization throughout Asia. On his death the empire he created was split up among his generals, Egypt falling to the share of Ptolemy, who founded a dynasty (see under Egypt). In Greece itself the formation of leagues between cities was attempted, but Roman interference had commenced, and gradually increased, until in B.C. 146 Greece became a Roman province.

2. ARCHITECTURAL CHARACTER.

The general architectural character of the earliest works is archaic, heavy, and severe, the influence of the early Pelasgic period being at once apparent.

A gradual change toward refinement and beauty is observable, and in the later periods the proportions of the columns were more slender, and the mouldings more refined. Carving and sculpture of the highest class then completed the effect of their great buildings.

Proportion was of the first importance to the Greeks ; they built in truth, construction was apparent, and no mixture of principles was allowed, trabeated construction being always paramount. Thus in Greek buildings we find simplicity, harmony, and unity.

The Grecian style is essentially a columnar and trabeated

(trabs = a beam) style, one in which a column of stone supporting a lintel of the same material is the main feature.

The arch was never used by the Greeks, who seem, if they knew of its existence, as it is believed they did, to have strongly objected to the mixing of constructive principles.

In considering this columnar architecture, we shall have to take notice of the so-called "orders of architecture," classified as the **Doric, Ionic,** and **Corinthian,** each with their distinctive features. We may explain here that an "order" in Greek and Roman architecture consists of the column, including base and capital, and of its entablature, which is the part supported by the column ; the entablature is divided into the architrave, or lowest portion ; the frieze, or middle member ; and the cornice or uppermost part. All of these parts vary in proportion in the different orders as do the mouldings and decorations applied to each part (Nos. 15, 31).

We shall be able to trace the **Doric** column, the oldest, plainest, and most sturdy, to its probable Egyptian prototype as exemplified at Beni-Hassan ; the **Ionic** column, especially noticeable for its scroll-like spiral capital, to its probable prototype in Asia Minor, and the **Corinthian** column and capital to a probable Egyptian and Assyrian prototype ; or else, as it has been assumed by some, to a natural development of the Ionic. The characteristics of each order are well expressed in the following lines :

> "First, unadorn'd,
> And nobly plain, the manly Doric rose ;
> Th' Ionic, then, with decent matron grace,
> Her airy pillar heaved ; luxuriant last,
> The rich Corinthian spread her wanton wreath.
> The whole so measured, so lessen'd off
> By fine proportion, that the marble piles,
> Form'd to repel the still or stormy waste
> Of rolling ages, light as fabrics look
> That from the wand aerial rise."—THOMSON.

The disposition of the triglyphs is important in the setting out of the order, for the point to be noticed is that the end triglyph is not over the centre of the column, as the intermediate triglyphs are.

iii. The cornice has subdivisions of—

    (*a.*) Bed moulding.

    (*b.*) Crowning part, or corona.

The mutules recall the feet of sloping timbers, from which many suppose them to be derived.

Remains :

> In Greece and Sicily, where all the more important remains of this order are to be found, we should notice :
>
> **The Temple of Corinth** (B.C. 650).
>
> **The Temple of Zeus, at Ægina** (B.C. 600).
>
> **The Temple of Theseus at Athens** (B.C. 465).
>
> **The Parthenon at Athens** (B.C. 438) (No. 22).
> See the fine model in the British Museum.
>
> **The Temples at Agrigentum,** erected in the fifth century B.C.
>
> **The Propylæa,** or Entrance-gate to the Acropolis at Athens, designed by Mnesicles.
>
> **The Temple of Jupiter at Olympia** (B.C. 435).
>
> **The Temple of Apollo Epicurius** (" The Ally "), at Bassæ, near Phigaleia in Arcadia, built by Ictinus in B.C. 420.

The Parthenon was erected from designs of Ictinus and Callicrates in the time of Pericles, Phideas being the superintendent sculptor (Nos. 15 and 22).

Notice how carefully all optical illusions are corrected : as the entasis or graceful swelling of the columns was applied to correct an appearance of weakness in the supports, while the outer intercolumniation was narrowed for the purpose of making the angle of the temple appear stronger. The slight hollowing of the underside of beams over the openings served to prevent them from appearing to "sag," or drop in the middle. The steps of the stylobate are also raised in the middle to prevent any appearance of sagging in them at the centre. The leaning inwards of all the columns prevented an appearance of falling outwards (the axes of the angle columns would meet if prolonged at a distance of over a mile above the horizon).

" Earth proudly wears the Parthenon as the best gem upon her zone."

EMERSON.

THE IONIC ORDER

(No. 23) is of a lighter character and more ornate than the Doric.   It was principally used by the Greeks in Ionia, Asia Minor, hence its name; and is probably founded on the wooden types of the Euphrates Valley.   The shafts are fluted with twenty-four flutes, separated by fillets. The column has a base.   The height of the column is generally about nine diameters; it has a distinctive capital of spiral-shaped scrolls probably from an Asiatic prototype as exemplified at Persepolis (No. 13).   The form has also been traced to the early Mycenean jewellery; either origin would be sufficient to account for its adoption in the later period.[1]

The method of striking volutes is a geometrical process easily acquired, and given in all books of the orders.

The **entablatúre** is $\frac{2}{7}$ of the column in height, and consists of:

Architrave: in faces.

Frieze: sometimes plain, but often with sculpture, or carving of continuous frieze-like character.

Cornice: with no mutules, but with characteristic dentil ornament, and sometimes also with the egg and dart.

N.B.—The Doric order provides a setting for sculptor's work.   The Ionic incorporates it with the order itself, usually in the form of carved enrichments on its main lines.

The most numerous **Remains** of the Ionic order are found in Asia Minor, while the Doric examples are chiefly in Greece and Sicily. We may mention as examples of the Ionic:

The Temple on the Ilissus (B.C. 484), destroyed by the Turks in 1780.

The Temple of Nike-Apteros ("Wingless Victory") (B.C. 469).

The six internal columns of the **Propylæa at Athens** (B.C. 432).

[1] For an interesting paper on the origin of the Ionic Volute, see R.I.B.A. Journal, 19 Dec., 1895.

The Erechtheion at Athens (B.C. 420), of which St. Pancras Church, London, is a modified copy.

The internal order of the **Temple at Bassæ**, in Phigaleia, in which note the angular treatment of capital.

The Temple of Diana at Ephesus (B.C. 330), which was reckoned as one of the seven wonders of the world.

The Temple of Minerva Polias at Priene, erected by Pythius (B C. 320).

In the plate (No. 23) is shown the Ionic order of the Temple on the Ilissus at Athens and the Roman treatment of the order after Scamozzi (No. 24).

THE CORINTHIAN ORDER

(No. 25) is still more ornate. It was little used by the Greeks. It is generally about 10 diameters high.

The base and shaft resemble the Ionic order.

The distinctive capital may have been based on the Ionic, or borrowed from the bell-shaped capital of the Egyptians, to which was added the spiral of the Assyrians; it has a deep "bell" below, on which is worked a plain circlet of acanthus leaves in tiers. The Assyrian honeysuckle ornament occurs in the capital of the order that decorates the monument of Lysicrates at Athens (No. 25).

We may here note Prof. Baldwin Brown's opinion that the foliage ornament carved on capitals is a copy of actual foliage, wreathed for festal purposes, round the heads of the posts of a porch.

The abacus to the capital is generally moulded, and the entablature, which is $2\frac{1}{2}$ diameters high, bears a general resemblance to the Ionic, but with the addition of modillions, and increased enrichments in the mouldings.

Remains:

The Choragic Monument of Lysicrates at Athens, B.C. 335 (No. 27).

The Tower of the Winds at Athens, B.C. 159, where notice should be taken of the Egyptian type of capital used.

THE THEATRES

were the largest buildings the Greeks attempted.   They were
unroofed, the performances taking place in the daytime.
There were few actors, and therefore they had only a shallow
stage.   A permanent architectural background with doorways answered for the scene.

The chorus executed dances, and chanted, in a circular
inclosure in front of the stage.

The auditorium was rather more than semicircular in
plan, in rising tiers, as at the Theatre of Dionysos at Athens,
where the seats are hollowed out of the Acropolis rock.

The Theatre at Epidaurus is one of the most perfect in
Greece, and apparently retains its original Greek arrangement.   The circle in which the orchestra was placed is
complete.   There was apparently no raised platform for the
stage, which was level with the orchestra.   Chambers and
passages are placed behind the fixed architectural scene.
The cavea, or auditorium, is rather more than a semicircle
in plan, and the seats are in rising tiers, cut out of the solid
rock, and faced with marble.

THE PALACES AND DOMESTIC BUILDINGS.

At Tiryns and Mycenæ, the former situated by the sea-coast
to the south-west of Athens, remains have been discovered of
recent years which are of the greatest interest in showing
the general arrangement of these buildings.

At Mycenæ, flights of steps lead to an outer courtyard, from
which, by traversing a portico and vestibule, the *megaron*, or
principal men's apartment, is reached ; this was surrounded
by a roof, open to the sky in the centre.   From the
megaron other chambers, whose uses are not defined, are
entered.   The women's chambers are planned so as to
afford the greatest seclusion, and are reached from the other
side of the outer court.   The plans of domestic buildings
seem to have resembled, on a smaller scale, the general
arrangement of the palaces.[1]

[1] Many of the *stele* or tombstones, in the design of which the Greeks
excelled, remain in the "Street of Tombs" at Athens.   The upper part is
generally treated with an anthemion design (No. 31 B).   Examples may
be seen in the British Museum.

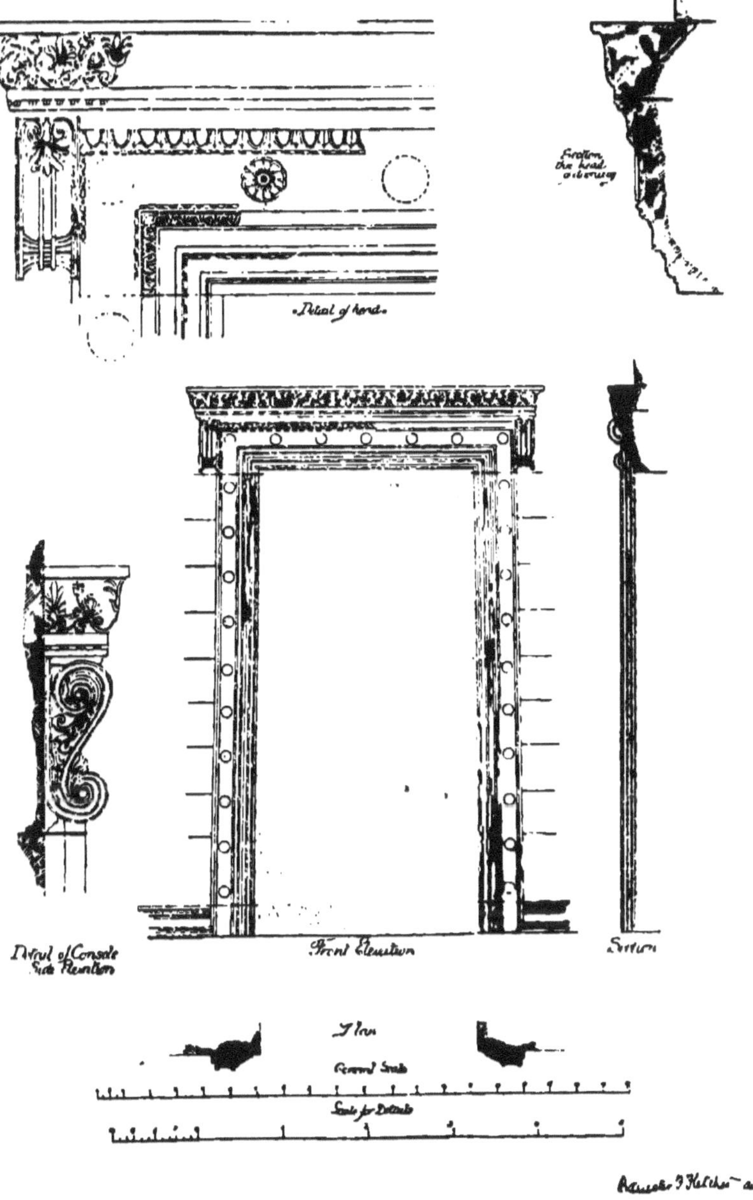

28. GREEK DOORWAY FROM THE ERECHTHEION.

32.   THE CLASSIC SIDE, ARCHITECTURAL LECTURE ROOM,
KING'S COLLEGE, LONDON.

4. COMPARATIVE.

A. The **Plans** (No. 18) of Greek buildings were simple, well-judged, nicely balanced, and symmetrical. (Exceptions to symmetry of plan: the Erechtheion, and the Propylæa, at Athens, and probably the private houses.) Plans involving the use of the orders were rarely extensive or complicated, being generally very regular; yet certain departures were made from the general rules, either for the purposes of effect or from necessity, as when columns were placed nearer together at the angles of Doric temples. Moreover, the central inter-columniation at the Propylæa at Athens was wider than the others, probably for the passage of chariots.

Greek temples might be described as Egyptian turned inside out ; the courtyard, porticoes, and columned halls being replaced by a small cella colonnaded on every face. The relations and proportions of these columns constitute the charm of Greek exteriors.

Circular planning was also adopted, as in the theatres and choragic monuments, and octagonal planning, as in the Tower of the Winds at Athens.

B. **Walls.**—The construction of walls was solid and exact. No mortar was used, the joints being extremely fine, and the finished surface of the walls was obtained, by a final rubbing down of the surface, by slave labour. The material was marble, which was accountable for the fine smooth face and exact jointing displayed. Hollow wall construction in the entablature was practised at the Parthenon, to lessen the weight upon the architraves, and perhaps for economy of material. In temples the cella walls were mostly masked behind columns. The base of a temple was always well marked and defined by steps, giving a real and apparent solidity to the structure. The top of the walls was always finished by a cornice.

No towers were used in Greek architecture, the nearest approach to towers being the lofty mausoleum at Halicar-nassus,[1] and the Lion Tomb at Cnidus, both in Asia Minor.

C. **Openings.**—Greek architecture was essentially a trabeated or beam-construction style. All openings were

[1] For a model and remains of this structure, lately re-arranged, the British Museum should be visited.

spanned by a lintel, *i.e.* are square-headed. The trabeated construction necessitated great severity in treatment; the supports were of necessity close together, because stone lintels could not be obtained beyond a certain length. Openings are often sloped inwards towards the top, as at the doorway to the Erechtheion (No. 28). Relief to the façades of temples was obtained by the shadow of the openings between the columns.

D. **Roofs.**—These coincided with the outline of the pediment. In temples they were carried by internal columns or by the walls of the cella, and were framed in timber and covered with marble tiles. Internal ceilings were probably also framed into deep coffers.

E. **Columns.**—They are generally the whole height of the building. As the orders have been fully treated under Examples, we summarize only as follows :

The forerunner of the **Doric** type is probably exemplified at Beni-Hassan and Deir el-Bahari, Egypt, and the most perfected form is seen in the Parthenon (No. 22).

The **Ionic** was probably introduced from Assyria; its origins can be traced in the Assyrian bas-reliefs in the British Museum; the most perfected form is to be found at the Erechtheion, Athens, and the Temple on the Ilissus (No. 23).

The **Corinthian** is considered by some as the natural outcome of the Ionic; it was sparsely used by the Greeks, the finest example being the monument of Lysicrates at Athens (No. 25), in which the student may see that the spiral scroll of the Ionic is retained in a somewhat modified form, while the lower portion of the capital is surrounded by acanthus leaves.

Caryatides, or carved human figures used in the place of columns, are of Asiatic origin, and were employed by the Greeks. Ex. : The Erechtheion at Athens, a cast of which is seen in the illustration from King's College Museum (No. 71).

F. **Mouldings.**—Refer to sketches of Greek Mouldings compared with Roman (Nos. 29, 30, 31). A comparative selection will be found at the Architectural Museum at King's College, London (No. 32).

"Mouldings are the means by which an architect draws a line upon his building."

A true knowledge of the effect of contour is to be best obtained from actual work rather than from drawings, and the examples at the British Museum must be studied.

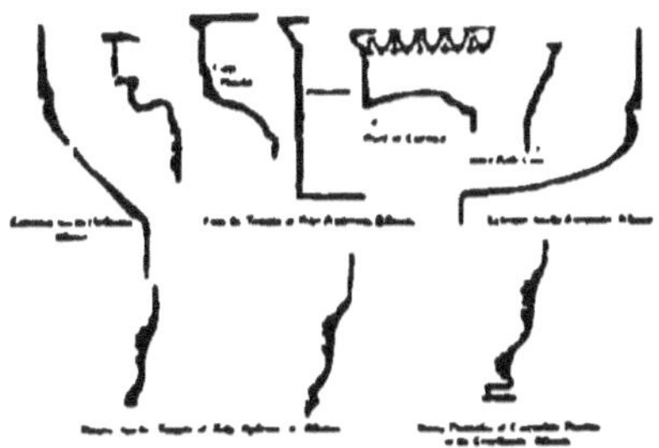

29. GREEK MOULDINGS.

The principal characteristic of Greek mouldings was refinement. The influence of an almost continuous sunshine, a clear atmosphere, and the hard marble material, had naturally great influence in the production of these delicate contours.

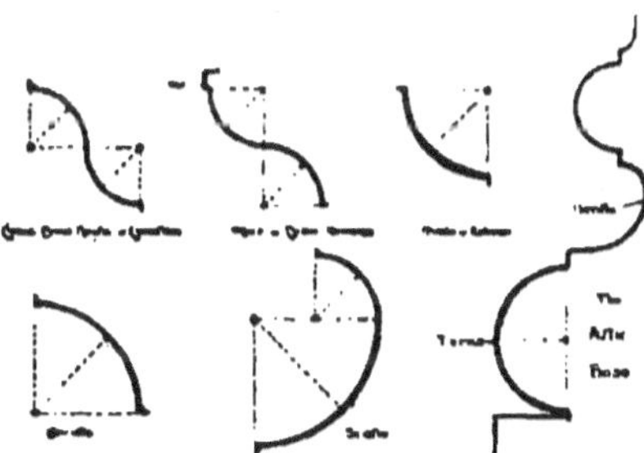

30. ROMAN MOULDINGS.

Grecian mouldings are not parts of circles; they were probably drawn by hand, but approach very closely to various conic sections, as parabolas, hyperbolas, and ellipses.

Note.—As a general rule the lines of the enrichment or carving on any Greek moulding correspond to the profile of the moulding on which it is carved. This is a rule that was rarely departed from, and therefore is one worthy of notice. The profile of the moulding is thus emphasized by the expression in an enriched form of its own curvature.

Notice the examples given from full-size sections taken at the Parthenon and the Erechtheion (No. 29).

The following are the most important mouldings in a classified list:

(*a.*) The **cyma-recta** (Hogarth's "line of beauty"). When enriched it is carved with the honeysuckle ornament, whose outline corresponds with the section.

(*b.*) The **cyma reversa.** When enriched it is carved with the water-lily and tongue.

(*c.*) The **ovolo** (egg-like), when enriched is carved with the egg and dart, or egg and tongue ornament.

(*d.*) The **fillet,** a small plain face to separate other mouldings.

(*e.*) The **bead** serves much the same purpose as the fillet, and approaches a circle in section. When enriched it is carved with beads, which in fact gave the name to the moulding.

(*f.*) The **cavetto** is a simple hollow, and is the upper part of the cyma-recta.

(*g.*) The **scotia** is the deep hollow occurring in bases, and is generally not enriched.

(*h.*) The **taurus** or **torus** is really a magnified bead moulding. When enriched it is carved with the guilloche ornament.

(*i.*) **bird's-beak** moulding is emphatically Grecian; it occurs in antæ-caps only, has great value for the deep shadow it gives; as a section it is very suitable for the English climate.

(*j.*) The **corona,** the vertical face of the crowning portion of the cornice, was often painted with a Greek "fret" pattern.

G. **Decoration** (No. 31).—The acanthus leaf and scroll play an important part in Greek ornamentation. The leaf grows wild in the south of Europe, in two varieties: (F) That with broad blunt tips, and (D) that with pointed and narrow lobes. Note the Greek preference for the pointed form.

The acanthus is found in the Corinthian cap (Nos. 26, 31), and is also seen in the crowning finial of the choragic monument of Lysicrates. The scroll which accompanies the leaf acts as a stalk, and is square in section with sharp edges; the leaf has deeply drilled eyes.

The sculpture employed by the Greeks was of the highest order.

Ex. in the Parthenon : The great frieze round the cella, the tympana of the pediments, and the metopes, or square spaces, in the frieze (No. 20). In later work the Caryatides, as at the Erechtheion.

Colour appears to have been largely used, and many traces are left.

5. REFERENCE BOOKS.

Stuart and Revett's "Athens." (The large folio volume, and also the small 8vo handbook.)

Wilkins' "Magna Græcia" and "Prolusiones," the latter for drawings, etc., of the Erechtheion.

Penrose's "Principles of Athenian Architecture."

Cockerell's "Ægina and Bassæ."

Inwood's "Erechtheion."

"Die Architektonischen Ordnungen der Griechen und Römer," by Mauch.

"History of Art in Primitive Greece," by Perrot and Chipiez.

"The Fall of Athens," by A. J. Church. (Historical Novel.)

The student should visit the Greek Court at the Crystal Palace for the sake of a splendid model of the Parthenon façade, and also the British Museum for actual fragments of the sculpture from the temples.

ROMAN ARCHITECTURE.

1. INFLUENCES.

i. **Geographical.**—The map (No. 33) will show that the sea coast of Italy, although the peninsula is long and narrow, is not nearly so much broken up into bays, or natural harbours, as the shore line of Greece, neither are there so many islands studded along its coasts. Again, although many parts of Italy are mountainous—the great chain of the Apennines running from one end of the peninsula to the other—yet the whole land is not divided up into little valleys in the same way as is the greater part of Greece.

We may therefore with fair accuracy compare the Greek and Italian nations in these respects: (*a.*) The Romans never became a seafaring people as the Greeks did, nor did they send out colonists of the same description to all parts of the world that they knew. (*b.*) There were never many equal and rival cities in Italy as in Greece, and the small Italian towns, being less jealous of their separate independence, and more ready to join in leagues, the Roman power could be built up by a gradual absorption of small states, a process that was never completed by Athens or Sparta.

ii. **Geological.**—The geological formation of Italy differs from that of Greece, where we find the chief and almost the only building material is marble; because in Italy besides marble we note that stone, brick, and terra-cotta, especially the two former, are largely used even for their more important buildings. The quarries of Tivoli (near Rome) supplied the stone for many of the principal buildings erected in Rome. Brick was used in bulk for walling, with a stone or marble casing. Roman architecture, as it spread itself over the whole then known world, would be influenced naturally by the materials found in the various parts where it planted itself, but bricks or concrete in conjunction with brick casing or banding were the favourite materials.

iii. **Climate.**—The north has the excessive climate of

33. MAP OF THE ROMAN EMPIRE.

the temperate region of continental Europe, central Italy is more genial and sunny, while the south is almost tropical.

iv. **Religion.**—The heathen religion of ancient Rome being looked upon as part of the constitution of the state, eventually the worship of the gods was only kept up as a matter of state policy. The emperor then received divine honours, and may almost be described as the leader of the Pantheon of deities, embraced by the tolerant and wide-spreading Roman rule. Officialism naturally stamped its character on the temple architecture.

v. **Social and Political.**—At the beginning of civilization we find three chief nations dwelling in the peninsula. In the central portion (or Etruria) lived the Tuscans, whose origin is doubtful; they were probably an Aryan people, who appear to have been settled in Italy before authentic history begins; they were great builders, as we shall notice later. In the south of Italy, the Greeks had planted many colonies, which were included in the name of " Magna Græcia." The remainder of Italy (exclusive of Cisalpine Gaul) was occupied by tribes sprung from the same Aryan stock as the Greek, and the common forefathers of both must have stayed together after they had parted off from the forefathers of the Celts, Teutons, and others. But long before history begins the Greeks and Italians had separated into distinct nations, and the Italians had also split up into distinct nations among themselves. The common form of government in ancient Italy resembled that of Greece, consisting in towns or districts joining together in leagues. Rome was firstly governed by chosen kings, aided by a senate and an assembly of the people. The kings appear to have been driven out about B.C. 500. The commonwealth succeeded, and was followed by the Empire, which commenced with Augustus Cæsar in B.C. 27.

vi. Historical.—The foundation of Rome is an uncertain date. The republic which succeeded the Kings engaged in wars with its neighbours, and conquered several Etruscan cities, meeting, however, with defeat in B.C. 390, at the hands of the Gauls, who continued to hold the northern part of Italy. In about B.C. 343 began the Roman conquest of the whole of Italy, which was effected in about sixty years, the dominion of a city over cities. Then came the wars with peoples outside of Italy, Pyrrhus, King of Epirus, being subdued, and the first great war against Carthage brought to a conclusion, in B.C. 241. The beginning of the Roman provinces is made with Sicily in B.C. 241.

The second Punic war with Carthage was the most severe struggle in which the Romans had engaged; Hannibal, entering Italy from Spain, defeated all the Roman armies, and maintained himself in a hostile country, until recalled by a counter attack of the Romans upon Carthage itself under Scipio.

The third Punic war (B.C. 149-146) ended in the total destruction of Carthage, whose territory became a Roman province. The conquest of Macedonia and Greece was also proceeding, and was effected in the same year as the destruction of Carthage. Greece formed a stepping stone to Western Asia, which gradually acknowledged the Roman power, until in B.C. 133 it also became a province. The conquest of Syria followed, the Roman empire extending from the ocean to the Euphrates, while Cæsar's campaigns in Gaul in B.C. 59 made the Rhine and the Bristol Channel its northern boundaries. In B.C. 55 Cæsar crossed into Britain.

This tide of conquest swept on in spite of civil war at home, and rendered the empire a political necessity owing to the difficulty of governing so many provinces under the previous system. On Pompey's defeat at Pharsalia, Cæsar remained without a rival, and his murder in B.C. 44 only produced fresh disturbances, until on the defeat of Antony at Aktion, Augustus Cæsar (his nephew) was made emperor B.C. 27, and governed till his death, B.C. 14.

That period was the "Augustan age" of literature; the poets Virgil, Horace, and Ovid, and Livy the historian were all contemporaries. Following Augustus came the long line of emperors, and under Trajan (A.D. 98-117) the empire reached its greatest extent. Italy went out of cultivation and depended on imported corn; a turbulent populace, and the huge armies required to keep in check the barbarian tribes on every frontier, dominated the government. Emperors soon chosen were sooner murdered, and the chaos that gradually set in weakened the fabric of the empire.

Architecture fell into complete decay until the vigorous efforts of Constantine did something to revive it. The force, in fact, that had been growing up was Christianity, which obtained under the latter emperor official recognition. (See section on Early Christian Architecture.)

2. ARCHITECTURAL CHARACTER.

Roman architecture proper may be said to have lasted from the first to the fourth century A.D.

The Romans adopted the columnar and trabeated style of the Greeks, and joined it to the Arch, the Vault, and the Dome, which it is presumed they borrowed from the Etruscans, and the union of these two elements of **arch and beam** is the keynote of the style.

The Colosseum (No. 36) at Rome is a good example of the junction of these two great constructive principles. As it has been pointed out, the piers between the arches on the different storeys are strengthened by the columns applied to them ; and thus the columns without doubt act the part of buttresses; the column has become part of the wall, and does not any longer carry its entablature unaided.

This introduction of the arch as an architectural form led, through the basilica, to the construction of those glorious Gothic cathedrals, which were erected in the Middle Ages.

We have been accustomed, in Greek architecture, to buildings of only one storey in height ; now, however, owing to the varying needs of the Romans, we find buildings of several storeys ; and the orders, with column and entablature complete, are piled one on top of the other. Thus the orders ceased to be a constructive element, and became decorative features.

The Temples follow in the main the Greek type, but with far less refinement in design and detail. The great Baths for recreation and study, the Amphitheatres, Aqueducts, Bridges, Tombs, Basilicas, and the Fora, are the proofs of Roman greatness. Herein was shown great constructive ability, and a power to use the materials to hand, with the best possible results (see page 61 in Examples as to the Baths of Caracalla).

Conquest, wealth, and power were the ideals of the Roman, and these are well expressed in the architecture which has come down to us.

3. EXAMPLES.

The Etruscans were great builders, and knew the full value of the arch for constructive purposes, using it extensively in their works.

The architectural remains of the Etruscans consist chiefly of walls and tombs, which have a great similarity to the early Pelasgic work at Tiryns and Mycenæ. The walls are remarkable for their great solidity of construction, and for the cyclopean masonry, where huge masses of stone are piled up without the use of cement, or mortar of any kind. The Cloaca Maxima, or great drain of Rome, admittedly an Etruscan work, has a semicircular arch of from 10 to 13 feet span, in three rings of arch stones. Moreover, in bridges, aqueducts, and city gates, the radiating arch was used by them at an early date.

THE BUILDINGS OF THE ROMANS,

which were many and varied, are difficult to summarize in a short space. Remains are found throughout Europe, as at the Roman settlements of Nîmes and Arles in France; also at Tarragona and Segovia in Spain, at Trèves in Germany, at Constantine, etc., in North Africa, and at Baalbec and Palmyra in Asia. See map of Roman Empire (No. 33).

In England there are many remains. See under English Architecture, page 133.

THE TEMPLES.

Note.—The orders are described in the comparative table at the end, page 76.

The Roman temples resembled in many respects, and were founded on, those of Greece. We give a sheet of Greek plans giving the technical names for many of these, which it is hoped will be useful to the student (No. 18).

The characteristic Roman temple has no side colonnades, as are found in Greek examples, the order of columns being attached to the flank walls. Such temples had steps at the portico ends only, the flight being inclosed by wing walls, continued along the flanks as a podium to the order, and finished at their extremities as pedestals for statues. This class is known as pseudo-peripteral (No. 34), meaning a temple where the encircling colonnade is replaced by three-quarter columns.

Such temples could be built on a larger scale than the Greek examples, and with greater ease, as the architraves unsupported by the walls are few in number. A loss of unity resulted, in comparison with Greek work, in conse-quence of the abolition of the side colonnades, and the stopping of the steps by the wing walls, for the steps when carried round formed a base to the whole structure.]

The more important Remains of Temples in Rome are:

The Ionic Temple of Fortuna Virilis at Rome (pseudo-peripteral).

The Temple of Jupiter Stator at Rome. ⎱ Only three co-
(2nd cent. B.C.)   ⎰ lumns of each

The Temple of Jupiter Tonans at Rome. ⎰ remaining.

The Temple of Antoninus and Faustina, which is now the Church of St. Lorenzo. (Pseudo-peripteral.) (A.D. 141.)

The more important Remains of Temples out-side Rome are:

At Athens. ⎰ The Temple of Jupiter Olympius, completed by Hadrian in A.D. 117. It is decastyle in front with twenty Corinthian columns on each flank, 58 feet in height. It equalled in size the great hypostyle hall at Karnac, and was the third largest temple in existence (No. 18 x.).

In France. ⎰ Hexastyle temple at Nîmes (No. 34 and 18, vii.), erected during the reign of Hadrian in the second cent. A.D.

In Syria. ⎰ At Baalbec are a group of temples of great interest. The great temple stood in a court 380 feet square with recessed porticoes. In front of this was a hexagonal cortile entered by a decastyle Corinthian portico 260 feet long. The smaller temple equals the Parthenon in size, and there is also an unique circular temple.

CIRCULAR TEMPLES

are another form used by the Romans, the shape being probably borrowed from the Etruscans.

Ex. Temple of Vesta at Rome.
„   „   „   „   Tivoli (near Rome) (No. 18, iii.).
Probably both erected during the reign of Augustus, B.C. 27—A.D. 14.

Both of these consist of a circular cella surrounded by a peristyle of Corinthian columns. The cella was probably carried up above the roof of the peristyle and separately roofed, but restorations vary as to the crowning features.

The difference in design of the two examples, and the reasons for the same, are instructive. The Roman example being placed in a low and flat situation, required all the height that could be given it; hence the columns are of slender proportions; while the temple at Tivoli being placed on the edge of a rocky cliff, and thus provided with a lofty basement, required to be low and sturdy in proportion, lest it should look insecure.

The Pantheon at Rome (No. 18, xiii.), the date of which was formerly doubtful, is now known, by recent investigations, to have been built during the reign of Hadrian, probably A.D. 123, on the site of a three cell temple of Etruscan type, built, during the reign of Augustus, by Agrippa in A.D. 27. The portico is that of the old temple taken down, and re-erected as the frontispiece of the new building. This portico consists of sixteen Corinthian columns of Egyptian marble, planned in three bays, in the same manner as the Etruscans formed the entrances to their three-cell temples. The exact date of the circular portion was discovered by the inscription on the bricks, which were opened out during the work of restoration in 1892.

The Pantheon is a circular building, the internal diameter being 145 feet 6 inches, which is also the height of the interior. The walls of brickwork are 20 feet in thickness. Hollowed out of these thick walls are eight great recesses, one of which forms the entrance; three of the remaining seven are semicircular exhedræ, the other four are rectangular on plan. The cupola has been discovered by M. Chedanne to be formed, not of concrete, as was formerly supposed, but of brick laid horizontally, each course overlapping the one beneath, so that no thrust is exerted on the walls which support it.

The internal surface of the cupola is coffered (No. 35), and note should be taken of the way in which the mouldings or sinkings of these coffers are regulated, so as to be seen correctly from below by the spectator.

Externally the cupola was originally covered by tiles of bronze, and gilded. The portico also had a bronze ceiling, since removed for the sake of the metal.

The old Roman bronze doors and frame, however, still remain (No. 41).

The structure was probably faced externally with white, and internally with coloured, marbles; the present internal casing has been assumed by Mons. Chedanne to be original.

The lighting is effected by one circular unglazed opening (No. 35), 27 feet in diameter, placed in the crown of the dome.

This method of lighting produces an effect which is most impressive and solemn; and there may have been a symbolic purpose in thus imitating the appearance of the vault of the heavens in this temple of all the gods, the idea being that the worship of Jove should take place in a building open to the sky. "One great eye opening upon heaven is by far the noblest conception for lighting a building to be found in Europe."

Diocletian's Temple at Spalatro (A.D. 284) is a further development of the last named. Internally it is circular, 28 feet diameter, decorated with columns placed in its angles, and crowned with a dome constructed in tiers of brick arches. Externally it is octagonal, surrounded by a low peristyle of columns.

The Christian baptisteries erected in the following centuries, were adapted from such circular temples, which are therefore extremely interesting and instructive.

PUBLIC PLACES.

The **forum** in a Roman city corresponds with the **agora** in the Greek city; and was an open space usually surrounded by porticoes, colonnades, public buildings, and adorned with pillars of victory, and statues to great men. The basilica, or hall of justice, was generally entered from the forum.

The forum corresponds to the " place " of the French towns, and to the " market place " of English country towns.

In our metropolis, the Royal Exchange corresponds to the ancient forum, as a place where the merchants could meet, and discuss matters of business.

THE BASILICAS, OR HALLS OF JUSTICE,

comprise some of the finest buildings erected by the Romans, bearing witness to the national love of government and justice. They are interesting as a link between classic and Christian architecture, as will be explained later on.

The usual plan was a rectangle, whose length was two or three times the width; two or four rows of columns ran its entire length, thus creating three or five avenues. Over the aisles were usually placed galleries.

The entrance was at one end, the tribunal at the other on a raised daïs, which was generally placed in a semicircular apse, partly cut off from the main body of the building by columns. In the centre of the apse at the extreme end sat the president, and on his right and left the assessors.

In front of the apse was the altar, where sacrifice was performed before commencing any important business.

The building was generally covered with a wooden roof, and the exterior seems to have been of small importance, being sacrificed to the interior.

Remains :

Example of a basilica with wooden roof.

The Ulpian, or **Trajan's Basilica at Rome**, of which Apollodorus of Damascus was the architect (B.C. 98). It was 180 feet wide, 360 feet long; the central nave being 87 feet wide, the side aisles 23 feet 4 inches.   Total internal height 120 feet.

It had a semicircular apse, raised by means of steps, and in front of the apse was the altar of sacrifice.

The basilica was entered, from the Forum of Trajan, by a central and two side doorways.

In connection was the celebrated Trajan's column. 92 feet in height, of which there is a full-size cast in the South Kensington Museum.   It stood in a court with storeys of galleries around, from which the elaborate sculpture could be viewed (see page 66), "group winding after group with dreamlike ease."

Example of a vaulted basilica.

The Basilica of Maxentius, or Temple of Peace, at Rome.   (A.D. 312.)

It was 195 feet wide, and 260 feet long.

The central nave was 83 feet between the piers, and 120 feet high.

The side aisles are roofed as three great semicircular archways, each 72 feet in span, and the nave is covered by an immense intersecting vault in three compartments.

The division walls to the side aisles are the supports of the central cross vaulting, the three bays communicating by arches through them.   Monolith columns, attached to the face of these piers, received the springers of the main vaults. Light was obtained for the nave from above the aisle vaults by means of lunettes, or semicircular windows, placed in the spandril of the main cross vaults.

The building is a prototype in many respects of a Gothic vault, all the thrust and weight of the superstructure being, by means of the intersecting vaulting, collected and brought down to various points, where piers are built to receive them.

Provincial basilicas.   Ex. at Trèves in Germany, and Silchester in Kent, England.

THE THERMÆ OR BATHS

are quite as characteristic of Roman civilization as the amphitheatres, though probably in origin derived from the Greek "Gymnasia."

Uses.—They were used for the purposes of bathing, the process being very similar to the modern Turkish bath. First, a hot-air bath in the so-called Tepidarium ; second, a hot-water bath in the Caldarium, next a cold plunge in the Frigidarium, or Piscina, and finally the "rubbing down," or shampooing, in the drying room.

They were also used for lounging, for various athletic exercises, and for the hearing of lectures and discourses ; thus supplying the place of the daily paper of to-day for the dissemination of news. They answered, moreover, in a great measure to our modern "club" as a rendezvous of social life. A small charge (equivalent to one farthing) was made to the populace, and in later days they were opened free, as a bribe, by emperors in search of popularity.

The Baths of Caracalla at Rome are the most important of all the remains, and give one a splendid idea of the size and magnificence of these structures. They accommodated 1,600 bathers.

The buildings are contained in an inclosure of 1,150 feet each way, or about one-fifth of a mile, not counting the segmental projection on three of the sides.⌐

Along the road front was a row of small chambers, probably used as shops.

The spaces within the inclosure were laid out for wrestling and games, halls being provided, in the segmental projections, for dramatic representations and lectures.

The central building (730 × 380 feet) was used entirely for baths, and had only four openings on the side exposed to cold winds (N.E.). It was, however, supplied with large columned openings on the south front, giving access to the gardens.

This central block is now in ruins, but restorations have been made, by French architectural students and others, which show the position of the dressing rooms ; of the Piscina (or swimming bath) ; of the Sphæristeria for gymnastics; of the Frigidarium, or cold-water bath; of the Tepidarium, or warm bath; and of the Caldarium, or hot bath, with its Sudatio.

The great central vaulted space, and the Rotunda, or circular hall, are sufficiently preserved to enable one to gain an idea of the immense size of those apartments. As a comparison, we might mention that the Houses of Parliament, including Westminster Hall, cover about the same area as the central block of these baths.

The **architectural character** of these immense structures indicates a further secession from Greek principles, in that the exterior treatment was neglected, all their glory depending on the adornment and colour of the interior.

The exteriors of these baths may have been treated in stucco, or more wisely left as impressive masses of rough brickwork, perhaps banded or dressed with bricks of a better colour.

Internally, however, where there is no question but that sumptuous magnificence was aimed at, the pavings were patterned in mosaic cubes of strong colours the lower parts of the walls were cased with marble, the upper parts with enriched and modelled stucco, bright with colour; the great columns, on which rested the vault springers, were of the finest porphyry or rare marbles; while the surface of the vaults was sunk with rich cofferings, or covered with bold figures, or decorations, in black and white, or in coloured mosaic. In the halls thus decorated were placed the finest sculpture of antiquity, brought from Greece itself, or executed in Rome by her artists.

The Vatican and Roman museums contain the results of the first and fruitful excavations in these thermæ, during the Renaissance period.

In **plan** alone, the baths are worthy of study, for while providing for the practical requirements of the bathers, care is taken to lead on from room to saloon and on to the great hall, which is the largest and most lofty apartment. Moreover, by a system of exhedræ or recesses, and by screens of columns, and by the relation of parts, any loss of scale was provided against, and the grandeur of the whole impressed

36.

THE COLISEUM. ROME.
Exterior

upon the spectator. (In Viollet-le-Duc's lectures, there is a drawing of the Frigidarium restored, which gives one a good idea of the effect produced.) In the construction of the vaults the system was that described on page 60 for the Basilica of Maxentius; while the Caldarium, or hot room, followed that given on page 58 for the Pantheon, so that the latter has been sometimes mistaken for part of Agrippa's Baths.

St. George's Hall, Liverpool, is a reproduction, both in scale and design, of the great hall of Caracalla's Bath, but with five bays instead of three.

Other Remains.—The Ephebium, or Great Hall, of Diocletian's Baths at Rome (A.D. 314), converted by Michael Angelo into the Church of Santa Maria degli Angeli.

The small private bath or balneum was also much used, as at Pompeii, where a painting now existing exhibits their manner of use ; they were heated by flues under the floors, in the walls, and lining the vaults, through which passed air, heated in the basement by the hypocaust or furnace.

THEATRES AND AMPHITHEATRES.

The design of the **theatres** was taken from the Greeks, but altered to suit Roman requirements as mentioned below.

The plan consisted of a semicircular auditorium—thus differing from the Greek theatre, which was rather more than semicircular—of tiers of seats one above the other, with wide passages and staircases communicating with the external porticoes on each storey. On the ground, separating the auditorium from the stage, was a semicircular area in which the Greeks placed the orchestra, while in Roman times this portion was occupied by the Senators.

Remains.—At Orange, South France, are the remains of a theatre, which must have been an important example; the auditorium being 340 feet in diameter. The stage is rectangular, being inclosed by shallow return walls, at right angles to the great scene or back wall. A ceiling, of wood probably, bounded by these walls, sloped outwards to the auditorium, and must have aided the voices of the actors. The great wall at the back of the stage, 340 feet long by 116 feet high, remains. The Odeion of Herodes Atticus at Athens is also a fine example.

The amphitheatres are truly Roman buildings, remains being found in every important settlement. They are good exponents of the character and life of the Romans, who had greater love for mortal combats between men and beasts, between men and men, or between beasts alone, than for the tame mimicry of the stage. Such combats were considered to be a good training for a nation of warriors.

These buildings were also used for naval exhibitions, as the drains for introducing the water for flooding the arena still exist.

Note.—The Spanish bull ring to some degree gives us an idea of the arrangement and uses of a Roman amphitheatre.

The most important example is the **Flavian Amphitheatre** at Rome, also called the Colosseum (No. 36).

The date of erection by Vespasian was A.D. 70.

By an examination of the model at the Crystal Palace, a better idea can be obtained of the general distribution of its parts than from any written description.

In plan it is a type of all the examples, consisting of a vast ellipse 622 feet × 513 feet. The height of the original façade (the three lower storeys of arcades) is 120 feet; including the later addition of the blank upper storey, it is 162 feet. The arena proper is 287 feet × 180 feet. The seats, in solid stone, rise up on all sides from the oval arena; underneath them are corridors and staircases. The dens for the wild beasts are immediately under the lowest tiers of seats, and consequently opened on to the arena as at Verona (No. 37).

The construction is strong and solid, and of an engineering character. The supports have been calculated at one-sixth of the whole area of the building. The system is one of concrete vaults resting on concrete walls, two feet three inches thick, faced with travertine stone four feet thick, and having an internal lining of nine inches of brickwork, making seven feet in total thickness. The details of the exterior orders are roughly executed; many of the plinth moulds, etc., are only roughly worked to a 45° splay.

37. AMPHI-THEATRE AT VERONA.

Interior View.

The radiating walls are cleverly constructed, concrete being used where least weight, tufa stone where more weight, and travertine stone where the most heavy pressures have to be supported.

The constructional idea consists of wedge-shaped piers radiating inwards, the vaults running downwards to the centre from the high inclosing walls (No. 36); consequently no building is more durable or more impossible to destroy— a feeling well expressed by the proverb:

" When falls the Colosseum, Rome shall fall."

If it has not come down to us in a perfect condition, it is because it was used as a stone quarry for Rome for centuries, many of the later buildings being erected with stones taken from this building alone.

In criticising the general architectural character of this wonderful building (No. 36), we may especially note: first, the multiplicity of its parts, three tiers of apparently count-less arcades encircling the exterior,. divided and united by three tiers of orders. Second, the grand sweeping lines of the unbroken entablatures running entirely round the building. Third, that the classic orders of architecture are purely decorative, and are piled one over the other, in strong contrast to the Grecian method of single orders. Fourthly, the weight of the structure is supported by the wall behind, the oval being divided into eighty arches en-circling the building.

There are other remains of amphitheatres, especially one in splendid preservation at **Verona**, in North Italy (No. 37), at **Nîmes** and **Arles** in France, and **Pola** in Istria, and also remains of a roughly-made example at Dorchester in Dorset.

TRIUMPHAL ARCHES AND PILLARS OF VICTORY.

The former were erected to generals and emperors, in honour of their victories, and were often placed at the entrance to cities.

In general arrangement they consisted of a lofty semi-circular central arch resting on an impost, with columns on either side. Besides architectural decorations they were also adorned with statuary.

An attic (or surmounting mass of stonework) was placed above, inscribed with the warlike deeds of the general to whom the monument was erected.

Ex. of single arch.—The Arch of Titus at Rome (A.D. 81).

The larger examples, *e.g.*, the Arch of Septimius Severus (No. 38), and that of Constantine, have smaller arches on either side of the central one.

> *Note.*—The Marble Arch in London will give a general idea of the arrangement in three arches; while that at Hyde Park Corner has but one.

Rostral columns were erected to celebrate naval victories, in which rostra, or prows of ships, are used in the ornamentation. In the time of the emperors they were numerous; a recital of the deeds which led to their erection was carved upon them.

Pillars of victory were usually placed in open courts, or in the Forum, and were surrounded by porticoes, whence the spectator could obtain views at various levels, and was thus able to read the inscriptions, and sculptured figures, with which some were decorated. Ex.: Trajan's column (page 60).

> "The sculptures wind aloft
> And lead, through various toils, up the rough steep
> The hero to the skies."

THE TOMBS

bear considerable similarity to Etruscan examples, whose influence should be noted.

(*a*.) **Caves** were hewn in the rock, or subterranean vaults, called Columbaria, were built and adorned with paintings and mosaics; internally were divisions or cells 3 feet by 3 feet, containing the sepulchral urn, in which the ashes of the deceased who had been cremated were placed, and upon which his name was carved.

(*b*.) **Monumental tombs.** These consisted of tower-

38. Arch of Septimus Severus, Rome.

shaped blocks, square or round, resting on a quadrangular substructure.

The Tomb of Cecilia Metella (B.C. 60), at Rome, has a basement, 100 feet square, on which rests a circular tower 94 feet in diameter, crowned probably with a conical roof.

One of the next important of these monumental tombs is the Tomb of Hadrian, now called the Castle of St. Angelo, on the banks of the Tiber at Rome.

It consists of a square basement, 340 feet each way, and 75 feet high, on which rests a circular tower 235 feet in diameter, and 140 feet in height. The sepulchral apartment is in the centre of the solid mass, and approached by a circular inclined plane, starting at the centre of the river front.

Some of these tombs must have appeared as artificial hills, being ascended by inclined roads, and planted with trees.

The Temple of Minerva Medica at Rome, whose origin is unknown, as also its date, is placed here, although Mr. Fergusson is inclined to think it was erected in later times. It was probably a Christian building, erected in the third century A.D. It has semicircular niches to nine of the sides, the tenth being the entrance; above are ten windows at the base of the dome to light the interior. The dome is polygonal on the exterior and interior, of concrete, ribbed with tiles, and bears a remarkable similarity to that of San Vitale at Ravenna.

> *N.B.*—The rudiments of the pendentive system are to be seen in the manner in which the dome is set on to the polygonal base; a system afterwards carried to great perfection by the Byzantines. The buttresses are placed at points where they are required, therefore thinner walls were used; this is an important step to Gothic principles. Compare in this respect the Pantheon.

(*c*.) The Egyptian **pyramidal form** is also used.

Example.—The Pyramid of Cestius at Rome.

(*d*.) **Smaller tombs** of various forms are generally erected at entrances to cities. Many are sarcophagus-shaped, resting on high basements; others resemble small temples.

Example.—The Street of Tombs at Pompeii.

> " Those ancient roads
> With tombs high verged, the solemn paths of Fame ;
> Deserve they not regard ! o'er whose broad flints
> Such crowds have roll'd ; so many storms of war,
> So many pomps, so many wondering realms."—DYER.

THE AQUEDUCTS AND BRIDGES

were really of a more engineering than architectural character, being in the main utilitarian. Rome had to be supplied with water from a distance, because of the badness and scarcity of the water on the spot, the Tiber being unfit for drinking purposes.

In any views of the Campagna round Rome, the ruined aqueducts are striking features. On approaching the Eternal City in the days of its glory, from all directions these enormous arched waterways must have seemed to the stranger to be converging into the centre. A view, from Windsor Castle ramparts, of the S.W.R. arched train-way winding across the valley of the Thames will give a faint idea of one only of such structures.

The principle of all the examples is similar—a level channel, lined with cement, is carried on arches, often in several tiers, and sometimes of immense height (say 100 feet) from the high ground, across valleys, to the city reservoir. Some examples have channels one above the other.

The **Aqua Claudia**, 45 miles long, and the "Anio novus," 62 miles long (date A.D. 48), entered the city on the same arches.

Perhaps the finest remaining, however, is the **Pont du Gard**, near Nîmes in France. It has three tiers of arches of rough masonry, spanning a valley at about 180 feet above the stream. The arches are rather lower in proportion than usual, the top tier being much smaller than the two below. It is strikingly impressive by the very simplicity of its bold design.

Bridges were firstly of wood, but on the introduction of the arch, stone was employed in their erection.

The characteristics of Roman bridges are that they are solid, sturdy, and built to last for ever. Many still remain, principally in the Roman provinces. A general feature is that the roadway was kept level throughout.

There are two types of Roman bridges in Spain, which equally impress the traveller, as for instance the extreme length of the many-arched example at Cordova; or the romantic sweep of the single arches that span the rocky valley of the Tagus at Toledo.

THE PALACES.

The ruins of the Roman palaces only remain, but there is enough to show their enormous extent and imposing character.

Examples.—The Palace of the Cæsars on the Palatine Hill, Rome, excavated largely by the Emperor Napoleon. The plan shows the reception and state apartments only, as the Tablinum, or throne room; the Basilica, or hall for administering justice; the Peristylium, a square garden surrounded by a colonnade; the Triclinium, or dining-hall, commanding a view of gardens beyond. These are all features which we may expect in each example, in addition to the many minor chambers of service, etc., whose uses cannot now be ascertained.

The Palatine remains are in fact a group of palaces, added to or reconstructed, by successive emperors, but the student of architecture visiting the site will most likely be more impressed with the giant remains attributed to Severus. Nero's golden house, preceded by an experimental palace, the "Transitorium," would seem to have exceeded the bounds of possibility, judging solely by the descriptions which alone have come down to us.

The Palace of Diocletian at Spalatro in Dalmatia (third century A.D.) is another famous example.

The **plan** consists of a parallelogram 592 feet × 698 feet, placed in an area of $9\frac{1}{2}$ English acres; the palace itself thus practically equalling in extent the Escurial in Spain.

It may be described as a royal country house, or better perhaps, as a château by the sea. It has a colonnade from end to end of the sea front, resting on a basement washed by the waves; terminated by towers, which, placed also along the landward façades, gave it the character of a Roman camp. On each of these façades, between such towers, were rich gateways; viz. the golden, iron, and brazen, ending the porticoed streets; which divided the inclosed area into four parts, each assigned to a particular purpose. The two northern portions were probably for the guests and principal officers of the household; while the whole of the southern portion was devoted to the palace, including two temples (see under circular temples, page 58). A circular vestibule formed an entrance to a suite of nine apartments overlooking the sea; here were placed the private apartments and baths of the emperor. The state rooms include an Imperial Basilica, or Hall of Justice.

Lining the inclosing walls of the whole area, on three sides, internally, were the cells that lodged the slaves and soldiers of the imperial retinue. The temple, and the more lofty halls of the palace proper, must have been visible above the inclosing walls in distant views by land and sea.

In architectural character it is noticeable for the debased style, in which broken and curved pediments with rococo detail occur. Its value, however, as a transitional example must not be overlooked. (It has been well illustrated in Adam's " Spalatro.")

THE DWELLINGS OF THE GREEKS AND ROMANS.

Allusions to these may be found in the Odyssey of Homer. Drs. Schliemann and Dörpfeld's discoveries at Tiryns and Mycenæ in Greece, and more especially the excavations at Pompeii, are the chief authorities on the subject.

In the early **Grecian** dwellings (see page 44) the rooms were grouped round an atrium or courtyard open in the centre. The women's quarters were singularly private, reached by tortuous passages and carefully planned door-ways, as evidenced in the excavations at Tiryns and Mycenæ. The women were placed in one part of the house, as in Turkish harems, and the men in the other.

The principle of seclusion was sought after, although there are no traces of doors having being used, the doorways

being probably hung with curtains. There were, it is supposed, windows, possibly unglazed.

The front part of the early Grecian house was the men's
portion, while in the Roman it was the public part of the
building. The back or secluded part of the Grecian house was
the women's abode, while in the Roman it was set aside for
the use of the family (No. 39).

From these comparisons we may note that the Romans
were not so seclusive as the Greeks.

Pompeii and Herculaneum.

The excavations at Pompeii have thrown considerable light
on this important subject. It has been supposed that these
remains differ little from the later Greek dwellings, as
Pompeii on the Bay of Naples was a Greco-Roman city. It
was overwhelmed by an eruption of Vesuvius in A.D. 79, and
buried by ashes, ten feet above the top of the houses.

Lytton's great novel, "The Last Days of Pompeii," will be
found of interest to the student as a description of the habits
and life of the Romans.

The streets of Pompeii were narrow, *i.e.*, 8, 12, or 15 feet
wide. The widest is 23 feet 6 inches, the roadway being
13 feet 6 inches, with two paths 10 feet. The houses had
plain fronts to the street, the frontage on either side of the
passage entrance being let off as shops.

The rooms are lighted from an internal courtyard called
an "atrium," as are Eastern houses to this day, and in
former days the inns of France and England.

The Pompeian houses are mostly of one storey in height,
but stairs and traces of upper floors exist, for such upper
storeys probably wood was used, but as a decree was passed
in the time of Augustus limiting the height of houses in
Rome to 75 feet, brick or masonry buildings must have
been carried out to a great height. The openings were
small, because the light is strong in the sunny climate of
Italy.

In the **House of Pansa** (No. 39), which may be taken
as a type of all, on entering from the street you pass
through a vestibule (see plan), and reach the atrium; which

serves as the public waiting-room for retainers and clients; from which the more private parts of the house were shut off. The atrium was open to the sky in the centre, with a " lean-to " or sloping roof round all four sides supported by brackets.

The impluvium, or " water cistern," for taking the water from these roofs, was sunk in the centre of the pavement, while round the atrium were grouped the front rooms, lit

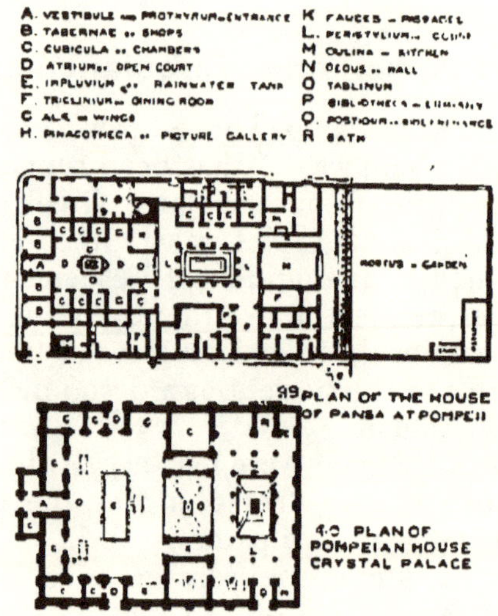

39 AND 40. PLANS OF POMPEIAN HOUSES.

through the doors, and probably used by servants or guests, or as semi-public rooms, *e.g.* libraries, etc.

An open saloon, or tablinum, with narrow passages, called " fauces," on either side, led to an inner court, or peristyle, often the garden of the house.

On the left of the peristyle are smaller rooms called "cubicula," or bedrooms, and the position of the triclinium, or dining-room, should be noted, with three couches for nine people to recline upon, the recognized number for a Roman dinner party, "not less than the Graces nor more than the Muses." Two such rooms were often required with differing aspects for winter and summer use.

The kitchen and pantry are in the side of the peristyle, furthest from the entrance.

The peristyle is the heart and centre of the private part of the house, and corresponded to the hall of Elizabethan times. Often a small shrine is placed in this part.

The Pompeian House at the Crystal Palace (No. 40), designed by the late Sir Digby Wyatt, is an exceedingly good reproduction of an ordinary Pompeian house. Notice especially the painted decorations, which are copies of original paintings at Pompeii. The darkest colours are placed nearest the ground, though sometimes the whole room was black, with centres of painted subjects in strong colours. The walls, at other times, are richly and fantastically painted with slender shafts, as of metal, with entablature, etc., in perspective; or else adorned with figure subjects of a gay character. The floors of these houses are of mosaic in black or white, or of rich and varied colouring.

4. COMPARATIVE.

GREEK.

A. **Plans.**—Their designs had refinement and beauty, proportion being of the first importance, and there was a dignity and grandeur of effect irrespective of the smallness of scale.

Unity was attained in the self-contained temples, while variety of grouping and some picturesqueness was attempted in the Propylæa and Erechtheion (No. 18, xii.).

Purity and severity of outline caused by the simple method of post and beam, which did not lend itself to such variety and boldness of planning as resulted from arcuated Roman style.

ROMAN.

A. **Plans.**—Designs bear a vast and magnificent impression, characteristic of a powerful and energetic race. The Romans were eminently great constructors, and knew how to handle the materials to hand. This constructive skill was acquired by the building of utilitarian works, such as aqueducts, bridges, etc., on a large scale; hence buildings have size and impress of power, which are their chief characteristics.

The arch, vault, and dome are the keynote to the whole system of Roman, and constitute a step toward Gothic

GREEK.	ROMAN.

No mixture of constructive principles is seen in the buildings of the Greeks, and the limits of their style have not been yet successfully expanded.

architecture. By the use of the arch, wide openings are rendered possible, and by vaults and domes large areas and complicated plans could be roofed (No. 18, xiii.).

Boldness and variety is introduced by the use of the vault, or continuous arch, leading to the system of intersecting vaults, by which the concentration of weights on piers is effected.

B. **Walls** constructed of large blocks of marble, without any mortar, allowing of refinement of treatment, and perfection of finish in construction. One-sixteenth of an inch was rubbed off the buildings on completion, this polishing being performed by slave labour. Jointing was not reckoned as a means of effect. Stability was achieved solely by the judicious observance of the laws of gravity, for mortar was unused, the adherence of the blocks of marble not being necessary, for the weights in these structures only acted vertically, and needed but vertical resistance. In fact, the employment of hewn stone or marble directly shaped the development of the style.

B **Walls** often constructed of small, mean, and coarse materials, such as brick, rubble, and concrete, with brick or marble facing, bond courses for strength being introduced. Such walls executed in rough materials as mentioned, are thus often coarse in character. Notice also haste in execution ; in the Colosseum, plinths will be noticed axed off at forty-five degrees. In the haste to complete for occupation, doubtless many buildings were never perfectly finished. By their extended use of concrete, it may be said that they inaugurated the employment, in large masses, of irregular materials, reduced into fragments and bound together by mortar. The materials which they made use of were not special to any country, but consisted of fragments of stone or hard rock and quarry *débris*, all of which sufficed for the most important projects.

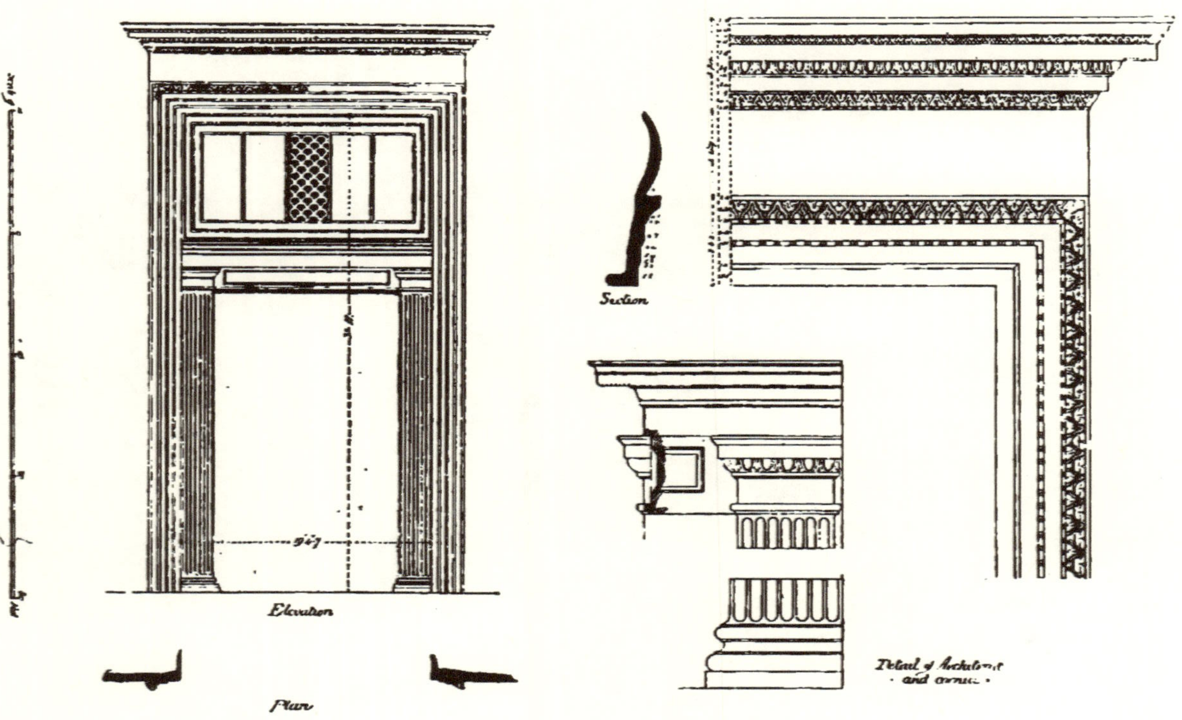

41. ROMAN DOORWAY FROM THE PANTHEON.

GREEK.

c. **Openings** are of minor importance, the columnar treatment giving the necessary light and shade. Doorways are square-headed, and often crowned with a cornice supported by consoles (No. 28).

D. **Roofs.**—Extreme care was bestowed upon the elaborately constructed, and highly finished, roofs of the temples. Large slabs of marble were joined by cover pieces, which at the eaves were finished with beautifully designed and carved antefixæ (Nos. 15, 25, 27). Ceilings were coffered in stone, with effectively carved members in the angles of the square recesses. Probably coffered ceilings in framed timber roofed over the large spans of the cellæ.

E. **Columns.**—The orders are a *structural* necessity wherever used. The column and beam are the keynote of Greek architecture.

The **Tuscan Order** was not employed by the Greeks.

ROMAN.

c. **Openings** form an important feature in the building, and are square-headed (No. 41) or circular, principally the latter. The semicircle divided vertically by two mullion piers is a favourite type of window.

D. **Roofs.**—Bronze was employed in some notable buildings, as in the Pantheon and some other temples. As the Etruscans roofed like the Greeks, but with terra cotta, the Romans may have continued the practice. Flat terrace roofs were certainly used (see Vitruvius, and the remains at Pompeii). It is thought that built-up trusses of T iron and concrete forming such terraces, covered some of the large halls of the baths.

For ceilings, the noble vaults described before constituted the greatest Roman development. From Horace we learn that splendid coffered wooden ceilings were used in the houses of the rich.

E. **Columns.**—The orders are used in connection with the arch, and gradually lose their structural intention, being used in a *decorative* manner, as in the Colosseum at Rome.

The **Tuscan Order** is a variation from the Doric; the column has, however, no fluting, and there are no triglyphs in the cornice.

GREEK.

The **Doric Order** (No. 20) was largely used by the Greeks, their most important buildings being erected in this order. It was used without a base, the capital having a plain square abacus, beneath which is the echinus (No. 29), whose outline varies in different examples. The proportions of the columns proceed from extreme sturdiness in the early examples to great refinement in the late ones, and the shaft is always fluted. The architrave overhangs the face of the column (No. 20). In the frieze, the triglyphs are over the central axis of the columns, except to those bounding the façade, where the columns are brought closer together, and the triglyph is placed at the angle of the frieze (No. 20).

The **Ionic Order** (No. 23) was used with great refinement by the Greeks. The distinctive capital has the scrolls showing on two sides only, although an example of the method adopted by the Romans is found in a special case at Bassæ.

The **Corinthian Order** (No. 25) was little used by the Greeks; the examples remaining are thought by some to indicate the decline of Greek art, in that sculpture, as such, now gave way to mere carving.

ROMAN.

St. Paul's Church, Covent Garden, is a good modern example by Inigo Jones.

The **Doric Order** (No. 21) was little used by the Romans, not being suited to their ideas of splendour and magnificence. The Romans added a base, varied the capital by adding extra mouldings to the abacus, altered the outline of the echinus, and modified the cornice by reducing its importance. The flutes were sometimes omitted in the shafts of the columns, and the proportions are less sturdy. The architrave does not overhang the face of the column, but is in a line vertical with it (No. 21). In the frieze the triglyph comes over the central axis of the column even at the angle.

The **Ionic Order** (No. 24) has its cornice further enriched. The capital is made uniform all round by the volutes being placed angleways, thus showing the face of the scrolls on each side.

The **Corinthian Order** (No. 26) was the favourite of the Romans; it was used in the largest temples, as those of Jupiter Stator and Jupiter Tonans at Rome. The capital is rich, though often coarse, the acanthus leaves

GREEK.

In Greece, the order was not introduced till the later age, and then appears to have been used in small buildings, only such as the choragic monument of Lysicrates and the octagonal Tower of the Winds at Athens. The Temple of Jupiter Olympius at Athens may be considered a Roman building. (See page 56.)

The **Composite Order** was never used by the Greeks.

F. **Mouldings.**—The Greeks relied for effect on the graceful contour of their mouldings, which approach conic sections in profile. The mouldings, though often covered with delicately carved enrichments, never lose the idea of grace of outline which the decoration seems but to enhance. Being executed in a fine grained marble, it is often so much undercut as to produce a lace-like effect. (See Nos. 29 and 31.)

G. **Decoration** (No. 31).—In sculpture the Greeks have never been surpassed,

ROMAN.

often bordering on naturalism.

The entablature is over-ornamented, especially the architrave, or lower member. An explanation for this has been found in the supposition that the Romans carved in ornamental patterns what the Greeks had only painted.

The cornice has carved consoles, which also tend to enrich it, and which do not appear in the few Greek examples which are left to us.

The **Composite Order** was invented by the Romans by placing the upper portion of the Ionic capital upon the lower part of the Corinthian. In other details the order follows the Corinthian, but with additional ornamentation.

F. **Mouldings.** — The Romans relied on the rich carving cut upon their mouldings ; ostentation replaces refinement. In the latest examples, every member being carved, a certain rich picturesqueness of fretted surfaces is produced in cornices and dressings.

Roman mouldings are nearly always parts of a circle in section, while the execution is often very careless. (See Nos. 30 and 31.)

G. **Decoration** (No. 31).— The Romans did not excel in either sculpture or paint-

GREEK.

whether in isolated groups or in works within the boundaries of an architectural framing, as at the Parthenon. In painting we know of Polygnotus and other great artists being employed upon the temples and other buildings. Part of the Propylæa was known as the Painted Loggia. The early frescoes were probably in the style of the vase painters of that period, while the later, if we may judge from the provincial imitations of Pompeii, must have been grand in style and decorative in effect.

ROMAN.

ing. Greek artists were employed, and Greek examples were prized and copied. In later times both vaults and floors worthy of note were produced in mosaic, but many examples show great vulgarity of sentiment. In the case of marble, for wall facings and floors, it is probable that rich and good effects were produced, as the Romans were connoisseurs in marbles, which they sought out and imported from all countries. The origin of the ox-heads connected with garlands, so frequently carved on Roman friezes, is supposed to be copied from the actual skulls and garlands which were hung for decoration on altars at which the beasts to which they belonged had been slain.

5. REFERENCE BOOKS.

Taylor and Cresy's "Antiquities of Rome."
Adam's "Spalatro."
Isabelle's "Edifices circulaires."
Wood and Dawkins, "Palmyra and Baalbec."
Piranesi's "Architectura di Romani."
Viollet-le-Duc, "Habitations of Man in all Ages."
Tatham, "Classic Ornament."
Spiers, Mauch, and Chambers for the Classic "Orders."
Vulliamy's "Classic Ornament."
"Roman Life in the Days of Cicero," by A. J. Church. (Historical Novel.)
A visit should be made to the Roman and Pompeian Courts at the Crystal Palace; also to the British Museum.

EARLY CHRISTIAN OR EARLY ROMANESQUE IN ROME AND ITALY.

1. INFLUENCES.

i. **Geographical.**—See under Rome. The position of Rome as the centre of a world-wide empire should be remembered. " All roads lead to Rome," and Christianity, to become universal, had to grow up at the capital, however eastern its birthplace.

ii. **Geological.**—The quarry of the ruins of ancient buildings influenced the work of the period, both in construction and decorative treatment; the "opus Alexandrinum" pavement is based on the nuclei of slices of old columns, bound together by patterns, formed of fragments of ancient marbles and porphyries.

iii. **Climate.**—See under Roman Architecture.

iv. **Religion.**—In A.D. 313 Constantine issued his celebrated decree from Milan, according to Christianity equal rights with all other religions. Constantine professed Christianity himself in A.D. 323, which then became the religion of the empire.

This step led to the practical establishment of Christianity as the State religion, and the Christians, who up till then were a persecuted sect, and had worshipped in the Catacombs, or burial-places of the early Christians, were now able to hold their services openly and freely.

The Council of Nice, A.D. 325, is called by Constantine, and was the first of several Councils of the Church, for the settlement of disputes about heresies.

A temporary reaction takes place in A.D. 360-363, under Julian, known as the " Apostate."

v. Social and Political.—On changing the capital of the empire from Rome to Byzantium in A.D. 324 Constantine practically reigns as an absolute monarch, the old Roman political system coming to an end.

The series of emperors in the West came to an end in A.D. 476, and the empire was nominally reunited, Zeno reigning at Constantinople over the Western and Eastern Empires.

Theodoric the Goth reigns in Italy A.D. 493-526, and this was a period of peace and prosperity.

From the Roman or common speech several of the chief languages of modern Europe commenced to arise, and in consequence are called *Romance* languages.

vi. Historical.—The Early Christian period is generally taken as lasting from Constantine to Gregory the Great, or from A.D. 300 to 600. The period of the Teutonic invasions of Italy commenced about A.D. 376, and Teutonic settlements took place within the empire about this time, these movements being caused by the incursions of the Huns into Germany.

The West Goths sacked Rome under Alaric in A.D. 410. The rise of a Gothic kingdom took place in Spain and Southern Gaul. The defeat of Attila, king of the Huns, at the battle of Châlons, A.D. 451, aids in consolidating Christianity in Europe.

Note.—One style evolves from any other so gradually, that it is impossible to say exactly where the one ended and the next began. This gradual growth characterizes progress in other departments as well as Architecture. Each age feels its way towards the expression of its own ideals, modifying the art of the past to meet the fresh conditions under which it lives. The reign of Gregory the Great (A.D. 590 to A.D. 603) is that in which the Latin language and Roman architecture in its latest forms ceased to exist in this distinctive type of Early Christian architecture.

For the next two centuries architecture was practically at a standstill in Europe, at the end of which period the old Roman traditions were to a great extent thrown aside, and the later Romanesque architecture was gradually evolved.

2. ARCHITECTURAL CHARACTER.

Naturally little money was at the command of the early Christians; therefore, where possible, they adapted the ancient basilicas, which were ready to their hand, for their own places of worship; and in cases where they erected new ones, such were generally built from the remains of ancient Roman buildings in the vicinity; and were often situated over the entrances to their former hiding-places or crypts. Thus in these early Christian basilicas in Rome we find columns with various ancient capitals, with shafts of various lengths, with or without bases, and made up by the addition of new pieces of stone, or even by double bases.

On this account, although extremely interesting from an archæological point of view, the buildings can hardly have, in the architect's mind at least, the value for study, which a new manner in architecture, arising from new structural necessities, is certain to possess.

The earlier basilicas had their columns closely spaced, and were crowned with the entablature which supported the main wall, on which rested the wooden roof (No. 46).

As the arch came more into general use these columns could be spaced further apart, being connected by semi-circular arches (No. 45).

The architectural character is impressive and dignified; the apparent size of the basilicas is increased by the long perspective of the columns, and the comparative lowness of the interiors in proportion to their length.

3. EXAMPLES.

EARLY BASILICAN CHURCHES.

The remarkable manner in which the basilicas, or Roman halls of justice, lent themselves to the purpose and uses of the early Christians, made them the stepping-stones from the Classic of pre-Christian times to the Gothic architecture of the Middle Ages, which thus may be said to commence with these basilican churches.

It should here be mentioned, however, that some authorities believe the early Christian churches to have grown out of the Roman dwelling-house, where at first the community were in the habit of assembling, or from the class-room where philosophers used to teach.

How suitable the Roman basilica was for Christian worship is easily seen from the plan of the well-preserved example of St. Clemente at Rome (Nos. 42 and 43).

The **bishop** took the place formerly occupied by the "**prætor,**" or "**questor,**" until in subsequent ages the seat was moved to the side, becoming the bishop's throne.

The **presbyters**, or members of council of the early Church, took the seats on either side of the bishop formerly occupied by the **assessors**. The apse became the chancel, whose form remained circular-ended in North Europe.

The **altar** in front of the apse, formerly used by the Romans for the pouring out of libations, or sacrifices to their gods, was now used for the celebration of Christian rites (No. 44). A *baldachino*, or canopy, was erected over the altar, which after a time was moved back, and placed against the east wall of the apse.

A **choir** was introduced, abutting into the nave (No. 43). It was inclosed by low screen walls, or "cancelli" (from which the word chancel is derived), and provided with two pulpits, or "ambos," from one of which the gospel was read, and from the other the epistle (No. 44).

A **transept**, called the "bema," or "presbytery," which existed in a modified form in the basilicas themselves, was occasionally introduced, converting the plan into a Latin

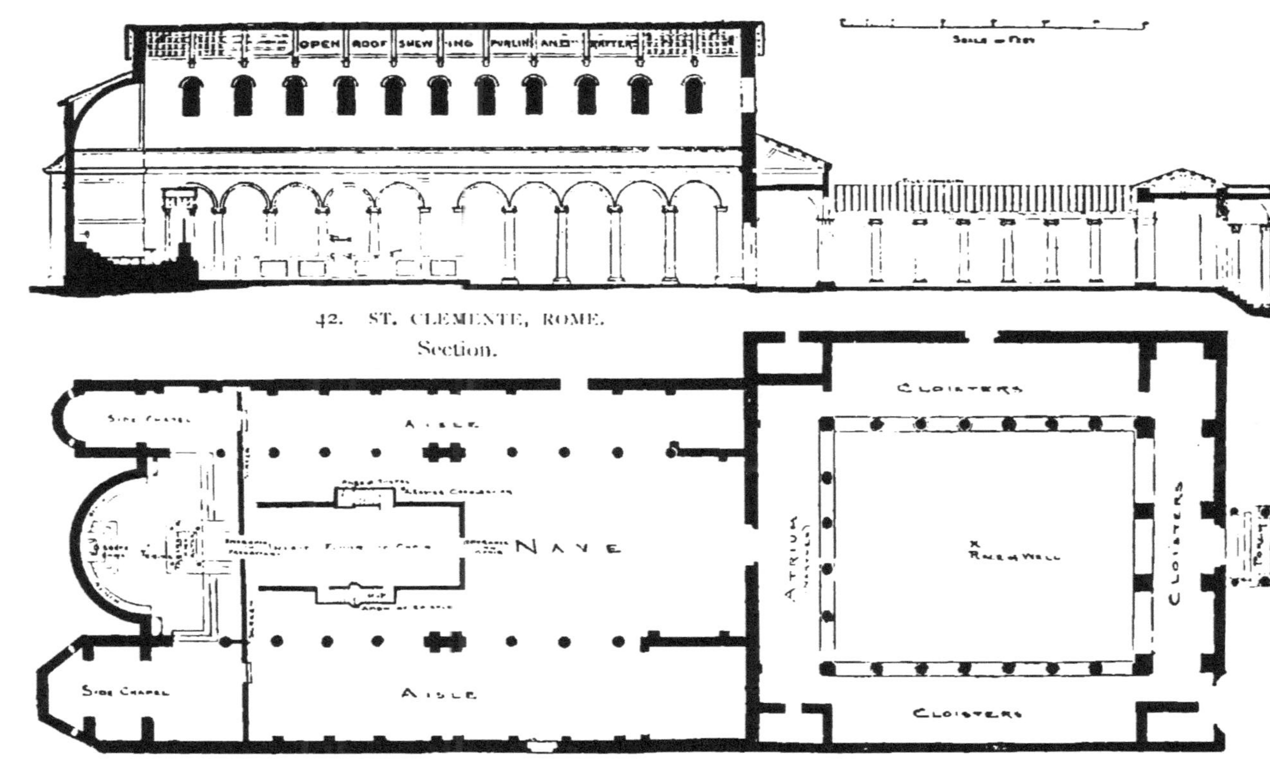

42.   ST. CLEMENTE, ROME.
Section.

44.　THE BASILICA CHURCH OF S. CLEMENTE, ROME.
Showing projecting choir and apsidal treatment

cross, of which the nave was the long arm.   Some consider, however, that this cruciform ground plan was derived from the buildings erected for sepulchral purposes as early as the age of Constantine.

In a few examples, **galleries**, sometimes called "tribunes," were introduced for women.   Where none existed, the women were seated on one side of the nave and the men on the other.   These Basilican churches have usually three aisles, but St. Paul's, St. Peter's, and St. John Lateran have five aisles.   St. Agnes and St. Lorenzo have their side aisles in two heights.   The aisles are generally half the width of the nave, or central aisle, the latter being lit by a clerestory of small windows.

Among the glories of these ancient buildings are the mosaics.   The apse was generally vaulted with a semi-dome (No. 44), and covered with mosaics, having a central figure of Christ seated in glory relieved against a gold background.

> " Below was all mosaic choicely planned,
> With cycles of the human tale."

The pavements of marble and mosaic are extremely fine and characteristic, as at St. Clemente.   These pavements were made out of the abundant store of ancient marbles existing in Rome.   Slices of old columns formed the centres, round which bands of geometrical inlay were twisted in intricate designs.

The grand decorative effect of these accessories must not be forgotten in criticising the buildings of this style.

Externally the building was approached through an " atrium," or fore-court, probably derived from the Roman "forum ;" the covered portion next the church was the "narthex," or place for penitents (No. 43).   In the centre of the atrium stood a fountain or well, used by the pilgrims to wash their hands before entering the holy place, a custom which survives in an altered form, as when Catholics dip their fingers into the stoop, or holy-water basin, placed against the entrance of a church.

The atrium survived through the Gothic ages in England, but was placed, as will be seen, in a different position, and called the " cloisters."

Remains.—The old Basilica of St. Peter's had a
"transept," or "bema," 55 feet wide, and of the height of
the nave (113 feet). Five arches, the centre called the
arch of triumph, gave access from the body of the church.
At the end was a semicircular apse on a raised floor, in the
centre of the back wall of which was the Pope's seat. The
priest stood behind the altar, and thus the orientation was
the reverse of the English practice.

Other examples :

There were in all thirty-one Basilican churches in Rome,
mostly made up of fragments of earlier pagan buildings.
The interior of these basilicas is impressive and severe, the
repetition of the long rows of columns being grand in the
extreme, as in the interior view of St. Paul's (No. 45), and
S. Maria Maggiore (No. 46).

There are also important remains at **Ravenna**, a city well
situated for receiving the influence of Constantinople, and at
one time the seat of an Exarch of the Empire. The
principal building is the octagonal church of San Vitale
(see page 94), which has been included in the Byzantine
style.

At **Torcello**, near Venice, the foundations of the original
bishop's throne, surrounded by six rows of seats in the apse,
still exists, giving one a good idea of the Early Christian
arrangements.

BAPTISTERIES

are another description of building met with in Early
Christian architecture. They were originally used only for
the sacrament of baptism; hence the name "Baptistery."
The form was derived from the Roman circular temples
and tombs, already described. Until the end of the sixth
century A.D. the baptistery appears to have been a distinct
building; but after this period the font came to be placed
in the vestibule of the church. There was generally one
baptistery in each city, as at Ravenna and Florence, and it
was as a rule a detached building, but usually adjoined the
atrium or fore-court.

In adopting the Roman tombs as their models for these

46. BASILICA OF S. MARIA MAGGIORE, ROME.
Interior.

buildings, the early Christians modified them to some extent, *e.g.*, in the Pantheon, and elsewhere, the columns were *not* used internally for constructive purposes, but simply for decoration. The early Christians, however, supported the walls carrying their domes by means of columns used constructively. It will be seen that to cover a large area with one dome was difficult, and if we imagine the addition of an aisle in one storey round a moderate-sized circular tomb, the inner walls being replaced by columns in the lower half, we shall arrive at just such a building as these early baptisteries (No. 47).

Examples in and near Rome.

The Baptistery of Constantine at Rome is octagonal, the roof is supported by a screen of eight columns two storeys in height.

St. Stephano Rotundo (sixth century A.D.) (No. 47) is 210 feet in diameter, and has its roof supported on two circular rings of columns, all taken from older buildings.

The Baptistery of St. Agnese, between Naples and Salerno, is circular; it has two rows of columns, is 80 feet in diameter, and has a central elliptical dome. This building is vaulted and covered with a wooden roof, and it appears that this is the first time that the latter is introduced in conjunction with the former, as the Roman architects always allowed the stone vault to show externally (ex. the Pantheon). In the case of St. Agnese, however, the vault is merely an internal ceiling which is covered with an external wooden roof. This is similar to the practice of Gothic architects, who, in the mediæval period, covered the stone vaults of their churches with timber roofs.

4. COMPARATIVE.

A. **Plan.**—The early Christians adopted the Basilican form for their churches (Nos. 42, 43). See also page 83.

Besides the basilicas, the halls, baths, dwelling-houses, and even the pagan temples were used by the Christians for places of worship.

An isolated circular church (see above), generally attached

to the chief Basilica (or cathedral), was used as a baptistery.[1]

B. **Walls** were still constructed according to the Roman methods, which, however, became more and more debased as time went on. Rubble or concrete walling was used, faced with plaster, brick, or stone; mosaic was used internally, and sometimes externally on the west façades for decorative purposes.

C. **Openings.**—In regard to the doors and windows, we find they were generally arched, the use of the lintel being dispensed with. The form of the arch was semicircular, and the window openings were small; the aisles were lighted by windows in the aisle wall, and the nave by clerestory windows, a feature to be further developed in the later Gothic architecture. (See Nos. 42, 45.)

D. **Roofs.**—Wooden roofs (Nos. 42, 44, 45) covered the central nave, a simple form of construction such as King and Queen post trusses being employed. Fergusson considers that these roofs were ceiled in some ornamental manner, the decoration of a visible framework being of a later date, as at S. Miniato, Florence (No. 62). The side aisles in the later basilica churches were occasionally vaulted,

---

[1] In later Romanesque and Gothic periods, these early baptisteries, themselves founded on the Roman circular temples and tombs, were treated as follows in the different European countries :

In **Italy**, where the churches are not derived from a combination of a circular eastern church with a western rectangular nave, as in France, but are direct copies of the Roman basilica; we find that the circular Roman building develops into a baptistery, which always stands apart, not becoming part of the church.

In **France**, circular churches were built to stand alone, and when it was necessary to enlarge them, the circular building was retained as the sanctuary or choir, and a straight lined nave was added for the use of the people. Thus the circular church originated the apsidal choir of later times.

In **Germany**, the earlier baptistery was joined to the square church, and formed a western apse. The Germans also built circular churches, and then added choirs for the priests, that they might pray apart from the people.

In **England**, the Romanesque and Gothic builders generally preferred a square east end, except where French influence made itself felt, as at Westminster. Circular churches were erected, as the Temple Church, London, but they were few in number, and due to the Knights Templars, being built as copies of the Holy Sepulchre at Jerusalem.

47.   ST. STEPHANO ROTUNDO, ROME.
Interior.

and the apse was usually domed and lined with mosaic (Nos. 44, 45, 46).

E. **Columns** are the most interesting feature of what we may call the Basilica style; they were mostly fragments of earlier Roman buildings which had either fallen into ruins or were destroyed for the purpose. For this reason on visiting an interior you will often find them of different design, size, and treatment (No. 47). It was natural that the early Christian builders, not being good craftsmen themselves, should use in their buildings the materials and ornaments which were ready to hand, and which had been left by the pagan Roman. The rich and grandiose effect which is the character of these buildings was thus easily obtained, but often at the expense of fitness in the details of the design.

F. **Mouldings** are coarse variations of Roman types, and the carving is of the rudest kind, though rich in general effect. Technique, or the power of handling tools, had been gradually declining since the time of the Greeks, and the progressive decay continued.

Enrichments were in low relief, and incised upon mouldings. and the acanthus leaf, although copied still from the antique, became more conventional in form.

G. **Decoration.**—The introduction of much colour into interiors is a feature of the period.

The apse, as has been mentioned, was domed and lined with mosaic, the subject generally being Christ surrounded by angels and saints (No. 44).

The arch of triumph preceding the apse is occupied with appropriate subjects, and long friezes of figures line the wall above the nave arcades. The wall spaces between the clerestory windows have subjects drawn from Christian history or doctrine (Nos. 44, 45, 46).

The figures are treated in strong colours on a gold background. The design is bold and simple, both in form and draperies, and an earnest and solemn expression, fitting well the position they occupy, characterizes the groups. The method of execution is coarse and large, and no attempt is made at neatness of joint or regularity of bedding. The interiors, while bright and free from gloom, are, by the aid of these mosaics, full of solemnity.

It will be seen that besides having regard to the internal effect of the walls, thus coloured with mosaics, they also employed pavements of coloured marbles, laid out in geometrical patterns, adding greatly to the rich effect of their interiors.   These pavements were formed largely of slices from the old Roman porphyry columns, which were worked into designs by connecting bands of geometrical inlay on a field of white marble. A good idea of this work, called "opus Alexandrinum," may be seen in the chancel of Westminster Abbey.

Of a finer and more delicate expression was the glass mosaic used to decorate the ambos, screens, and episcopal chairs. Ex. : the furniture of the church of San Clemente at Rome (No. 44).

5. REFERENCE BOOKS.

Hubsch, " Monuments de l'architecture Chrétienne depuis Constantin jusqu'à Charlemagne."
Bunsen's " Christian Basilicas of Rome."
Prof. Baldwin Brown's " From Schola to Cathedral."
" Hypatia," by Charles Kingsley (historical novel dealing with the period).

BYZANTINE ARCHITECTURE.

" So fair a church as this had Venice none :
The walls were of discolored Jasper stone
Wherein was Christos carved ; and overhead
A lively vine of green sea agate spread."—CHAUCER.

1. INFLUENCES.

i. **Geographical.**—Geographically speaking, Constantinople occupies the finest site in Europe, standing on a bold peninsula between the Sea of Marmora and the curved inlet called the "Golden Horn." It is called "Rome" by the Turks of Asia, and, like the other Rome in Italy, it rests on seven hills. It occupies one of the most important commercial sites on the globe, standing at the intersection of the two great highways of commerce— the water high-road from the Black Sea into the Mediterranean, and the land high-road from Asia into Europe : a position which, in the times of which we are writing, gave it power and influence.

ii. **Geological.**—As far as possible the materials upon the spot had to be employed. The cupola of Santa Sophia is of pumice and bricks from the island of Rhodes. The walling consists of brick, faced with marble. The bulk of the marble used in Santa Sophia and in Constantinople generally, is local as regards the Mediterranean.

A writer on the subject, Mr. Brindley, is of opinion that quite seventy-five per cent. of the coloured marble used in Santa Sophia, and the other churches and mosques in Constantinople, is Thessalian green (Verde Antico). He supposes that the architect was influenced by the kind of column likely to be at once obtainable, as the quarries were situated in different parts of the empire, and were worked by convict labour, the monolith columns being worked in groups of sizes such as the quarry could produce.

iii. **Climate.**—Being further east than Rome, and having a hotter climate, Oriental customs in building had to be assimilated by the Romans, on settling at Constantinople.

iv. **Religion.**—It was Constantine who first made Christianity the state religion. The political division that came to pass between east and west was followed by a separation of churches also. The east declined to go with the west in adding to a creed (the Filioque controversy) and still claims to be the orthodox church. The iconoclastic movement ended in the admission of painted figures in the decoration of churches, but all sculptured statues are excluded. These and other points of ritual difference have vitally affected eastern church architecture.

v. **Social and Political.**—The geographical position of Constantinople insures the presence of a large trading community. Constantine removed the capital there from Rome in A.D. 323. His system of government was an expansion of the despotic methods introduced by Diocletian. After his death rival emperors troubled the state, and disputes in the church were rife—the Council of Nice in A.D. 325 was the first of the general councils called to suppress heresies. During the eighth and ninth centuries the iconoclastic movement was in force. The eastern emperors lost all power in Italy, by endeavouring to force their policy in this matter upon the west. By the election of Charlemagne, chosen Emperor of the West in A.D. 800, the Roman empire was finally divided.

vi. **Historical.**—Byzantium was a Greek colony in the fourth century B.C. Byzantine architecture is that which was developed at Byzantium, or Constantinople, on the removal of the capital of the Roman Empire to that city, in the fourth century A.D. by Constantine. This style was carried on until the city fell into the hands of the Turks in 1453, when it became the capital of the Ottoman empire. During the reign of Justinian (A.D. 527-565), who erected Santa Sophia at Constantinople, the whole of Italy was recovered to the Eastern Empire, accounting for the style of some of the buildings in Italy which we shall notice.

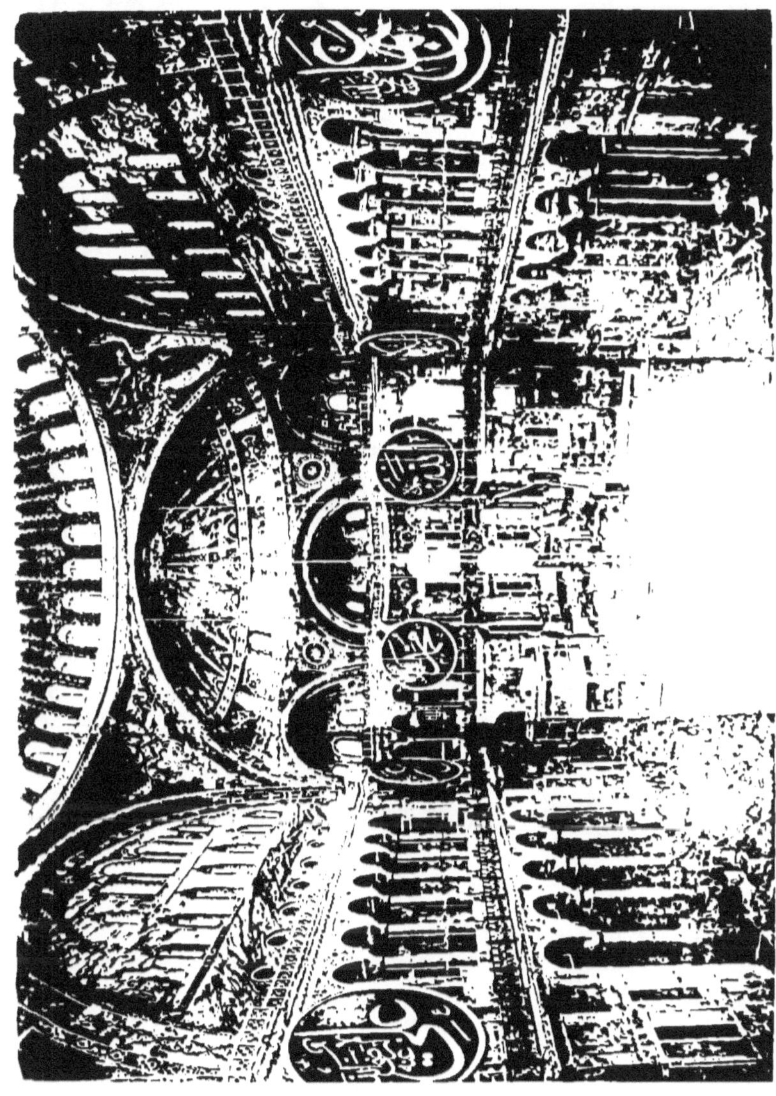

50.   SANTA SOPHIA, CONSTANTINOPLE.

Thus the Byzantine style includes not only the style developed in Byzantium itself, but also those buildings which were erected elsewhere under her influence, the chief of which we shall notice in this section. After the defeat of the Visigoths, Italy was placed under the rule of a delegate of the Byzantine Emperor, who had his seat at Ravenna, a city which during this period rivalled Rome in importance, and where consequently we find some important examples of the style.

2. ARCHITECTURAL CHARACTER.

The change from the old Roman forms was of course gradual, but in the course of 200 years the East asserted herself, and under Justinian, in the sixth century, the Church of Santa Sophia (Nos. 48, 49, and 50) was erected, and remains the greatest achievement of the style—being perhaps the most satisfactory of all domed interiors.

The general architectural character depends on the development of the dome, in contrast with the Romanesque style, which we shall see developed the vault in Western and Northern Europe.

The **dome** is the prevailing *motif* or idea of Byzantine architecture, and had been a traditional feature in the old architecture of the East. M. Choisy, in his "Art de Bâtir chez les Byzantins," traces the influence of this Oriental tradition on Greek architecture, to show how from this fusion the later imperial architecture proceeded. The classic orders are dispensed with, and the arches (semicircular) rest directly on columns. In the interiors, carving and sculpture give way to grand decorative work in coloured mosaic on a background of massive gold, covering the whole surface of the wall.

In the exteriors (Nos. 50 and 53) the grouping of the smaller domes round the larger central one was very effective, one of the most remarkable peculiarities of these churches being that the tunnel vault retains its form externally, as in the case of a dome (No. 50). In no style does the elevation so closely correspond with the section, as in the

Byzantine.   An attempt was made to render the rough brick exteriors of Roman times more pleasing, by the use of bands and relieving arches of an ornamental character.

Byzantine art was carried westward by traders through the needs of commerce, and we find at St. Mark's, Venice, at St. Vitale, Ravenna, at St. Front Périgueux, France, and elsewhere, Byzantine influences at work, which account for, and largely direct, the architecture of those districts.

3. EXAMPLES.

Santa Sophia at Constantinople

(Nos. 48, 49, 50) was built by order of Justinian in A.D. 532-537, the architects being Anthemius of Tralles and Isodorus of Miletus.

The plan (No. 48) consists of a central space bounded by four massive piers, 25 feet square, connected by semi-circular arches, and supporting a dome of 106 feet in diameter, rising 180 feet above the pavement.   The base of this dome is pierced by forty small windows, lighting the centre area (No. 49).   Against the eastern and western arches of the dome abut half-domes; thus a long oval interior is formed.   Within the depth of the south and north arches are galleries in two storeys, the upper being for women.   In the spandrel walls, which stand up on the front line of the gallery arcades, are ranged tiers of narrow windows giving additional lighting to the interior (No. 49). The two storeys of arcaded galleries, the numerous small windows, all these in the relation of their parts, give scale to the interior.   The abutment of these side arches of the dome, not having half-domes resting against them, is taken by huge external buttresses.   Out of these half-domes grow smaller semi-domes.   The floor space is made rectangular by the angles being filled in with domes.

"Simple as is the primary ideal, the actual effect is one of great intricacy, and of continuous gradation of parts, from the small arcades up to the stupendous dome, which hangs, with little apparent support, like a vast bubble over the centre, or as Procopius, who witnessed its erection,

is two storeys in height, the lower storey being a decagon containing a cruciform crypt. It is 45 feet in diameter; each face is pierced with a niche. Traces remain of an external arcade round the lower portion, standing on the decagonal basement. The roof consists of one slab of stone, hollowed out in the form of a flat dome, 35 feet

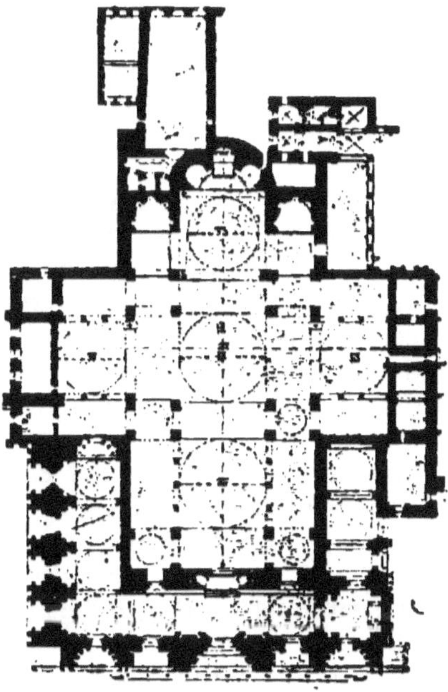

51. ST. MARK'S, VENICE. PLAN.

in diameter, and round the edge of this block are stone handles, originally used to place this immense covering in position. The ashes of the founder were placed in an urn on the top of the covering.

St. Mark's at Venice

(Nos. 51, 52, 53) was erected A.D. 977-1071. Venice was by situation the connecting link between the Byzantine and Franconian empires, and the great depôt of the traffic between the East and West. This influence is shown in her buildings.

The **plan** of St. Mark's (No. 51) is in the form of a Greek cross, of equal arms, covered by a dome in the centre (42 feet diameter), and one over each arm of the cross. It is derived from the Church of the Holy Apostles at Constantinople (the second type of Byzantine plan), which was pulled down by Mahomet II. in the fifteenth century. A point in the plan is that the square piers, which carry the dome, are pierced on the ground floor and gallery levels; the gallery arcade connects the piers on either side, the depth of the gallery being that of the pier.

Notice the vestibules filling out the western arm of the cross to a square.

The interior (No. 52) is rich with coloured marbles casing the lower part of the walls; above, and extending in one great surface over vault and dome, is a lining of richly coloured glass mosaic, in which are worked figures of saints mingled with scenes from their lives, set off by a broad background of gold. Mosaic, in fact, is the real and essential decoration of the church, to which all architectural detail is subordinated.

The exterior façade (No. 53) has five entrances enriched with shafts of many-coloured marbles, brought from Alexandria, and the ruined cities of the East, forming a rich and beautiful portal. Mosaic panels also serve to enrich with colour the spandrels of the arches. It must be remembered that this and the external domes are a later casing upon the original exterior of the usual Byzantine type.

Note.—"The effects of St. Mark's depend not only upon the most delicate sculpture in every part, but, as we have just stated, eminently on its colour also, and that the most subtle, variable, inexpressible colour in the world—the colour of glass, of transparent alabaster, of polished marble, and of lustrous gold."—RUSKIN.

4. COMPARATIVE.

A. The **plans** of Byzantine churches are all distinguished by a great central square space covered with a dome, supported by means of pendentives, clearly shown in No. 49.

On each side extend short arms, forming a Greek cross on plan, which with the narthex and side galleries make the plan nearly square. The narthex was placed within the main walls.

| Compare : | AN EARLY CHRISTIAN |
A BYZANTINE CHURCH.	BASILICA.
The eye is drawn to the centre of the building to the great central dome.	The form compels us to look towards the apsidal termination.
The leading thought is vertical by the grouping of domes round a principal central dome.	The leading idea is horizontal by a long perspective of columns.

B. **Walls.**—In general we find that all the oriental love of magnificence was developed internally, while externally the buildings are comparatively plain. Internally, marble casing and mosaic were applied to the walls, often constructed of brick. Therefore a flat treatment and absence of mouldings prevailed. Externally the façade is sometimes relieved by alternate rows of stone and brick, in various colours.

C. **Openings.**—Doors and windows are semicircular headed, but segmental and horse-shoe arched openings are sometimes met with.

The windows are small and grouped together. The universal employment of mosaic in Byzantine churches, and the consequent exclusion of painted glass, rendered the use of such large windows as the Gothic architects employed quite inadmissible, and in such a climate very much smaller openings sufficed to admit all the light that was required. Tracery was, in consequence, practically non-existent as a northern architect would understand it.

The churches depend largely for light on the ring of windows at the base of the dome, or in the "drum," or circular base on which the dome is raised, and upon openings grouped in the gable ends.

Such windows, grouped in tiers within the semicircular arch beneath the dome, are a great feature in the style (Nos. 49, 52).

D. **Roofs.**—The method of covering these buildings consisted of a series of domes formed in brick, stone, or concrete, with frequently no further external covering. In S. Sophia the vaults are covered with sheets of lead, a quarter of an inch thick, fastened to wood laths, resting on the vaults without any wood roofing.   Hollow earthenware was used in order to reduce the thrust on the supporting walls.

A good idea of a Byzantine dome (No. 49) is obtained by halving an orange, cutting off four slices, each at right angles to the last, to represent the four arches; scoop out the interior; then the portion above the crown of these semicircles is the dome, and the intervening triangles are the pendentives.   At first the domes were very flat; in later times they were raised on a drum or cylinder.

E. **Columns** were often, in the earlier buildings, brought from more ancient structures.   These were naturally not so numerous in the East, as in the neighbourhood of Rome, consequently the supply was sooner exhausted; and thus an incentive to design fresh ones was provided.   Capitals generally took the form shown in the illustration (No. 54), and consisted in the lower portion of a cube block with rounded corners; over this was placed a deep abacus, or block, representing the expiring classic architrave, and which aided in supporting the springing of the arch, naturally larger in area than the shaft of the column.

An altered shape of capital was advisable, as an arch instead of a beam had to be supported, for which a convex form was better adapted.   The surfaces of these capitals were carved with incised foliage of sharp outline, having drilled eyes as a relief (No. 54).

Columns were always subordinate features, and often only introduced to support galleries, etc., the massive piers alone supporting the superstructure.

F. **Mouldings.**—Internally these were subordinate to the decorative treatment in marbles and mosaic.   Flat splays, enriched by incised or low relief ornamentation, are used. Externally the simple treatment of the elevations in flat expanses of brickwork, etc., did not leave the same scope for mouldings as in other styles.

G. **Decoration** is the most interesting feature in the style; the walls being lined with costly marbles, and with figures in glass mosaic, in contrast to the painted frescoes which were more generally adopted in western Romanesque churches.

Mosaic was used in a broad way as a complete lining to a rough carcase. Architectural lines are replaced by decorative bands in the mosaic, worked on rounded angles. One surface melts into another as the mosaic sheet creeps from wall, arch, and pendentive up to the dome. The gold of the background is carried into the figures, thus unity of surface is always maintained.

In carving, Greek, rather than Roman precedent, was followed. It was executed in low relief, and effect was obtained by sinking portions only of the surfaces. In fact, the **drill** instead of the **chisel** was adopted by the Byzantine masons, and is responsible for the character of the carving. The acanthus leaf, deeply channelled and adapted from Roman architecture, became more conventional.

The great characteristic of Byzantine ornament as compared with the classical, is that the pattern is **incised** instead of seeming to be **applied**. The surface always remained flat, the pattern being cut into it without breaking its outline.

Grecian and Asiatic feeling strongly pervades Byzantine ornamentation. This is accounted for by the fact that Constantinople was a Greek city, and in close contact with the East.

> *Note.*—A good general idea of the exterior of a church in this style is to be gained from the Greek Church in the Moscow Road, Bayswater, erected by Gilbert Scott. The mosaics and casts in the South Kensington Museum should also be inspected.

5. REFERENCE BOOKS.

Didron's " Christian Iconography."
Salzenberg's " Byzantine Architecture."
Texier and Pullan's " Byzantine Architecture."
"L'Art de Bâtir chez les Byzantins," by M. Auguste Choisy.
"Sancta Sophia; a Study of Byzantine Building," by W. R. Lethaby and Harold Swainson.
Also the great work on St. Mark's by Ongania.
"Count Robert of Paris," by Sir W. Scott. (Historical Novel.)

ROMANESQUE ARCHITECTURE IN EUROPE.

GENERAL INTRODUCTION.[1]

1. INFLUENCES.

i. **Geographical.**—The style which grew up on the decay of the Roman empire, and which we know as Romanesque, was carried on throughout practically the whole of the Western empire—that is, in those countries which had been directly under the rule of Rome. The position of each country will be slightly touched upon under its own heading.

ii. **Geological.**—In these early times a rough use of the material at hand characterizes the style in each country, and will be referred to under the same.

iii. **Climate.**—Local styles were favoured by the variations of climate north and south of the Alps. Refer to Rome in Classic and France and Germany in Romanesque sections.

iv. **Religion.**—The Christian Church was striving to extend its boundaries in Northern Europe. It represented the civilizing and educating agency of the age. The erection of a church was often the foundation of a city. The papacy had been rising to great power and influence, and, directed with great skill, it rivalled or controlled such civil government as existed. As East and West drifted apart their architecture developed on opposing lines. Work done in Western Europe under Eastern influence has to be classed as Byzantine. The West looked to Rome at first until each

[1] Before treating of the development of each division of the style peculiar to each country, an outline sketch is given of the style in general.

country developed its own style. Religious enthusiasm prevailed, and was manifested in magnificent edifices. As evidencing the same zeal we should note that when the Turks overran Palestine, the loss of the Holy Places brought on the long warfare between the Christians of the West and the Mahometans of the East, known as the Crusades (1096-1270).

v. Social and Political.—The system of feudal tenure, or the holding of land on condition of military service, was growing up, and caused important changes in the social and political organization of states. While through its operation the class of actual slaves died out, still the poorer freemen gradually came to be serfs, bound to the land and passing with it, on a change of ownership.

The growth of the towns as civilization advanced is noticeable, and the privileges which they acquired, amounting almost to independence, rapidly gave them importance.

Constant warfare rendered the condition of the people during this period barbarous, and skill in craftsmanship was at the lowest ebb. Christianity and civilization gradually extended from southern to western Europe. The clergy—the scholars of the period—directed the building of the churches, while the influence of the freemasons produced important results.

vi. Historical.—In the year A.D. 799 the Roman Empire in the West practically passed from the hands of the Romans, by the election of the first Frankish king, Charlemagne, whose election is a convenient date to mark the end of the Roman Empire as such. Till the time of Charlemagne very little building was done, but he in a great measure restored the arts and civilization to Western Europe, before his death in A.D. 814.

After the year A.D. 1000, buildings sprang up in all parts, with many local peculiarities, which we shall notice under each country; but the change was, as ever, slow; traditional forms were firstly transformed in general design and detail, and then new forms created.

Nearly all the nations of Europe had at this time come into existence; the states of Europe, including France, Germany, and Spain, etc., were growing up, and tending to set aside the rule of the Holy Roman Empire, which now had become only a title.   In northern Europe, Denmark, Sweden, and Norway were distinct kingdoms, and England had become welded into one by the Norman kings at the end of the eleventh century.

2. ARCHITECTURAL CHARACTER.

The term **Romanesque** may be said to include all those phases of architecture, which were more or less based on Roman work, and which were being carried out, in a rough and ready way, in various parts of Europe, from the departure of the Romans up to the introduction of the pointed arch in the thirteenth century.   Each country is described under its own heading.

The general architectural character is sober and dignified, while picturesqueness is obtained by the grouping of the towers, and projection of the transepts and choir.

3.   EXAMPLES (refer to each country).

4. COMPARATIVE.

A. **Plans.**—In church architecture further developments from the type of the Early Christian basilica took place. Transepts were usually added, and the chancel prolonged further east than in the basilicas, the church partaking more and more of a fully-developed cross on plan, as at S. Michele at Pavia (Nos. 55, 56, 57).   The transepts were the same breadth as the nave, which was usually twice the width of the aisles.

The choir was raised considerably by steps ; under it was the crypt, where the saints and martyrs were buried, this portion being supported on cross vaults as at S. Miniato, Florence (No. 62).   In later periods the aisles were continued round the choir.

The cloisters in connection with the churches are often of great beauty and elaborately carved.

The towers are special features, and of great prominence in the design, as at the Church of the Apostles at Cologne (No. 67).   They are either square, octagonal, or circular, with well-marked storeys, having windows to each.   The

west and east end, and the crossing of nave and transepts
are all favourite positions.

B. **Walls.**—Roman work and precedent, of course, influenced all constructive art in Europe, although technical
skill was at a very low ebb during this period.   Walls were
in general coarsely built.   In the exterior are pilaster strips
of slight projection, connected at the top by horizontal
mouldings, or by a row of semicircular arches resting on

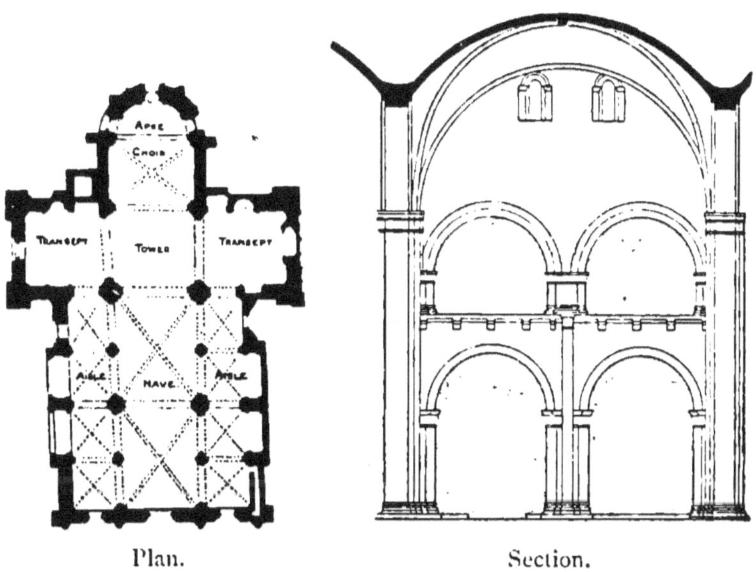

Plan.   Section.

55, 56. St. Michele, Pavia.

a corbel table projecting from the wall.   Semicircular
arches, resting on rudely formed capitals, also occur.   Other
peculiarities are noted under each country.

c. **Openings.**—The door and window openings are very
characteristic.   The principle upon which the jambs were
formed was in receding planes, or rectangular recesses, in
which were placed circular columns or shafts (No. 58).   A
continuous abacus often runs over these columns, and the
profile of the jamb is carried round the semicircular portion
of the arch, in southern examples.

The principal doorways are in general placed in the transepts.

Note.—The characteristic rose, or wheel, window occurred over the principal door of the church in the west front, as at Iffley Church, Oxon (No. 75). Also in Southern Italian examples, as at Palermo.

D. **Roofs.**—The introduction of vaulting, in the second half of the eleventh century, was a great advance in construction over the flat wooden roof.

The form of arch universally employed was semicircular, often raised above the semicircle, *i.e.* stilted (No. 74).

In early buildings rib mouldings were used in the vaulting (No. 59). These ribs were at first plain, and afterwards moulded in a simple manner. Intersecting barrel vaults (No. 85) are common, and the difficulty in constructing these in oblong bays, led to the use of pointed arches in later times.

E. **Columns.**—The shafts of the columns have a variety of treatment; flutings,—vertical, spiral, or in trellis work form, —are used.

The capital in early times is of a cubiform shape, as in St. John's Chapel in the Tower of London (No. 74), with lower corners rounded off and no carving. In later times it becomes richly carved and scolloped.

In some cases the scroll of the ancient Ionic cap is shown —as in the third column from the right in St. John's Chapel, Tower of London (No. 74), where classic influence is apparent.

F. **Mouldings** are often carved elaborately, as will be seen in noticing English Romanesque or Norman architecture.

The abacus over the capital (No. 74) is always distinctive in form; it is higher, but projects less than in the classical style, and is moulded with alternate fillets and cavetti.

The base to the column (No. 74) is generally an adaptation of the old classical form, or Attic base, resting on a square plinth, at the angles of which flowers or animals are occasionally carved to fill up the triangular part. The lower moulding often overhangs the plinth.

St. Michele, Pavia.

57.

58. ROMANESQUE DOORWAY FROM ST. CHRISTOPHORO, LUCCA.

G. **Decoration.**—In regard to carving and ornaments notice that many types are borrowed from the vegetable and animal kingdom, and treated in a conventional way, often but rudely carved.   For interiors fresco is more

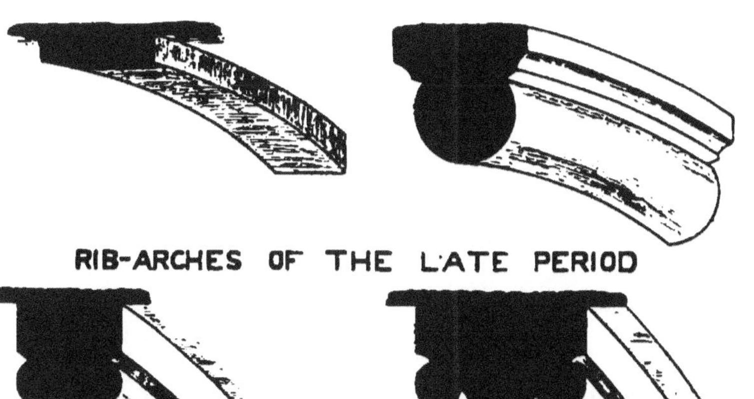

59. COMPARISON OF RIB ARCHES.

common than mosaic, which required great technical skill. Early stained glass is influenced by Byzantine mosaic.

Note.—The above are the principal characteristics of the style as a whole.   Local influences of taste, of climate, of geographical and geological formations must be looked to for the different characteristics in each country.   These will be now briefly alluded to.

ITALIAN ROMANESQUE.[1]

ITALY (Central).

"In Middle Rome there was in stone working
The Church of Mary painted royally
The chapels of it were some two or three
In each of them her tabernacle was
And a wide window of six feet in glass
Coloured with all her works in red and gold."

1. INFLUENCES.

i. Geographical.—The boundaries of Central Italy, in this section, would include Florence and Pisa on the north and west, and extend to Naples on the south. Pisa, by position, was a maritime power, while Florence lay on the great route from south to north, commanding the passage of the Arno.

ii. Geological.—Tuscany possesses greater mineral wealth than any other part of Italy. Building stone was abundant. The ordinary building materials of Rome were bricks, volcanic stone (tufa or peperino) on the spot, and Travertine stone from Tivoli, a few miles off. Marble was obtained from Carrara, or Paros and the other Greek isles.

iii. Climate.—(See under Rome, page 51.)

iv. Religion.—It was during this period that, although the Popes had no temporal dominions, they began to make their power felt in civil government, and the disputes with the emperors began. Gregory VII. rules that the clergy may not marry, and that no temporal prince shall bestow any ecclesiastical benefice. The struggles of the Guelphs and Ghibellines (see hereafter) are in large part the result.

[1] The style is divided into three—central, north, and south. The comparative table of the three together is given on page 116.

v. Social and Political.—In Italy an artistic movement took place in the eleventh century, in which architecture took the lead; painting and sculpture being in a state of stagnation. The Tuscan towns were the principal scene of this movement. An industrial population gradually arose, commerce spread, independent views were acquired in active party conflict, and education became more enlightened.

vi. Historical.—At the commencement of the eleventh century, Pisa was the great commercial and naval power in the Mediterranean, and a rival of Venice and Genoa. Pisa took the lead in the wars against the infidels, defeated the Saracens in 1025, 1030, and 1089 at Tunis. The trade of Pisa, in the twelfth century, extended over the entire Mediterranean. Their policy was Ghibelline. They were defeated by Genoa, 1284, which led to their decline. The rise of Florence dates from 1125, when, Fiesole being destroyed, its inhabitants moved there. In the following century its growing commerce causes it to rival Pisa. Florence, though divided in policy, favoured the Guelphs.

Lucca was an important city at this period, being also a republic. It was rent by the feuds of the two parties. Its architecture is influenced by that of Pisa.

2. ARCHITECTURAL CHARACTER.

ITALIAN ROMANESQUE.

New ideas rarely found. Constructive boldness not sought after, less departure being made from the ancient Basilica type. The Italians have always possessed a greater capacity for beauty in detail, than for developing a bold and novel construction into a complete style.

NORTHERN ROMANESQUE.

The principal aim is perfection in the construction of vaulting, which influences the whole design—as in Normandy and the Rhine provinces, where vaulting was now being developed.

3. EXAMPLES.

The **Cathedral of Pisa** (No. 60) (A.D. 1063-1092) is a fine example. The interior, with rows of columns and the flat ceiling, recalls the Basilica (No. 61).

The cathedral has transepts with a segmental apse at each end, which is an advance on the Basilica plan. The side aisles, externally, have blind arches running all round, built in stripes of red and white marble.

The west façade has small open pillar arcades, one above the other, producing a fine effect (No. 60).

But it will be seen that the architectural character of the church has not the promise of logical development into a style, that a northern example possesses. It depends for artistic effect upon the beauty and interest of its ornamental features.

The **Leaning Tower** at Pisa (No. 60) (A.D. 1172), which is circular on plan, consists of storeys of arcades one above the other. The tower leans one in twelve, and is capped by a small semicircular tower, 27 feet in height, in which are placed the bells. Total height is 183 feet. The foundations gave way during the building, and the cornice overhangs the base by 13 feet.

The **Baptistery** at Pisa (No. 60), designed by Dioti Salvi in A.D. 1153, is circular on plan, 129 feet in diameter. It is also entirely of marble, surrounded on the lower storey by half columns, connected by semicircular arches; above is a gallery in two heights, supported on smaller detached shafts. It was not completed till A.D. 1278, and has Gothic additions of the fourteenth century, in consequence of which it is not easy to ascertain what the original external design really was. Compare with the church of S. Donato, at Zara in Dalmatia, ninth century.

The dome is 60 feet in diameter, and is supported on four piers and eight columns. It is a cone in shape, the top appears above the external dome in a rather singular way. If it had an internal cupola it would resemble the scheme of construction at St. Paul's. (See No. 154.)

Other examples :

    San Michele, Lucca (A.D. 1188). This city belonged to Pisa when most of the churches were erected, hence their similarity to the Pisan work.

    Lucca Cathedral (A.D. 1288).

    The Cathedral at Pistoia, twelfth century A.D.

All of these have more or less the same characteristics.

Rome. In the Romanesque period, *i.e.* from A.D. 600—

62.   ST. MINIATO, AT FLORENCE,
Interior.

1100, while the rest of Europe was slowly developing towards the Gothic style in architecture, Rome was continuing to use the remains of classic buildings, utilizing their columns and features in any new buildings.

The **Cloisters of S. John Lateran**, twelfth century. The small twisted columns are inlaid with mosaic in patterns of great beauty, evidencing the patient skill of the workmen. The cloisters are formed in square bays, the vault arches inclosing the arcades, in groups of five or more openings.

Towers. In Rome during this period a series of towers were erected, which may be regarded as prototypes of the Mediæval towers and spires. Their origin is not clear, as the custom of bell ringing was not then in existence.

Florence. S. Miniato (No. 62) is a leading example of this central Italian style. The principal features are the division of the church into three main compartments longitudinally; and the raised eastern portion, under which is a crypt, open to the nave. The division of the church by piers seems as a prelude to the idea of vaulting in compartments, and is an evident departure from the basilica type of long unbroken ranges of columns or arcades. The marble panelling, of exterior and interior, is to be noticed; it was carried to a further extent in the next period.

For the Comparative table of Italian Romanesque, see at the end of the sections (page 116).

ITALIAN ROMANESQUE.

ITALY (North).

1. INFLUENCES.

i. Geographical.—Milan, the capital of Lombardy, has always had a high degree of prosperity, on account of its favourable situation in the centre of that state, and being near the beginning of several of the Alpine passes.

The city is surrounded by rich plains. The cultivation of the mulberry (for the silkworm), and the vine, adds to the general prosperity of the district.

ii. Geological.—Brick is the great building material of the plains of Lombardy, and the local architecture shows the influence of this material.

iii. Climate.—North Italy has a climate more resembling that of the continent of Europe, *i.e.*, climate of extremes. Milan is near enough to the Alps to experience cold in winter, while in summer the heat is often excessive.

iv. Religion.—At the end of the fourth century, Theodosius, the great emperor, had been forced to do penance on account of a massacre in Thessalonica, St. Ambrose closing the doors of the church against him. This is an instance of the great power the church had acquired. St. Ambrose's fame and influence maintained the Ambrosian rite, which differed in some points of ritual, as in the non use of side altars, etc. (See under Milan Cathedral, later.)

v. Social and Political.—The devastating wars in the North Italian plains leads to the gradual rise of the settlement of Venice, where the first form of government was republican. An oligarchy in which a Duke, or Doge, was invested with supreme authority gradually grew up. Italy

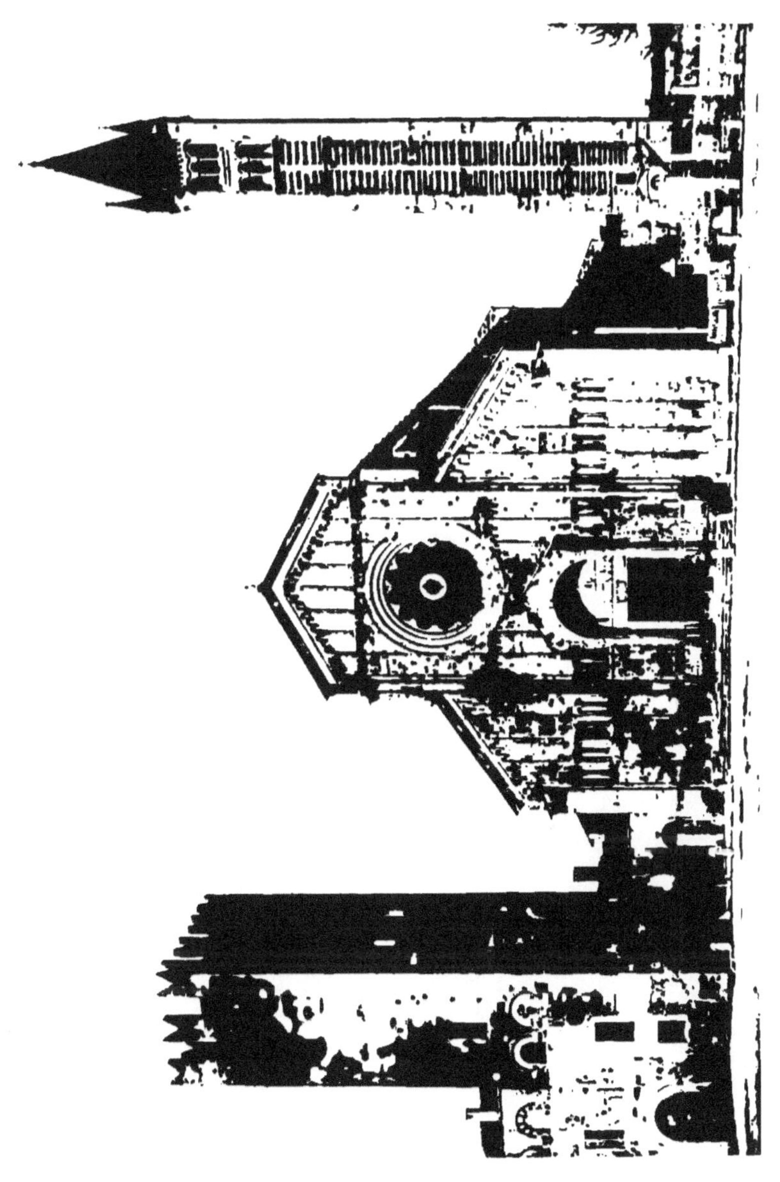

itself consisted of a number of separate cities which were independent commonwealths.

vi. Historical.—Venice from the first kept up a close alliance with Constantinople, by means of which the naval importance, and commerce, of the little state increased continually. Especially after the eleventh century, by which time their commercial relations gradually extended to the Black Sea, and all the coast of the Mediterranean ; while the outlying possessions included Dalmatia, Croatia, and Istria. The invading barbarians who occupied the valleys of the Rhine and Po pursued a similar development in spite of the intervening Alps. Milan was as much German as Italian. In Italy, the old population, that had to be absorbed, eventually caused barbarian influence to wane, but until this had come to pass little building was done. The eleventh and twelfth centuries were the great building epoch in Lombardy.

2. ARCHITECTURAL CHARACTER.

NORTH ITALIAN.

Galleries restricted to top of gables and of apses. The character of the style is more that of stonework than marble, and brick is also much used. Wide, flat, and severe façades are typical, covering the whole church, without marking in any way the difference of nave and aisles. A rose window and a porch resting on lions are often the chief relief (No. 63). Detail shows the tendencies that led to Gothic. In sculpture, scenes as of hunting, etc., reflecting the life of the northern invaders are common, and in these a grotesque element is prominent.

CENTRAL ITALIAN.

Façades covered with galleries (60). Marble facing carried to such an extent as to almost form a style in marble. Basilica type closely adhered to. Detail affected by classic remains and traditions. At Pisa ancient sarcophagi richly sculptured with figures existed, by whose study the Pisani were influenced.

3. EXAMPLES.

The **Churches** of

St. Antonio at Piacenza, twelfth century A.D.,
St. Michele at Pavia, eleventh century A.D.,
St. Ambrogio at Milan, twelfth century A.D..,
St. Zenone at Verona, nave, A.D. 1139, choir, thirteenth century A.D.,

may be mentioned as good examples.

San Zenone at Verona (No. 63). Notice the arcaded corbles, under the slope of gable, which are so characteristic of the work in this district, also the great western rose, or wheel, window, and the projecting porch of the main doorway, with columns supporting arches, and resting on the backs of crouching lions.

The origin of the arcaded galleries, as seen in many of the more important churches in the period (No. 57), is interesting, as illustrating how such architectural features have had, originally, a constructive meaning—thus, when a wooden roof is placed over a circular vault, the external walls must be carried up to the springing of the vault, but are not necessary above; the wooden roof only having to be supported. This portion was therefore arcaded (the arches running back on to the receding extrados of the vault in the case of the apses), giving a deep shadow in an appropriate position (No. 67). This arcading, from being used merely in this position, came to be employed, in every possible part of the building, as a decorative feature, so that it even entirely covered the western façade.

Note.—Similarly in late Gothic in England; the battlemented parapet, primarily of use for defence at the top of the building, eventually was employed as a decorative feature on window transoms, etc.

At **Venice** still remain some palaces of this period, with the characteristic cubiform capital, carrying semicircular arches often stilted.

Ex.: The **Palazzi Farsetti** and **Loredan** and the great warehouse on the Grand Canal used in the eastern trade, and hence called the **Fondaco dei Turchi.**

The **towers** (campanile = bell tower) are an important feature of the period. They are not joined structurally with the church to which they belonged, as in England, France, and Germany, but are placed at some little distance, and sometimes connected by cloisters.

In plan they are always square, and have no projecting buttresses, as on this side of the Alps. They are treated as plainly as possible, without breaks, and with only sufficient windows to admit light to the staircase, or sloping way, inside; the windows increase in number from one in the lowest storey to five or more in the uppermost storey, making this stage into what is practically an open loggia.

Ex. : The Campanile at San Zenone at Verona is typical (No. 63).

These campanili occur in most of the north Italian towns, and in many cases are more civic monuments than integral portions of the churches near which they are situated, as at St. Mark's at Venice. In these cases they were erected as symbols of power, or to commemorate certain events, being similar in purpose to the civic towers of Belgium (page 174).

For comparative table of Italian Romanesque, see at the end of the sections, page 116.

ITALIAN ROMANESQUE.

SOUTHERN ITALY AND SICILY.

"Therein be neither stones nor sticks,
Neither red nor white bricks;
But for cubits five or six
There is most goodly sardonyx,
And amber laid in rows."

1. INFLUENCES.

i. Geographical.—Being situated centrally in the Mediterranean sea, and being of triangular form, Sicily presents one side to Greece, another to Italy, and the third to Africa. Its history is a record of the successive influence of the conquests of each of these three powers.

ii. Geological.—The deposits of sulphur contributed to the wealth and prosperity of the island. The mountainous character of the island affords an abundant supply of a calcareous and shelly limestone. The influence of the geological formation of the island on its architectural character should be noted.

iii. Climate.—The climate of South Italy and Sicily is almost sub-tropical. Palms grow in the open air, and the orange and lemon groves near Palermo are celebrated. On the south-eastern coast of Italy, the towns have the general characteristics of Oriental cities, such as flat roofs, etc.

iv. Religion.—In Sicilian work, Mahometan influence is seen in the intricate geometrical patterns which cover the façades. These they invented, partly owing to the fact that their religion forbade the representation of the human figure, as tending to idolatry.

v. Social and Political.—The Mahometans introduced into Sicily valuable commercial products as grain, cotton, etc. Their civilization was, however, considerably

aided by the previous Byzantine influences.   Southern Italy
has always maintained a close connection with Sicily, and
has yet to be fully explored for traces of its architectural
development.

vi. Historical.—In A.D. 827 the Mahometans land
in Sicily, and gradually overrun the whole island.   The latter
part of the tenth century is the most prosperous period of
their sway.   Sanguinary struggles, amongst certain sects,
lead to the insurrection of several cities, and hasten the
downfall of the Mahometan dynasty.   From 1061-1090 the
Normans, under Robert and Roger de Hauteville, conquer
the island, and a descendant of Roger is crowned at
Palermo, 1130.   Sicily prospers, and her fleet defeats the
Arabs and Greeks.   Civil wars as to the succession lead to
the island passing in 1268 to Louis of Anjou.

2. ARCHITECTURAL CHARACTER.

We can trace the change from the **Byzantine** to the
Mahometan dominion, and from the latter to the supremacy of the **Norman** in the eleventh century, *e.g.*, the
Byzantine influence is shown in the plan of certain churches,
as in the Church of the Martorana at Palermo, where a
square space is covered in by four free columns carrying
a dome, and surrounding vaults.

Architecture develops considerably under the Norman
rule by the erection of cathedrals, and a school of mosaic
was maintained in the Royal Palace during this period.

The churches have either wooden roofs, or a Byzantine
dome, but are hardly ever vaulted.   Dark and light stone is
used in courses externally, and rich mosaics, and coloured
marbles, are employed as a facing internally.   The architectural features of the interior, in the buildings of which
the Cathedral of Monreale (No. 64) is the type, were subordinate to the mosaic decorations which clothe the walls.

3. EXAMPLES.

In Sicily the church at **Monreale** (begun 1174, No. 64)
on the high ground at the back of Palermo, illustrates the
mixed Byzantine and Mahometan influence.   In plan it

resembles a Roman basilica, the aisles being continued to form apses at the east end, which is raised above the nave. The nave columns have well carved capitals of Byzantine form, supporting pointed arches, which are square in section, and not in recessed planes as they would be in northern work. Pointed windows without tracery occur in the aisles. The walls are a background for mosaics in colour, representing biblical history, in scenes surrounded by arabesque borders. A dado, about 12 feet high, of slabs of white marble, is bordered by inlaid patterns in coloured porphyries. The open timber roofs, intricate in design, are decorated in colour in the Mahometan style. The interior is solemn and grand, the decoration is marked by severity, and by the employment of great richness in the material. Note the raised, oblong, crowning lantern, the early bronze doors, and rich cloisters.

The **Capella Palatina**, in the Royal Palace at Palermo, 1132, is the model of the above church, and though of small size, is unrivalled for richness of the effect of the mosaics.

In S. Italy the churches are small in comparison with their northern contemporaries. The church of San Nicolo at Bari (1197) is a good example and typical of the class. The entrance front was always distinguished with a projecting porch, with the columns resting on lions' backs, and supporting a projecting roof, above which is the characteristic wheel-window. The detail especially of these buildings is refined and graceful, which may be due to some extent to the Greek descent of the inhabitants. The crypts are a special feature, that at Otranto especially is to be noted for the numerous points of support, employed to carry the choir.

ITALIAN ROMANESQUE.

4. COMPARATIVE TABLE OF CENTRAL, NORTH, AND SOUTH ITALY.

A. **Plans.**—The plans of most of the churches were substantially the same as the basilicas, more especially in Central Italy; in the north are some attempts at vaulting, in which modifications are introduced on the lines of German work ; in the south, the low lanterns at the crossing, oblong in plan, are marked features, as at Monreale Cathedral (No. 64). A number of circular examples were built mainly as baptisteries, and an atrium at Novara connects such an one to the cathedral; there is also a fine specimen of an atrium at S. Ambroglio, Milan. In the north the galleried apses seen in conjunction with the low arcaded octagon lantern, usual at the crossing, constitute the charm of the style. Projecting porches are preferred to recessed doorways, and are bold open arched structures often of two stories, resting on isolated columns, standing on huge semi-grotesque lions, having a symbolic character. Towers are detached, being straight shafts without buttresses or spires. Such attempts at the latter as occur may be traced to German influence.

B. **Walls.**—The flat blank arcades of the northern style are developed by the Pisan (central) architects in their galleried façades. The west front, including the aisles, is carried up to a flat gable, with galleries following the rake, and other galleries carried across in bands. The northern façades are flatter, and sometimes have a large circular window to light the nave. In the south this feature is highly elaborated with wheel tracery, as in the churches at Palermo. Flank walls are decorated by flat pilaster strips, connected horizontally by small arches, springing from corbels.

C. **Openings.**—In consequence of the bright climate the openings are small, and opaque decoration was preferred to translucent. Window tracery is not developed. The wheel windows just described (No. 63) are only rudimentary in pattern, more attention being bestowed upon their decoration, as in the rich carving of the Palermo examples.

D. **Roofs.**—Where round arched cross vaulting, or simple barrel vaults, are not employed, the timber roofs of the basilica style are used, and often are effectively decorated with colour. In the southern examples, domes rather than vaults were attempted, but timber roofs are the rule in Palermo and Monreale (No. 64), and owing to Mahometan influence, great richness in timber ceilings is attained.

E. **Columns.**—Piers with half shafts are employed rather than columns, especially in the north, where vaulting was more in use ; coupled and grouped shafts were, however, seldom properly developed in relation to the vaulting ribs.   Buttressing was obtained by the division walls of an outer range of chapels, more often than not unmarked on the exterior. In Central Italy, as at Toscanella, rude Corinthian columns carry a round arched arcade, above which the plain walls are pierced, by the small arched openings of the clerestory, while the roof is of the simple basilica type.

F. **Mouldings.**—Flat bands are characteristic of northern work. Strings are formed by small connecting arches, running from one pilaster strip to another.   Rude imitations of old classical detail are met with.   Southern work is far superior in detail, possessing often good outline, grace, and elegance. Richness and elaboration are attempted in the doorways (No. 58).

G. **Decoration.**—Rude grotesques of men and animals, vigorous hunting scenes, and incidents of daily life are found in northern sculpture. In Central Italy greater elegance is displayed, and classic models were copied. The rows of apostles on the lintels of the doorways, as at Pistoia, would seem to be enlargements of Byzantine ivories.

In southern examples, elaborate bronze doors are a feature, as at Monreale Cathedral, etc. Elaborate decoration in mosaic exists as in the Palermo churches, and colour was the intention and object in the design of the interiors.

5. REFERENCE BOOKS.

Taylor and Cresy, " Pisa."
Street, " Brick and Marble of North Italy."
Gally Knight's " The Normans in Italy."
Hittorf and Zanth, " Sicilian Architecture."
Osten's " Bauwerke in Lombardie."
De Dartein's " Etude sur l'Architecture Lombarde."
Grüner's " Terra-cotta Architecture of North Italy."

FRENCH ROMANESQUE.

1. INFLUENCES.

i. **Geographical.**—Relative position has had much to do with the architecture of each district in France. France is practically on the high road between the south and north of Europe. When Rome was a great power it was up the Rhone Valley that civilization spread. Here it is that we find a strong classical element. The trade with Venice and the East, that passed *viâ* Périgueux, introduced into that district a masonic version of the Byzantine style.

ii. **Geological.**—France is exceedingly rich in building materials : most of the towns are built of stone, which is everywhere abundant. In the volcanic district of Auvergne walling is executed in a curious inlay of coloured material. The soft, fine-grained stone of Caen, used throughout Normandy, was also exported to England.

iii. **Climate.**—In France, three zones of climate are marked—(*a*) the northern slope resembles that of the south of England; (*b*) the western slope, the temperature of the Atlantic coasts being higher than the same latitudes further east, by reason of the Gulf Stream and warm S.W. winds; (*c*) the southern, or Mediterranean districts, have a climate and landscape almost African in its aspect.

iv. **Religion.**—Christianity, when introduced, took a strong hold in the Rhone Valley, Lyons contributing martyrs to the cause. In this southern district the most interesting event is the rise of the Cistercians, the severity of whose rules, as to church building, was a reaction from the decorative character of the later Romanesque, as in façades of St. Gilles, and the cathedral of Arles. Attention was thus concentrated upon the means of producing grand, if severe, effects, and the change to the pointed style was promoted, by the effort to solve the problems of vaulting.

v. Social and Political.—Hugh Capet ascended the Frankish throne towards the close of the tenth century, Paris being made the capital of the kingdom. At this period the greater part of the country was held by independent lords, and the authority of the king extended little beyond Paris and Orleans. Lawlessness and bloodshed were rife throughout the century.

vi. Historical.—On the death of Charlemagne the Northmen had invaded northern France, thus giving the name to Normandy, their leader, Rollo, being the ancestor of the Norman kings of England. The conquest of England in 1066 marked the transference of the most vigorous of the Normans to England. The hold, however, that they retained on their possessions in France was the cause of continual invasions and wars in the two countries, until the complete fusion of races in both was marked by the loss of the English possessions in France.

2. ARCHITECTURAL CHARACTER.

The southern style is strongest in rich decorative façades, and graceful cloisters. The style of Provence is a new version of old Roman features, here seeming to have acquired a fresh significance.

In Aquitania and Anjou it is the vast interiors in one span, supported by the massive walls of the recessed chapels, that impress us. In them we seem to see revived the great halls of the Roman Thermæ. In the north, however, the style, though rude, is the promising commencement of a new epoch, the first tentative essays of a new system. These interiors close set with pier and pillar, and heavily roofed with ponderous arching, are to lead to the fairy structures of the next three centuries, where matter is lost in the emotions expressed.

3. EXAMPLES.

France exhibits several varieties of the Romanesque style, in which different peculiarities are traceable. For this reason it may be divided into provinces.

The influence of Roman remains was naturally greatest in the parts where they more particularly occur, as at Nimes, Arles, Orange, etc., in the Rhone Valley.

In **Aquitania** two distinct styles occur; the first is the round-arched tunnel-vaulted style, of which St. Sernin at Toulouse is an example; and the second is a pointed-arched dome-roofed style, peculiar to this province, and indicating an eastern influence; as exemplified in **St. Front, Périgueux**, which had a large trade with Byzantium. This church may be described as a copy in stone of St. Mark's, Venice, but it must be remembered that the arches supporting the domes were pointed (they have in the last few years been changed to semicircular). Attached to the church is a magnificent campanile in stone, consisting of a square shaft, surmounted by a circular ring of columns, carrying a conical dome.

The plan of **Angoulême Cathedral** is of a different type. The long aisleless nave has four stone domes supported on pointed arches. The transepts are shallow, the choir is apsidal. A splendid square tower, with many storeys of arcaded openings, is attached to the north transept. The smaller churches in this district followed this type, and are full of interest.

In **Auvergne** the geological influence is frequently apparent. It is a volcanic country; inlaid decoration is formed with different coloured lavas, giving a local character to the buildings, as at Notre Dame du Port, Clermont.

In **Provence** pointed tunnel vaults are used. There are numerous remains of the eleventh and twelfth centuries, all showing classical influence. The portal of S. Trophîme at Arles, and that of S. Gilles, exhibit great richness of effect and beauty of detail. The cloisters specially require attention; they consist of columns, used in couples in the depth of the wall, and carrying semicircular arches. These arcades

are entirely open, and no attempt at tracery-filling is made,
The deep capitals are a special feature, and are sculptured
with sharp and distinctive foliage.

In **Normandy**, prosperous by reason of the power of
the Norman dukes, the vaulted basilica began at this time
to develop towards the complete Gothic style of the thirteenth
century, and the churches at **Caen** illustrate those difficulties
in vaulting which ultimately led to the introduction of the
pointed arch.

The **Abbaye-aux-Hommes** (or St. Stephen's, No. 65),
commenced in A.D. 1066 by William the Conqueror as a memorial of his victory at Hastings, is the best known example.
In plan it seems founded on the Romanesque church of
Spires (Germany).   It had originally an eastern apse superseded later by the characteristic *chevêt.*

The west end is flanked by two towers crowned by spires.
This façade is a prototype of the Gothic schemes to follow.
Internally the vaulting illustrates the problems that were
being solved.   The system of Sexpartite vaulting (No. 85)
adopted here, is a stage, soon to be superseded by the use of
the pointed arch, which solved the difficulty of the oblong
compartment.

OTHER EXAMPLES.

The Abbaye-aux-Dames, commenced in A.D. 1083.
The Church of St. Nicholas, commenced in A.D. 1084.
The former shows especially the progress of intersecting
vaulting, and is referred to in the Gothic section.
The style was introduced into England by Edward the
Confessor and William the Conqueror.

4. COMPARATIVE.

A. **Plans.**—In the south, internal buttresses, inclosing
the outer range of chapels, are preferred, as at Vienne
cathedral.   Round churches are rare in the south.   Towers
are detached, and resemble Italian examples.   Cloisters are
a feature treated with the utmost elaboration and richness.

65.   ST. STEPHEN'S, CAEN.
View of East end.

Generally, double columns with magnificent capitals receive the round arches of the narrow bays, which were entirely open; glazing or tracery were not required by the climate.

In the north, the increasing demand for vaulted interiors modifies the planning. The vaulting ribs are provided with individual shafts, which develop the pier plans. In the setting out of the bays important changes are introduced. In early plans the nave bay is square, including two bays of the aisles in its compartment. The possibility of vaulting oblong spaces once grasped, enabled every bay of the aisle to be a compartment of the church.

B. **Walls.**—Massiveness is the characteristic of all the early work. Elaboration is reserved for doorways in the arcaded lower portion of the façades, which are often models of simplicity and richness. Buttresses are often mere strips of slight projection, and the façades are arranged in storeys, with window lights in pairs or groups. The towers are mostly square with pyramidal roofs (No. 65).

C. **Openings.**—The earlier vaulted churches have no clerestory (see below). In the south, narrow openings suffice, while in the north a commencement in grouping is made, more especially in the direction of filling in the vault spandrels (clerestory), with arrangements of three and five light openings.

D. **Roofs.**—In Provence, the early treatment is a tunnel vault to the nave, buttressed by half tunnels over the aisles. No clerestory is thus provided. The pointed section is used doubtless to lessen the thrust upon the walls, and to carry the roofing slabs of stone direct upon the extrados of the vault. In the north, clerestories are obtained by means of intersections in the nave vaults, and arches across the aisles are developed towards the later flying buttresses. Note that the vault, in the northern examples, is a stone ceiling protected by a wooden roof.

E. **Columns** (No. 66).—In nave arcades, square piers, recessed in planes, have upon their faces half round shafts, that run up to carry the vaulting. Columns reminiscent of Roman times, circular or octagonal, are also used, often alternately, and then the vaulting shafts start awkwardly from the abacus of their huge capitals, imitated from the Corinthian order.

F. **Mouldings.**—In the south, the elegance due to classic tradition contrasts with the rough axed decoration cut upon the structural features of the Norman work. In the latter, arched jambs are formed in recessed planes, with nook shafts plainly fluted, or cut with zigzags. Capitals are cubical blocks, or carved with rude copies of the acan-

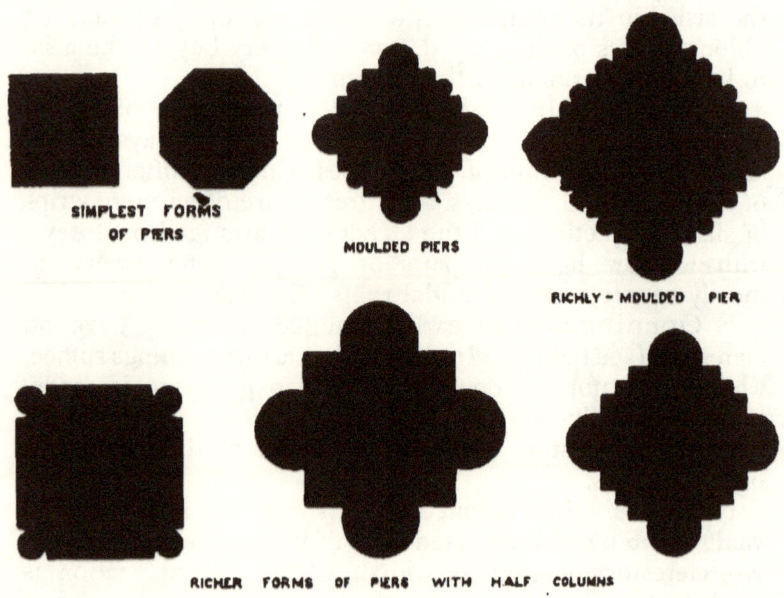

66. COMPARISON OF ROMANESQUE PIERS.

thus leaves from old Roman examples. Corbel tables, supported by plain blocks or grotesque heads, etc., form the cornices of the walls.

G. **Decoration.**—Painted glass is not favoured in southern examples, opaque colour decoration being preferred, with small, clear-glazed openings. The diaper work so common in the spandrels of arches, etc., in northern work is supposed to have arisen from the imitation, in carving, of the colour pattern work, or draperies that originally occupied the same positions. Stained glass favouring large openings is gradually developed in the North. Increased size in the clerestories is obtained by the use of the pointed arch.

5. REFERENCE BOOKS.

Revoil's "Architecture Romane du midi de la France."
Ramée, "Histoire de l'architecture."
Edmund Sharpe, "The Domed Churches of the Charente."
Viollet-le-Duc, "Dictionnaire Raisonné" (Article on Construction).

GERMAN ROMANESQUE.

1. INFLUENCES.

i. Geographical.—On the banks of the Rhine, and in the south, cities had been established during the Roman occupation, and it was in these parts that Christianity took root, while, in the north and east, paganism was still existing.

ii. Geological.—The existence of stone in the Rhine valley facilitated the erection of churches, rendered permanent and fireproof by the early introduction of vaulting No stone being found on the sandy plains of Prussia, brick was employed by the North Germans, and the style here is consequently varied from that of the Rhine valley.

iii. Climate.—The average temperature of Central Germany may be said to be the same as Southern England, but with wider extremes, as the heat in the summer is ten degrees greater, and in the winter correspondingly lower, so that carriages in Berlin are converted into sledges.

iv. Religion.—In the early period the Germans looked much to Rome. Charlemagne was a strong supporter of Christianity, forcing the people of Saxony to embrace that religion. Ritually, the most important local German differences are the double apse plan, and the number and importance of the circular churches, built as tombs, or more especially as baptisteries, the conversion of the tribes giving great importance to that ceremony.

v. Social and Political.—The Germans united under Charlemagne afterwards split up into principalities, etc., whereas the French, divided at first, became fused into an absolute monarchy and have remained, in spite of all changes, the least divided of continental powers. In the later portion of this period, Germany was troubled by the dissensions of the two rival parties, the Guelphs and Ghibellines, the one the supporters of the Church and municipal rights, and the other representing the Imperial authority. The conflict between the two took place mainly in Lombardy.

vi. Historical.—It must be remembered that Charlemagne, the first Frankish king who became Roman Emperor, being crowned by the Pope at Rome, ruled over the land of the Franks, which included all Central Germany and Northern Gaul. In addition he established the Frankish dominion over South Gaul and Germany. In a great measure, he restored the arts and civilization to Western Europe, resulting in the erection of many important buildings in his dominions.

On Charlemagne's death in A.D. 814 this empire crumbled into pieces through internal wars. In the unsettled state of the country, the German princes pushed themselves into prominence by demanding the right to elect their own sovereign—Conrad the First, reigning as King of Germany at the beginning of the tenth century. His successor, Otho, extended the boundary of the German Empire southwards into Lombardy, being crowned Emperor of the West at Rome. This shows the leading position of the Frankish emperors at the period, not without its influence on the architecture of these regions. The house of Hapsburg succeeded the Hohenstaufen dynasty in 1273, when French Gothic architecture was introduced, and henceforth copied.

2. ARCHITECTURAL CHARACTER.

The style bears a strong resemblance to North Italian Romanesque, and the reasons for this have been already noted (page 111).

The Rhine districts possess the most fully-developed Romanesque to be found anywhere, and the style has fewer local varieties than in France. The general architectural character is rich in the multiplication of circular and octagonal turrets, in conjunction with polygonal domes, and the use of arcaded galleries under the eaves. The most richly ornamented parts are the doorways and capitals, which are rude, yet bold and effective in execution.

The Germans may claim to be the inventors of the Lombard, or North Italian, Romanesque.   Their round arched style lasted till 1268.

3. EXAMPLES.

The churches at **Cologne** (dating from end of twelfth century) are some of the finest examples.

Ex.: **St. Maria in Capitolio, St. Martin, the Church of the Apostles** (No. 67), and **St. Cunibert** may be mentioned.   Besides which the Cathedrals at **Mayence** (tenth cent.), **Worms** (twelfth cent.), **Spires** (eleventh cent.), and the east end of **Bonn** (twelfth cent.) are important.

The **Church of the Apostles at Cologne** (No. 67) is one of a series which possess characteristic features.   In plan it consists of a broad nave, and of aisles half the width of the nave.   The eastern portion has three apses, opening from three sides of the central space, crowned by a low octagonal tower, giving richness and importance to this portion of the church.   The grouping externally is effective, the face of the wall being divided up by arcading, and crowned with the characteristic row of small arches under the eaves of the roof.   Compare the bold dignity of this church with the confused effect of the French *chevet*, as S. Stephen's at Caen (No. 65).

The **Cathedral of Worms**, erected in the twelfth century, vies with Mayence and Spires, as the representative cathedral of this period.   As usual, one bay of the nave occupies two of the aisles, both being covered with cross vaults.   Twin circular towers flank the eastern and western apses, the crossing of the nave and transept is covered with a low octagonal tower, with a pointed roof.   The entrances are placed in the sides, a position which is quite German. The façades have semicircular windows, framed in with flat pilaster strips as buttresses.

The **Cathedral at Aix-la-Chapelle**, built A.D. 768-814

67.   CHURCH OF THE APOSTLES, COLOGNE.
Exterior view of Apse.

by the Emperor Charlemagne as a royal tomb for himself, is interesting as resembling St. Vitale at Ravenna. In plan it is a polygon of sixteen sides, 105 feet in diameter. Internally, every two angles converge on to one pier, which thus number eight. These support a dome 47 feet 6 inches in diameter, rising above the side aisles, which are in two heights. It is of interest, historically, as the crowning place of the Western Emperors.

4. COMPARATIVE.

A. **Plans.**—The naves and aisles are vaulted in square bays, two bays of the aisle making one of the nave, as in the plan of St. Michele at Pavia, No. 55.

There is sometimes a triforium, and always a clerestory.

A tower occurs at the crossing with a high-pitched roof (No. 67). Western transepts are found, contrasting in this respect with Italy.

The choir is always apsidal, and western apses are frequent. (Ex. : at Trèves and the Abbey Church at Laach.)

Apses also occur at the ends of transepts. (Ex.: Church of the Apostles at Cologne, No. 67.)

We should especially note the multiplicity of towers, there usually being two at the east end flanking the apse, and also often two western towers, connected by a gallery. The towers rise in successive storeys, from square to circular and polygonal. A characteristic finish is four gables and steep roof, a hip rafter rising from each gable top (No. 67). These towers produce a rich and varied outline.

B. **Walls.**—The blank walls are cut up by flat pilaster strips, connected horizontally by small arches springing from corbels. Owing to the smallness of scale this favourite feature is to be considered as a string course or cornice.

Open arcades (see Italian Romanesque, page 112 for origin) occur under the eaves of roofs, especially round the apses (No. 67).

C. **Openings.**—No tendency to tracery is found. The windows are usually single, being rarely or never grouped. The doorways are placed at the side, rarely in the west front or transept ends.

D. **Roofs.**—In the Rhine district vaulting was intro-duced, a central semicircular barrel vault was supported by half-circle vaults over the aisles, a system which led by degrees to complete Gothic vaulting. Timber roofs were also em-ployed for large spans. Tower roofs, and spires of curious form, are a great feature of the style. A gable on each tower face, with high pitched intersecting roofs, is common, and is developed by carrying up the planes of the roof to form a pyramid, which leads on to further spire growth (No. 67).

E. **Columns.**—The nave arcades are generally con-structed of square piers, with half columns attached. The alternation of piers and columns is a favourite German feature. The capitals, though rude in execution, are well designed, being superior to the later Gothic examples.

F. **Mouldings** are not a strong feature of the style (see under walls), caps and bases take a distinctive form, leading from Roman through Romanesque and Gothic.

G. **Decoration.**—Internally the flat plain surfaces were decorated in fresco. The traditions and examples, of the early Christian and Byzantine mosaic decorations, were carried on in colour.

5. REFERENCE BOOK.

Moller's " Denkmaehler der Deutschen Baukunst," vol. i.

103.   ANTWERP CATHEDRAL.

104.   TOWN HALL, BRUGES.

BELGIAN AND DUTCH GOTHIC.

1. INFLUENCES.

i. **Geographical.**—This small kingdom lies across the country, wedged in, as it were, between the Germanic and Romanic elements of the European peoples. We shall expect to find, therefore, dual influences in its architectural development.

ii. **Geological.**—The district abounds with clay for the making of bricks. The consequent effect upon the architecture was of course considerable, being specially noticeable in domestic work, as in the small house façades in the towns.

Granite is also available, the cathedral at Tournai being wholly of that material.

Stone is used in Brussels Cathedral and other instances.

iii. **Climate.**—Resembles England, but is more excessive in heat and cold.

iv. **Religion.**—Refer to France and Germany.

v. **Social and Political.**—The mediæval architecture of these countries developed with the social progress of the people. Towns with independent municipalities rivalled each other in the arts of war and peace, hindering the development of an especially national style of architecture. The prosperity and wealth of the people gave rise to buildings, large in conception and rich in detail.

vi. **Historical.**—Flanders, as a fief of France, became by marriage joined to Burgundy. Under the dukes of Valois, themselves descended from the French kings, the whole of the Netherlands, and Belgium, were brought together under the rule of these dukes. During the Middle Ages the cities of the Low Countries were the richest and most powerful in Europe, and were constantly at war with one another.

2. ARCHITECTURAL CHARACTER.

The Dutch character of simplicity is translated into their architecture, their churches are barn-like, and contrast with the richly-treated town halls of Belgium.

The hilly, or eastern, portion of the country partook of the influence of German work, while the flat, or western, portion (Flanders) naturally fell under the influence of French work.

3. EXAMPLES.

CATHEDRALS.

The cathedrals of Tournai, Ypres, Brussels, and Antwerp (No. 103) are among the more important, and show a general inclination to French ideas, in their "short and wide" plan. The seven aisles at Antwerp are to be noted. The cathedral of Tournai well illustrates three successive periods. The nave is Romanesque; the transepts, with four towers and a lantern, and bold apsidal termination, is in the transition style; and the choir is fully developed Gothic, very light and elegant in character. The whole cathedral is built of granite.

CIVIL AND DOMESTIC ARCHITECTURE

shows still more the independent and prosperous condition of these mediæval towns. The possession of a "beffroi" (or belfry) attached to the town hall was an important privilege granted by charter; the lower portion was of massive construction, and was used as a record office. The beffroi at Bruges is one of the most picturesque of these towers; it is 300 feet high, and forms a landmark for many miles round (No. 104).

The **town halls** are also exceptionally fine; those at Brussels, Bruges (No. 104), Louvain, and Ghent (No. 105) being the more important. Many are designed on the same lines, and are of several storeys in height, surmounted by a high roof, with dormer windows in tiers. The central portion is carried up as a tower, with a richly ornamented spire (No. 104).

The illustration of the town hall at Ghent is a somewhat striking example of comparative architecture, the Gothic portion, on the right hand, contrasting with the Renaissance portion on the left hand (No. 105).

The **trade halls** for buying and selling merchandise, and specially cloth, for which the country was renowned at this period, are also very characteristic, as at Ypres.

The **guildhalls**, or meeting-places for the separate trades or guilds, which were very powerful, were also built, as in the market-place of Brussels, where several examples can be seen.

4. COMPARATIVE.

A. **Plans.**—As noted in the examples, short and wide plans after French models are adopted in the cathedrals. Antwerp has seven aisles. The French *chevet* is adopted.

B. **Walls.**—In domestic work the long unbroken façades are to be noticed, and the greater symmetry and regularity of the scheme which has somehow come to be regarded as a non-Gothic quality. In reality these great halls, as at Ypres, are a class of building that the condition of the people elsewhere did not necessitate. Compare their free and open appearance with the halls of Florence and Siena.

C. **Openings.**—The windows are richly ornamented with sculpture, tracery, and panelling. Similarity and regularity in position are marked features in these large buildings.

D. **Roofs.**—In domestic work roofs are of steep pitches, and are either hipped (No. 105) or ended by crow-stepped and traceried gables of picturesque outline. Numerous turrets, and bold chimney stacks, combine with the tiers of dormers, to complete the rich profusion of the walls below.

E. **Columns.**—The use of round pillars in the nave, instead of clustered piers, is well exemplified at St. Rombaut, Malines. In the town hall arcades a strange trick may be seen : a column is omitted by hanging up any two arches by means of a long keystone from a concealed arch.

F. **Mouldings.**—Coarse profusion is characteristic of Belgian Gothic, neither the vigour of French, nor the grace of English, mouldings must be looked for in the buildings of this style.

G. **Decoration.**—In St. Waudru, at Mons, blue stone is combined with a red brick filling-in of the vault, in a scheme of permanent decoration. St. Jacques at Liège is fully decorated with paintings of a rather later date.

5. REFERENCE BOOKS.

Haghe and Delepierre, "Ancient Monuments of Belgium."
Goetghebuer, "Monuments des Pays-Bas."
King's "Study Book of Mediæval Architecture."

GERMAN GOTHIC.

"Some roods away, a lordly house there was,
Cool with broad courts, and latticed passage wet
From rush flowers and lilies ripe to set,
Sown close among the strewings of the floor ;
And either wall of the slow corridor
Was dim with deep device of gracious things :—
Some angels' steady mouth and weight of wings
Shut to the side ; or Peter with straight stole
And beard cut black against the aureole
That spanned his head from nape to crown ; these
Mary's gold hair, thick to the girdle tie
Wherein was bound a child with tender feet ;
Or the broad cross with blood nigh brown on it."

1. INFLUENCES.

i. Geographical.—The boundaries of Germany are due to racial differences on the south, west, and east.

ii. Geological.—The plains of Northern Germany produce no building material but brick, and its influence on the architecture in these regions is to be noted.

The materials in the geological divisions are :

Brick,	Stone,	Timber,
N. and N.E.	Centre and S.	N.W., Hanover, etc.

iii. Climate.—See under German Romanesque (p. 126).

iv. Religion.—The most interesting feature in the religious life of Germany, prior to the Reformation, is the civil, as well as ecclesiastical, rule of many of the bishops. Some of these episcopal principalities were not finally abolished until the period of the French Revolution.

v. Social and Political.—Trade guilds acquired great importance during this period, that of the masons, an organization called the Freemasons, has been credited with

the design and working out of the style.   In the absence of
records, the truth as to the individuality of the architects
will not easily be made out.

vi. Historical.—In the twelfth and thirteenth centuries
Germany was the heart and centre of the Western Empire.
Under the Swabian Emperors long wars occurred with the
Lombard league of the north Italian towns.   The years
1254-1274, known as the "great interregnum," because no
king was universally acknowledged by all Germany, were
times of great confusion and lawlessness, until the house of
Hapsburg came into power in 1273.

2. ARCHITECTURAL CHARACTER.

The Gothic architecture of Germany was borrowed
directly from France, and is not a pure development of
the Romanesque, as in the latter country.

Gothic was reluctantly adopted in Germany, at the time
when it was attaining its great perfection in France.

3. EXAMPLES.

CATHEDRALS.

Cologne Cathedral should be regarded as the great
cathedral in this style, and the student should notice the
resemblance in plan No. 127 and dimensions with that of
Amiens (No. 95).   The date is 1322-1388.

Strasburg Cathedral has two western towers, a
large rose window at west end, and double tracery in the
windows (*i.e.* tracery in two planes).   The character of
the detail is somewhat "wiry."   The nave was finished in 1275.

It was built by

> "A great master of his craft,
> Erwin von Steinbach ; but not he alone,
> For many generations labour'd with him.
> Children that came to see these saints in stone,
> As day by day out of the blocks they rose,
> Grew old and died, and still the work went on,
> And on and on and is not yet completed.
> .   .   .   .   The architect

106. RATISBON CATHEDRAL.
West Front.

> Built his great heart into these sculptured stones,
> And with him toiled his children, and their lives
> Were builded with his own into the walls
> As offerings to God."—LONGFELLOW.

Ratisbon Cathedral (No. 106) has a regular plan, octagonal apse, and western towers.[1] Notice the peculiar little triangular porch.

Ulm Cathedral is noticeable for the small ratio of support in regard to its floor space. It is spacious and lofty; only one western tower is carried up. It has an arcaded gallery to the eaves, a remnant from Romanesque traditions, and fine choir stalls.

St. Stephens, Vienna.—This splendid church has the following peculiarities of the style: There is no clerestory or triforium; the three aisles are nearly equal in width and height, and one great roof covers the whole in one span. Tower porches occupy the position of transept; the completed one has a splendid spire, less open than usual in German work; the vaults are traceried, and the original stained glass exists. It was built between 1300-1510.

DOMESTIC ARCHITECTURE.

In domestic work of the period the roof was a large and important feature, and frequently contains more storeys than the walls below it. It was used as a "drying ground" for the large monthly wash, and planned with windows to get a through current of air.

In towns the planning of the roof-ridge parallel, or at right angles, to the street influenced the design considerably.[2]

Ex.: At **Nuremberg** the ridge is generally parallel to the street; dormer windows are plentiful; party walls are apparent, and artistically treated.

At **Landshut** and elsewhere, the ridge being generally at right angles to the street, gables are the result, and these exhibit great variety of design in scrolls, etc.

The dwelling-houses of early date in **Cologne**, with their stepped gables, are noticeable.

---

[1] Date, 1275-1534. The open spires added in 1859-1869.
[2] See German Renaissance, p. 249.

4. COMPARATIVE.

A. **Plans.**—Apses are often semi-octagonal, and found at the end of transepts.

The *chevet* is uncommon, though it occurs at Cologne.

Triapsal plans are a favourite feature. A square outline to the general plan is not uncommon.

Twin towers occur at west end, as in France, at Ratisbon (No. 106). In later work, sometimes only one central tower occurs, as in England.

Entrances are often on north or south, and not at the west end. They are sometimes carried up as towers, and take the place of transepts.

Towers are continued from the last period, the junction of the spire is often insufficiently marked, and the outline, though ornamented, is weak.

B. **Walls.**—The apsidal galleries of the Romanesque style are copied, without reference to their origin and meaning. Tracery is employed as an outer wall surface, and its mullions often cut across the openings behind.

Lübeck in the north is the centre of a brick district, and churches of this material abound; they are also found in Bavaria and at Munich.

C. **Openings.**—Tracery was elaborated, double tracery windows being used in later examples.

Excessive height is a characteristic. The use of two tiers of windows is due to the lofty aisles. In the north the clerestories are excessive in size, starting as low down as possible, to provide a great expanse of stained glass.

D. **Roofs.**—Churches nearly always vaulted, but are sometimes covered only with a wooden roof.

The special German feature is the immense roof, covering nave and aisle in one span. This is due to the side aisle being made as high as the nave. Tower roofs of the Romanesque form continue.

E. **Columns.**—Piers are usual in interiors, as in England, and not the columns found in early French work. The tendency is to make them lofty posts carrying the roof, again owing to the height of the aisles.

F. **Mouldings.**—Complexity rather than simplicity was striven after. Interpenetration of mouldings (fifteenth century) was a very characteristic treatment, *i.e.* in bases, etc., each member, after passing through another, is traced out and provided with its own base and cap, etc. Much patience is bestowed upon the intricacies that resulted from such interpenetrations.

Features such as pinnacles increase in size as they get higher, and therefore scale is destroyed, as at Cologne.

Features do *not* increase in size in English and French work.

G. **Decoration.**—Foliage was treated in a naturalesque manner, and the interlacing of boughs and branches is a common feature.

In fittings the Tabernacle, or Sacrament House, was developed as a separate structure placed at one side. Late examples are lofty and tower-like, tapering upwards in many stages of wonderfully complicated work. Stained glass and ironwork are well treated.

5. REFERENCE BOOKS.

W. Whewell, "Notes on Churches."
W. Lübke, "Ecclesiastical Art."
G. Moller, "Denkmaehler der Deutschen Baukunst."
"Anne of Geierstein," by Sir W. Scott. (Historical Novel.)

ITALIAN GOTHIC.

1. INFLUENCES.

i. **Geographical.**—We should note the German influence in Lombardy through the connection of this part of Italy and Germany, geographically by the Brenna Pass. The work at Venice is similarly influenced by an oversea trade connection with the East.

ii. **Geological.**—The influence of materials in the development of this style is important. The coloured marbles, of northern and central Italy, supplied abundant and beautiful material for the elaboration of plain wall treatment, as we see in Florence (No. 110), Siena, Genoa, Orvieto, Lucca, and other places. Red, black, and white marbles were used in stripes, and also in panels, the architect relying for effect upon their colour and disposition alone.

The brick and terra-cotta of northern Italy has left a decided impress on the architecture of that district, many large buildings, such as the Hospital at Milan and the Certosa at Pavia, having been erected in these materials.

iii. **Climate.**—The influence of climate is apparent in the small windows, which were necessary to keep out the glare and heat of the Italian sun. The development of tracery was of course hindered by the same cause.

The preference for opaque treatment, such as mosaic

work and fresco decoration, was inherited from the Romans, while the climate counteracted effectually any desire the Italians might have had for stained glass, for the reasons mentioned above.

iv. Religion.—The real power of the Pope as head of the Western Church died with Gregory X. (1271-1276). The following popes were under the influence of the King of France, and for seventy years they resided at Avignon, losing authority and influence, during their absence from Rome. Rival popes existed until a settlement was arrived at by the Council of Constance, held 1415. The factions of the Guelphs and Ghibellines (see under Germany) distracted Italy from 1250 to 1409, a subject well treated by Mr. Oscar Browning in his " Mediæval Italy."

v. Social and Political.—Italy at this period was cut up into small principalities and commonwealths, in which political life was full of rivalry and activity, and small wars were of constant occurrence. Tasso has a line to the effect that each holiday they blew the trumpets, and proceeded to sack the adjoining town. Yet other countries looked to Italy as the head in arts, learning and commerce. The poet Dante (1265-1321) lived during this period, and his great poem is a summarized picture of the age.

The revival of learning took place in Italy nearly a century in advance of northern Europe.

vi. Historical.—In the thirteenth century the Visconti ruled at Milan, and in consequence of the wealth and industry of the cities over which they ruled the Dukes of Milan were very powerful. The maritime commonwealth of Genoa considerably reduced the power of Pisa in 1284, and the latter was conquered by Florence in 1406. Florence became one of the chief states of Italy under the powerful family of the Medici (see under Renaissance, page 210).

2. ARCHITECTURAL CHARACTER.

The influence of Roman tradition, and classic forms, was so great that the verticality, which marks the Gothic architecture in the north, does not pervade the Italian or southern examples to the same extent as in those we have been considering.

In the exteriors of the churches we notice especially the flatness of the roofs (No. 110); the tendency to mask the aisle roofs on the west façade, by including the whole composition under one gable (No.107); the great central circular window in the west front lighting the nave; the flatness and comparative unimportance of the mouldings, their place being more than taken by the beautiful coloured marbles with which the façades were faced (No. 110).

The importance of the crowning cornice (No. 110), and the absence of pinnacles due to the unimportance of the buttresses, should be remarked; also the employment of elaborately carved projecting porches at the west end, the columns of which often rest on the backs of lions and other animals (No. 63).

> "Stern and sad (so rare the smiles
> Of sunlight) looked the Lombard piles:
> Porch pillars on the lion resting,
> And sombre, old, colonnaded aisles."—TENNYSON.

Sculpture wherever used partakes of classical purity, and is so far superior to that exhibited in northern examples, but it enters far less into the general composition and meaning of the architecture.

Mosaic was also used externally in panels, in continuation of early ideas and practice.

3. EXAMPLES.

NORTH ITALY.

Milan Cathedral is the most important work erected in Italy during the Middle Ages (A.D. 1385-1418) (No. 107), and we shall notice especially the German influence, both in character and details. It is the largest mediæval cathedral, with the exception of Seville, and is built entirely of white marble. The roof is very flat in pitch, being constructed of massive marble slabs, laid upon the upper surface of the vaulting.

107.   Milan Cathedral.

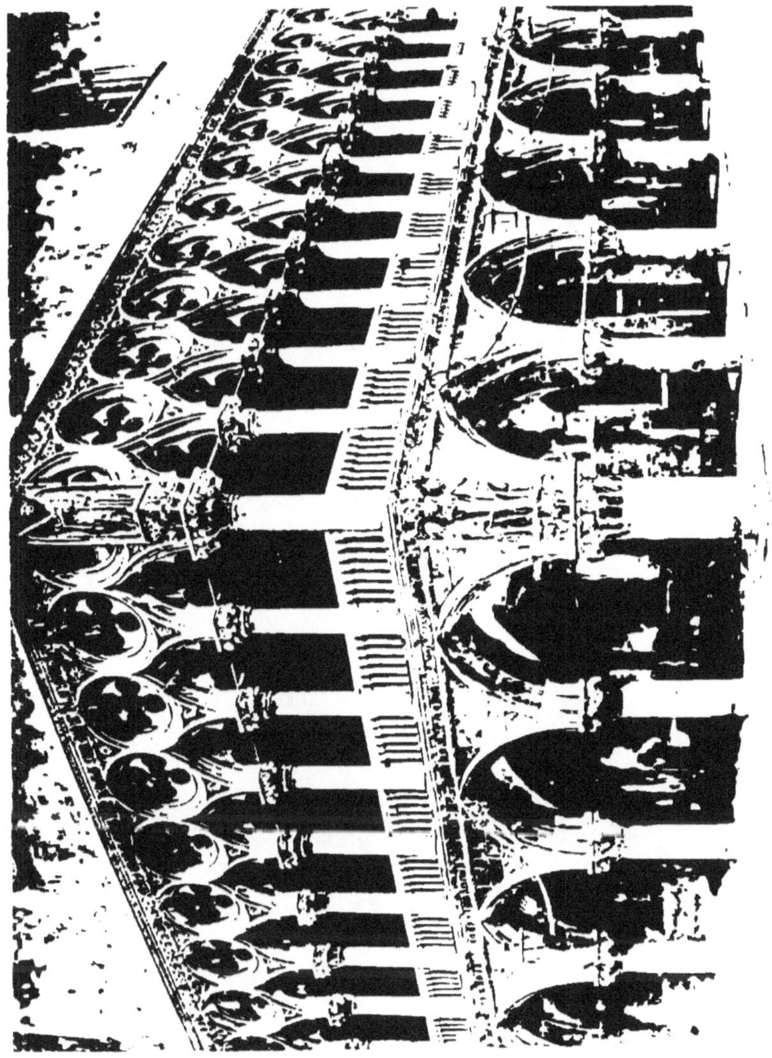

In plan it consists of a nave with specially small clerestory, and of double aisles of extreme height; the nave terminates with a circlet of columns in the French manner, but this is inclosed in a German polygonal apse. To the Ambrosian ritual is due the absence of side-chapels in the original scheme. At the crossing of the nave and aisles is placed a vault crowned with a marble spire, designed by Brunelleschi in A.D. 1440. The feature of the interior is the range of immense shafts to the nave, whose summits are treated with canopied niches, filled with statues, in the place of the ordinary capitals. Externally, the character of the whole design is expressive of richness and lace-like intricacy, which is aided in effect by the numerous pinnacles of glittering marble.

> "O Milan, O, the chanting quires;
> The giant windows' blazon'd fires:
> The height, the space, the gloom, the glory!
> A mount of marble, a hundred spires."—TENNYSON.

The absence of stone and influence of brick on the architecture of the district is exemplified in the **Certosa at Pavia**, erected in 1396, and the great **Hospital at Milan**, where terra-cotta is largely used. The churches and palaces at Bologna, Vicenza, Padua, Verona, Cremona, and Genoa, contain specimens of brick architecture with pleasing detail, moulded in this material.

Venice is remarkable for the civic and domestic architecture of this period. In this connection we must remember the prominent position Venice occupied as a great trading centre in the Middle Ages; also the supremacy of her navy, and, in consequence, her power and richness.

> "Where Venice sate in state, throned on her hundred isles."

Note.—St. Mark's, Venice, is described under Byzantine (p. 95).

The **Doge's Palace** (No. 108) (façade A.D. 1424-1442, by Giovanni and Bartolommeo Buon) is the grandest effort in civic architecture of the period. Each façade consists of an arcade of two storeys, one above the other, supporting the external wall of the upper storey, which latter is, however, supposed by Street to have been an addition. The structure is built with rose-coloured and white marble, the blank walls of the upper storey being a chequer of these colours broken by a few large and richly ornamented windows. The delicate and light carving in low relief, which occurs in the capitals of the arcades is justly celebrated. Notice that the lower columns seem to rise out of the ground, having no bases; also the solid and connected character of the tracery, which gives some stability to the design, so heavily loaded above.

The excellence of marble, as a material for carving, is largely responsible for the refinement of execution which we find in this example.

The **Ca d'Oro Palace** (No. 109) on the Grand Canal is another fine specimen of the domestic work with which Venice abounds. The tracery especially is Venetian in character; as is also the grouping of the windows towards the centre of the façade, the extremities of the design being left comparatively solid, thus producing the effect of a central feature inclosed by wings.

Note.—A good general idea of the treatment of Venetian Gothic is obtained from the old front of St. James's Hall and from the building in Lothbury, opposite the Bank of England.

CENTRAL ITALY.

The **Cathedral of Florence** (No. 110) is chiefly remarkable for the wide spacing of the nave arcades, the absence of pinnacles and buttresses, and for the marble façades in coloured panelling. The cathedral was erected (1294-1462) from the designs of Arnolfo del Cambio. The octagonal dome was added on in Renaissance times by Brunelleschi. Internally the fine effect promised by the plan is not realized. Vast masses of grey pietra serena stone, in piers and arches, are contrasted by blank spandrels of whitewash. The baptistery is an octagonal structure faced with pilasters and richly coloured ornamentation, being further remarkable for the fifteenth century bronze doors by Ghiberti.

110.   FLORENCE CATHEDRAL, AND GIOTTO'S CAMPANILE.

The adjoining **Campanile** (No. 110) by Giotto, A.D. 1324, is square on plan, 292 feet high, in four storeys of increasing height, and is built in red and white marble. Tracery of an elementary character is introduced into the

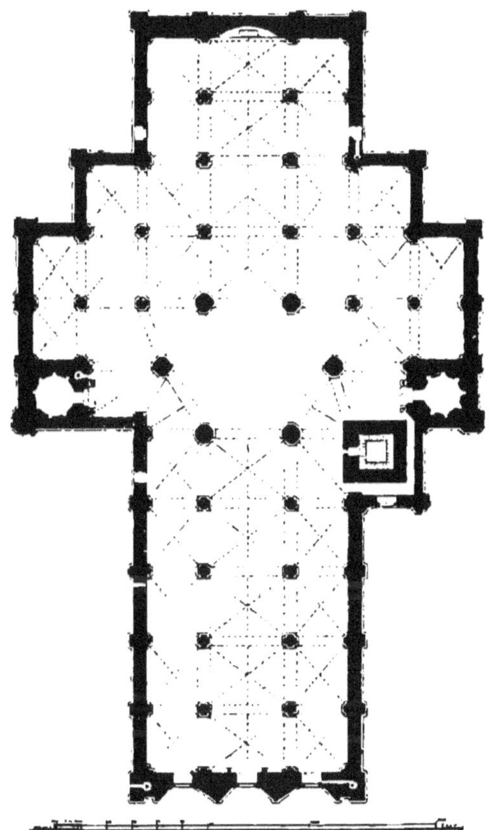

111. PLAN OF CATHEDRAL AT SIENA. ITALY.

windows in this example. Inserted in the solidly designed lower storey are sculptured panels of great interest and beauty. Below the present tile roof the start of the intended spire can be traced.

The **Cathedral of Siena** (No. 111), A.D. 1243, is to be

remarked for its dome which is hexagonal on plan, its façade in black and white stripes, the three portals of equal size, and for the characteristic rose window. The ground falling towards the east end, allows of a crypt being formed under the sanctuary, which is used as a baptistery. The unfinished elevation of this east end is a grand design.

Orvieto Cathedral (commenced in A.D. 1290) resembles Siena Cathedral, but is noticeable as being imbued more considerably with Northern Gothic feeling. It is mainly of one date, and more harmonious in design. The nave is now restored with an open timber roof of the basilican type.

The Church of St. Francis at Assisi was commenced in A.D. 1228, and finished in A.D. 1253. It consists of an upper and lower church, and is very northern in detail, but it depends much more on its frescoed interior, than upon its architecture proper, for its magnificence and character. Both churches are vaulted, built of brick and plastered, for a complete treatment in painted decoration.

SOUTHERN ITALY AND SICILY.

The influences at work in these districts have already been referred to in Romanesque (page 114). The style has been described as "Greek in essence, Roman in form, and Saracenic in decoration."

The Cathedrals at **Messina, Monreale,** and **Palermo.**

The plan of these churches is founded on the Roman basilica type; they are not vaulted, but have timber roofs of great elaboration and intricate construction, resembling in their effect the honeycomb work of Saracenic art. The pointed arch is used, but it is square in section, and without receding planes.

The main idea striven after in these churches is the unfettered display of mosaic decoration, in which the principal personages of the Bible are rendered in a stiff archaic style, with borders of arabesques in gold and colour.

The lower part of the walls has a high dado of white marble, with a border introducing green and purple porphyry in patterns.

Palermo Cathedral is a remarkable example of external architectural decoration in stones of two colours. The apses in particular should be noted. At the west end is a group consisting of a central and two lower towers of an arbitrary style in detail, but suggesting Northern Gothic in its vigour of skyline.

4. COMPARATIVE.

OF NORTH, CENTRAL, AND SOUTH ITALIAN GOTHIC.

A. **Plans.**—The endeavour to create a great central space in their churches is noteworthy, as at Florence and Siena cathedrals (No. 111), and shows the influence of Roman times, and Etruscan originals. The wide spacing of the piers in the nave arcades is specially noticeable.

These arcades are the feature of the interior, the triforium being usually omitted, and the clerestory reduced to the un-importance of a vault spandrel, pierced by a small, and generally circular, window. These lofty arcades practically throw the aisles into the nave, and give the effect of a single hall.

Towers are usually isolated, and are square shafts, sometimes beautifully decorated, continuing the Romanesque tradition, and developing no spire growth, like northern examples.

The central lantern tower, in diminishing stages as at Chiaravalle and Milan (No. 107), may be mentioned as an advance on the Romanesque crossing lantern, and should be compared with English work.

B. **Walls.**—The absence of large windows obviated the necessity for projecting buttresses, the walls being comparatively solid throughout their length, and able to withstand the pressure of a vault without them. From the absence of vertical features and shadows in the façade, we may note that flatness is the predominant characteristic of the style.

Iron tie-rods were used to secure roofs, vaults, and arches, as the constructive feeling in Italian Gothic is subordinated to the decorative.

Façades have often no relation to the structure or roofs behind. These façades are often incomplete, being compositions in marble facing, that had not seldom to be postponed, on the score of expense. The marble is used in bands of two colours at Siena and Orvieto, and in panelling at Florence. This surface treatment should be compared with northern methods, in which effect is obtained by deeply-moulded string courses, projecting buttresses, and lofty pinnacles.

C. **Openings.**—The windows are often semicircular headed, and are provided with shafts having square capitals, instead of the moulded mullions of northern Gothic. These slender shafts are often twisted, and even inlaid with *cosmato* work, while the caps are richly sculptured.

A moulded keystone is often provided to pointed arches, which are frequently inclosed by square lines as a panel.

D. **Roofs** are of low pitch, and play little or no part in the design. Often they are in flat contradiction to the steep gables of the façades, which seem to have been borrowed from the north, and then treated solely as a field for mosaic and other elaborate decoration.

E. **Columns.**—The piers of the arcades in the churches are at times surprisingly clumsy and rude in plan; four pilasters thrown together is a common section. Round piers, with caps and bases, recalling Roman work, are also used. We do not find the continuous sequence in design in such features, as may be traced north of the Alps.

In Milan Cathedral the circular moulded piers, by their height and size, produce the effect of a columnar interior.

F. **Mouldings.**—In mouldings notice the flatness and squareness, and the parts often little changed from Roman work. It should be observed that the section of an arch mould is often identical with that of the jamb, although there may be capitals at the impost. Mouldings are throughout subordinate to the decoration, and the most interesting are those due to the use of brick as a material.

G. **Decoration.**—Opaque decoration was preferred to translucent, the art of fresco by constant exercise upon the noblest subjects in the grandest buildings, led up to the golden age of Michael Angelo and Raphael. Some buildings, such as Giotto's chapel at Padua, and the Sistine chapel at Rome are shells for painted decoration, almost devoid of architectural features. In carving and sculpture classic tradition leads to a refinement and an elegance, which contrasts with the grotesque element found in northern work. On the other hand the general design is often lost sight of in the attention bestowed upon accessories.

5. REFERENCE BOOKS.

G. E. Street's " Brick and Marble of N. Italy."
Waring and Macquoid's " Italian Architecture."
Gally Knight's " Ecclesiastical Architecture."
Hittorf and Zanth, "Sicily."
Ruskin's " Stones of Venice."

SPANISH GOTHIC.

1. INFLUENCES.

i. Geographical.—The architecture of Spain cannot be understood without a knowledge of its geography. The existence of rival races and kingdoms within the peninsula was rendered possible by the mountainous character of some parts, and the subdivision of the country by sierras, or chains of low rocky hills. The kingdom of Granada, where the Moors held out until the close of the Gothic period, is surrounded by mountains which inclose a fertile plain, the pick of the whole country.

ii. Geological.—Stone was the material generally employed, but granite and some of the semi-marbles, which the country throughout possesses, were used in places. Rubble-work, with brick bonding courses and quoins, were used under Moorish influence with much taste and success. Ex. : Toledo, the towers and gates of the city.

iii. Climate.—This varies with the structure of the country, which is that of a series of table lands of varying elevations, divided by sierras.

Burgos, in the north, 3,000 feet above the sea, is cold, and exposed to keen winds even in the summer, while in the south of Spain the climate is African.

iv. Religion.—Constant warfare with the Moors gave a certain unity to Spain, the struggle was a war of religions as well as of races. Allegiance to the papacy has been a characteristic of Spain. Santiago was a pilgrimage centre of more than national importance. In ritual the arrangement of the choirs is to be noted, as well as the size and importance of the chapels attached to the cathedrals.

v. Social and Political.—In the Spanish peninsula,

the Christian states of Castile, Leon, Navarre, Aragon, and Portugal were all growing up and gradually driving the Mahometans into the southern part called Andalusia. After many reverses, the battle of Tolosa (1212), gained by the Christians, was the turning point, after which the Mahometan influence in Spain gradually decayed. St. Ferdinand (1217-1252) united Castile and Leon, and won back Seville and Cordova. James, called the Conqueror (1213-1276). King of Aragon, pressed into the east of Spain until the kingdom of Granada was the only portion left to the Mahometans.

vi. **Historical.**—The study of the history of a country, always necessary in order to properly understand the development of its architecture, is doubly required in the case of Spain, which has been occupied at different times by peoples of different races. After the Romans left Spain the Vandals and Visigoths took possession ; then the country was invaded by the Moors from North Africa, in the seventh century A.D., and for 800 years their influence was continuous. The evidence of this is to be seen in the southern part of the peninsula (the stronghold of their power), where the curious construction, the richness of the architecture, and the exuberance of intricate, and lace-like, detail are everywhere apparent. This influence occasionally reached far into the north. owing to the superior education and ability of Moorish workmen. We find Moorish and semi-Moorish work in northern towns because the Spanish conquests were gradual, thus Toledo was captured by the Christians in 1085, and the final expulsion of the Moors did not take place till 1492.

2. ARCHITECTURAL CHARACTER.

In the south, as already mentioned, there was always more or less of Moorish influence, and from Toledo (the Moorish capital) this influence made itself felt in Saracenic features, such as the horse-shoe arch, and, in later times, the pierced stonework tracery of Moorish design. These fretwork screens occupy the whole window, and are rich in detail. Elsewhere we find buildings, under Moorish influence, covered with intricate geometrical and flowing patterns and rich surface decorations, for which the Saracenic art is everywhere remarkable. Ex.: Jews' synagogue, etc., at Toledo.

The curious early churches of the Spanish conquerors seem to have been executed by the aid of Moorish workmen.

The Gothic style is best in Catalonia, where, though on French lines, it has a special character, owing to the grand scale of the single-span vaulted interiors.

Leon Cathedral in the North goes beyond its French original, in the expanse of window opening and the tenuity of support.

The exteriors generally are flat in appearance, owing to the space between buttresses being utilized internally for chapels.

In the later period, the grafting of classical details on to Gothic forms produced some of the most picturesque features imaginable.

3. EXAMPLES.

CATHEDRALS.

Burgos (A.D. 1220) is irregular in plan (No. 112). The view (No. 113) shows the two towers of the western façade, with their open-work spires. The richly-treated lantern in the background was completed in 1567. The "coro" or choir is in the usual western position. Note that the nave is reduced to a mere vestibule, also the extraordinary size and importance of the side chapels. Ex.: The chapel of the Connestabile, an octagon over 50 feet in diameter, which is specially remarkable for the beauty and richness of its late detail. The character of interior is shown in No. 114.

Toledo Cathedral (A.D. 1227) is a five-aisled church, and resembles Bourges in France in general idea. It is about the same length, but nearly fifty feet wider, and has the choir inclosure west of the crossing, with a singularly shallow apsidal sanctuary. Here is placed an immense retablo or reredos (wood), this being flanked by tiers of arcaded statuary upon the sanctuary piers.

Barcelona Cathedral (A.D. 1298) is remarkable in

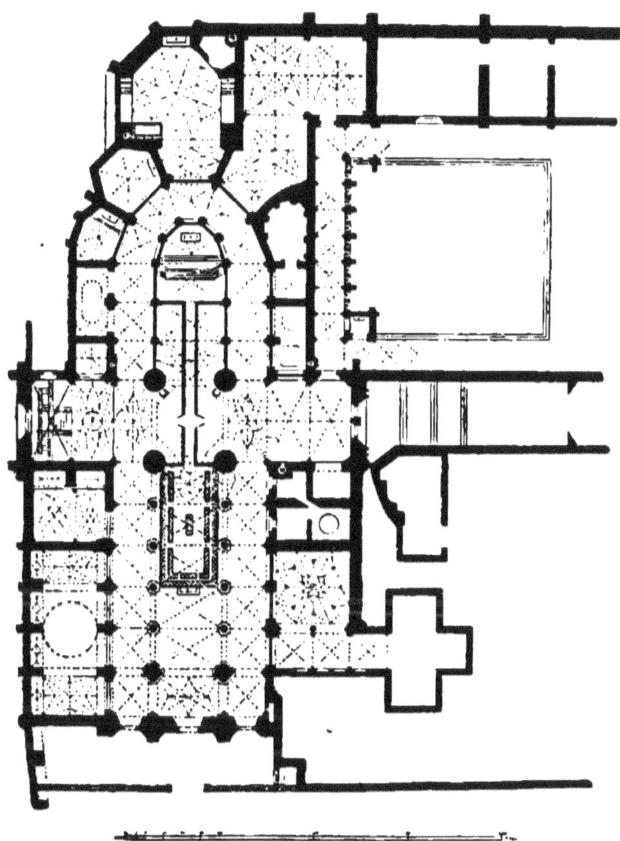

112. PLAN OF BURGOS CATHEDRAL.

that the thrust of the vaults is taken by buttresses, which are internal features, as at Albi in the south of France, the space between being used as chapels. This was developed at **Gerona**, where the aisles have disappeared, and the interior consists of one vaulted hall, 73 feet in width, in four compartments. The Central Hall of the Law Courts will give an idea of this interior.

The Church of S. Maria del Mar, in the poor quarter of Barcelona, is a splendid example of a town church. The vaults rest upon octagonal piers of granite about 4 feet diameter, the spacing being wide, and the aisles and nave of great height. There is no triforium, and only small clerestory windows in the spandrels of the vaults. Severe simplicity is the characteristic of the church ; both inside and out there are no features but a few well-studied mouldings.

Seville Cathedral (1401-1520), erected on the site of a mosque of the same size, is the largest mediæval cathedral erected anywhere. It bears a considerable resemblance to Milan Cathedral, but is less fanciful in detail, or, as some would prefer to say, of a purer Gothic style. The vaulting is rich, loaded with bosses in places, but confused and weak in its lines. Externally there is a certain shapelessness and absence of sky-line. *Note.*—The *parroquia* or parish church is separate, but included within the cathedral area.

The peculiarity of plan was no doubt caused by the structure being made to fill up the space occupied previously by a mosque. It is typically Spanish in having a rectangular outline ; it differs from most of the great Continental churches in having a square east end, and not an apse. Compared with Westminster Abbey (the highest stone-vaulted building in England) we find that the nave of the abbey is the same height and width (practically) as one of the four side aisles of Seville, while the bays of the nave arcade at Westminster are but half the span. The length of the Abbey is slightly under that of Seville. Thus one aisle of Seville represents the size of the nave and choir of the abbey, which is repeated four times at Seville ; in addition to which there is the great nave, 55 feet wide from centre to centre of pier, and 130 feet high. Surrounding the church, and of the same depth as the aisles, are the ring of chapels. From these comparisons we may obtain an idea of the immense size of this Spanish cathedral.

St. Juan de los Reyes, Toledo (No. 115) is a rich example of a sepulchral chapel, erected by Ferdinand and Isabella, comparing in its intended purpose with Henry VII.'s

BURGOS CATHEDRAL.
View from North West.

114. BURGOS CATHEDRAL.
View of the Choir.

Chapel at Westminster. In domestic work the best examples are to be found in Catalonia. Ex.: *Barcelona* municipal buildings, and *Valentia* town hall.

4. COMPARATIVE.

A. **Plans.**—In regard to the plan of the cathedrals, we remark that the great width of many of the naves is a prominent characteristic. The position of the choir is generally to the west of the crossing of nave and transepts, as at Burgos (No. 112); an arrangement probably derived from the Early Christian basilicas, as at St. Clemente, Rome (No. 42). Chapels are numerous and large. The *parroquia*, or parish church, is often included in the area of the cathedral, as at Seville.

The *cimborio*, or dome (No. 114) at the crossing of the nave and transepts, is similar in treatment to examples in the south of France. Compare S. Sernin, Toulouse, and Burgos Cathedral (see under Columns) in plan, and Valentia and St. Ouen at Rouen, in design. Internally these octagon vaults are characteristic; they seem inspired by Moorish work. They are intricate in design and ingenious in construction (No. 115).

B. **Walls.**—In design French models are favoured. The later work is characterized by extreme, and even wild, ornamentation. There is much flatness and absence of sky-line in the exteriors. Burgos has in place of gables effective horizontal terminations by arcades, on the lines of the façade of Notre Dame at Paris. Traceried spires, as in Germany, are favoured; those at Burgos are worthy of attention (No. 113).

C. **Openings** were carried to excess in Leon Cathedral, which has not only a glazed triforium, but also as much as possible of the wall surface of the clerestory glazed as well.

Even in the South, as at Seville, openings are of a large size, stained glass being much used.

D. **Roofs.**—Vaulting is used freely, but developed in decoration, rather than in construction. The tracery, bosses, ribs, etc., employed, produce a rich effect; but the lines are not always good, and nothing to compare in interest with English vaulting was accomplished.

In the South, wide interiors, in one span, were successfully vaulted in a simple style; that at Gerona is no less than 73 feet span, and compares with the hall at Law Courts, London. The boldest and most original vaults are the great flat spans, that form galleries across the western ends of the churches, extending through nave and aisles in three spans. Their rich soffites attract attention on entering, and their curves frame the view of, and give scale to, the interior of the church beyond.

E. **Columns.**—The favourite feature of a lantern at the crossing gives importance to the central piers. At Burgos (No. 112) they are circular in plan (rebuilt 1567), and contrast with the great octagons at S. Sernin, Toulouse.

In Seville Cathedral great column-like piers are employed for all the arcades, similar in effect to those of Milan, but without the tabernacle capitals.

F. **Mouldings.**—Refinement is not the usual characteristic of Spanish work. Original and arbitrary forms will be found, mingled with features borrowed from French work. In Catalonia the best and most artistic work, in a restrained manner, was produced; in S. Maria del Mar, Barcelona (see *ante*, page 196), every moulding has its purpose and expression; but this is far from being the character of other more numerous examples in Spain.

G. **Decoration.**—The most decorative feature in Spanish churches is the vast *retablo* or reredos, which is often as wide as the nave, and reaches up to the vaulting. They are constructed of wood, stone, or alabaster, and are crowded with niches, figures, canopies, and panelling (No. 115).

Painting and gilding are used to heighten the effect, the former naturalistic, and the latter sometimes solid, so that the effect of metal is obtained.

Sculpture in stone or marble is often life-size, naturalistic, and expressive, and however deficient in other qualities, it combines in producing the notoriously impressive, if sensational, interiors of Spanish churches.

Stained glass is used, as at Seville, Oviedo, etc. Usually

115.   SAN JUAN DE LOS REYES, TOLEDO.
Interior.

it is Flemish in style, is heavy in outline, and strong to gaudiness in colouring. *Rejas*, or rich and lofty grilles, (No. 114) in hammered and chiselled iron, must also be counted as decoration. The formality of the long and vertical bars is relieved by figures beaten in *repoussé*, in duplicates, attached back to back, and by crestings and traceries adapted to the material, and freely employed. Few things in Spain are more original and artistic than these *Rejas*.

5. REFERENCE BOOKS.

G. E. Street's "Gothic Architecture in Spain."
Waring and Macquoid's "Architectural Art in Spain."

RENAISSANCE ARCHITECTURE.

> " New structures, that inordinately glow,
> Subdued, brought back to harmony, made ripe
> By many a relic of the archetype
> Extant for wonder ; every upstart church,
> That hoped to leave old temples in the lurch,
> Corrected by the theatre forlorn
> That as a mundane shell, its world late born,
> Lay, and o'ershadowed it."--BROWNING.

GENERAL INTRODUCTION.

THE causes which led to the re-introduction, or re-birth, (Renaissance) of Classic Architecture in Europe at the beginning of the fifteenth century, are instructive, and must be grasped in order fully to understand so great a change.

In this section we shall treat of the Renaissance movement as affecting the whole of Europe.

1. INFLUENCES.

i. **Geographical.**—The Renaissance movement, arising in Italy in the fifteenth century, spread from thence to France, Germany, and England, and over the whole of Western Europe—over what had been, in fact, the Roman empire in the West. The Eastern empire did not come under its influence ; in fact, the Greeks in the East, who had been the most civilized people in Europe, were now falling before the Turks.

ii. **Geological.** } The reader is referred to each country.
iii. **Climate.** }

iv. **Religion.**—The invention of printing, which aided

the spread of knowledge, and the diffusion of freedom of thought, led, among the Teutonic races, to a desire to break away from Romish influence. This desire was originally fostered in England by Wycliffe (A.D. 1377), and by Martin Luther in Germany (A.D. 1517), in which countries Reformation in religion proceeded side by side with Renaissance in architecture. This renewed vigour in thought and literature was accompanied by a fresh building era in northern Europe. In England, civil and domestic architecture received a special impulse from the diffusion among laymen of the wealth and lands of the monasteries dissolved by Henry VIII.

In Italy, on the other hand, where the Reformation took no hold, and where comparatively few churches had been built in the Gothic manner during the Middle Ages, a revival of ecclesiastical architecture took place, and in every important town we find Renaissance churches, carried out on a grand scale and in a most complete manner. The Jesuits who headed the counter-reformation carried the style into all parts, giving to it a special character of their own.

v. Social and Political —A new intellectual movement manifests itself sooner in literature than in architecture, and thus the former influences the public taste. The fall of Constantinople in A.D. 1453, caused an influx of Greek scholars into Italy, whose learning was an important influence in an age which was ripe for a great intellectual change. Thus a revival of classical literature produced a desire for the revival of Roman architecture.

Again, among the MSS. of Greek and Latin authors brought to light about this time, was Vitruvius' book of Architecture, which was translated into Italian in A.D. 1521.

Erasmus (1467-1536), one of the few Greek scholars of the period, worked hard to direct the public attention to the original text of the New Testament, and to the Greek classics, as a set-off to the writings of the schoolmen, whose authority had for so long borne an exclusive sway.

Italian architecture was naturally the first to be affected, because the Gothic style had never taken a firm hold on the Italians, who had at hand the ancient Roman remains, such as the Pantheon, the Basilica of Maxentius, the

Colosseum, the remains of the great baths, and the Roman fora.　In Italy, therefore, practically a direct return was made to Roman forms.　(Refer to each section of Renaissance architecture.

vi. Historical.—We shall find that this section is exceedingly interesting.　At this period—the beginning of the sixteenth century—we note a general grouping together of the smaller states into independent kingdoms, under powerful rulers, who governed with authority, and kept large standing armies.　We find also that three great inventions came into being—gunpowder, which changed the whole method of warfare; the mariner's compass, which led to the discovery of new worlds beyond the sea, and the foundation of colonies by European states; and, lastly, printing, which favoured that stirring of men's minds which caused the reformation in religion, and the revival of learning.

2. ARCHITECTURAL CHARACTER.

The main features in the style, of course, are the revival of the classic orders, viz., the Doric, Ionic, and Corinthian columns or pilasters, with their entablature, which are used decoratively, in the same way as the Romans used them, and are of no constructive value.　Buildings designed for modern wants are clothed in the classic dress of ancient Rome.　It must not be supposed, however, that in this development no advance was made.　It is true that classic precedent was the basis, but the classic decoration of column and pilaster, entablature and details, was applied in many novel and pleasing forms.　System in their application was gradually evolved, and a style built up which has become the vernacular of all modern states.

It is in the decorative detail, also, that such an advance may be noted.　In metal work the bronze baptistery gates at Florence are won in competition by the sculptor Ghiberti, in 1404, and are the finest examples of a class of work for which these craftsmen-architects were famous.　These accessories of architecture were erected, or added to many old buildings, both in Italy and elsewhere.

Note.—Having now taken a rapid survey of the causes which led to the revival of classical architecture throughout Europe, and before proceeding especially to consider the development in each country, let us compare a few of the more prominent characteristics of the style, with the treatment which obtained in Gothic architecture.

3. EXAMPLES (see under each country).

4. COMPARATIVE.

RENAISSANCE.	GOTHIC.
A. **Plans.**—Symmetry and proportion of part to part carefully studied (Nos. 124, 125, 126).	A. **Plans.**—Picturesqueness and beauty of individual features more particularly sought after (Nos. 94, 95, 127).
Grandeur gained by simplicity (No. 121). Fewness of parts has a tendency to make the building appear less in size than it really is.	Grandeur gained by multiplicity (Nos. 80, 101). In consequence of the large number of parts, the building has a tendency to appear larger than it really is.
Towers are sparingly used, and when they occur are symmetrically placed. In England those by Sir Christopher Wren, at St. Paul's (No. 155), and Bow Church, Cheapside, are exceedingly fine. The dome is a predominant feature in the style (Nos. 130, 131, 138).	Towers are a general feature, and are often crowned with a spire (Nos. 78, 80. 93, 96, 103, 104, 106, 113). Small towers, turrets, and finials help to emphasize the vertical tendency (Nos. 101, 107). The tower and spire are predominant features (No. 65).
Interiors of churches are planned on Roman principles (Nos. 122, 124, 125, 126), and covered with flattish domes and pendentives.	Interiors are more irregular, and are covered with stone vaulting (Nos. 79, 81, 91, 102), or open-timbered roofs.
The parts are few, the nave being divided probably into three or four compartments (No. 122). In consequence of this, a general effect of grandeur is produced.	The parts are many, a nave of the same length as a Renaissance church probably divided into twice as many compartments. Compare St. Paul's, London, with Cologne Cathedral (Nos. 124, 127).

RENAISSANCE.

B. **Walls** are constructed in ashlar masonry of smooth-faced walling, which, in the lower storeys, is occasionally heavily rusticated (No. 118). Materials are large, and carry out the classic idea of fewness of parts. Stucco or plaster are often used as a facing material where stone is unobtainable. The idea of the use of the material according to its nature is lost, the design, as such, being paramount. Visible joints are considered a defect.

Angles of buildings often rusticated, as in Florence, *i.e.*, built in blocks of un-smoothed stone, or carefully indented with patterns (No. 120).

Gable ends of churches and buildings generally are formed as pediments, with a low pitch (Nos. 130, 138, 155).

Simplicity of treatment and breadth of mass are prominent characteristics (Nos. 118, 119, 120, 138).

c. **Openings.**—Door and window openings are semi-circular (No. 118, 119, 128, 133), or square-headed (Nos. 120, 134). *Note.*—The influence of climate is important. In Italy, which has a bright climate, the windows are small. In northern Europe, with a dull climate, in the earlier period windows are large, and often have stone mullions or solid uprights dividing the window

GOTHIC.

B. **Walls** are often constructed of uncoursed rubble or small stones (No. 74), not built in horizontal layers, also of brick and rough flint work. Materials are small in size, and carry out the Gothic idea of multiplicity. Stone-work is worked according to the nature of the material to a new and significant extent. It is not too much to say that, as in a mosaic, each piece in a wall has its value in this style.

Angles of buildings often of ashlar masonry or smooth-faced stone, the rest of the walling being of rough materials, as rubble or flint.

Gable ends are steep, occupied by windows, and crowned either with sloping parapet or ornamented timber barge boards (Nos. 75, 80, 89, 150).

Boldness and richness of sky-line and intricacy of mass are prominent characteristics (Nos. 96, 101, 103, 106, 107).

c. **Openings.**—Door and window openings usually pointed (Nos. 82, 83, 86, 93, 96, 102, 109), and of considerable size, and divided by mullions, though not necessarily so. This treatment is for the introduction of painted glass. The use or non-use of this means of decoration influences the size and number of the openings. Often little attention is paid to the axes, *i.e.*, the placing of open-

RENAISSANCE.

RENAISSANCE.

space vertically (Nos. 134, 153). Openings generally come over one another, and are symmetrically disposed with reference to façade.

The classic system of moulded architrave (Nos. 28, 41, 117) projecting from the wall face is revived. Doorways and other openings are surrounded by such architraves, often richly carved.

GOTHIC.

ings over one another. Windows and doors were placed where wanted, without much regard to symmetry of composition.

Openings formed in receding planes (Nos. 82, 86, 116), with mouldings of great richness, are often provided with small circular shafts and carved capitals.

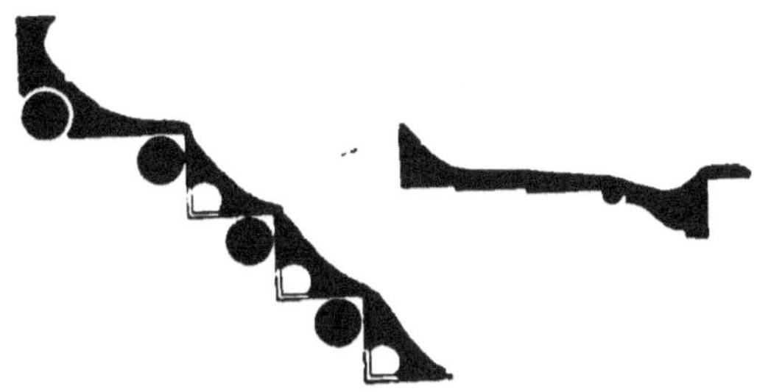

116. Gothic Doorway.   117. Renaissance Doorway.

Comparative Plans of Jambs of Gothic and Renaissance Doorways.

D. **Roofs.**—Vaults are of simple Roman form without ribs. Domes have usually an internal plaster soffit or ceiling, and are painted in coloured fresco, upon which they depend for their beauty. The dome over a large space is generally constructed with an inner and outer covering, as St. Paul's, London (No. 154). Open-timbered roofs occur, as in the Jacobean halls, but the tendency is gradually to plaster them up. All roofs but domes are neglected and hidden as far as may be.

D. **Roofs.**—Vaulting is developed by means of the pointed arch, and depends for effect on the richness of the carved bosses, on the setting out of the ribs, on which the panel of the vaulting rests, and on the grace and beauty of these curves (No. 85). Open-timbered roofs are a beautiful feature of the style, the most perfect specimen in England being Westminster Hall. Externally roofing is an important element in the design, and in conjunction with chimneys, must be reckoned as a means of effect.

RENAISSANCE.	GOTHIC.

E. **Columns.**—The classic columns and orders, revived and used decoratively in façades, as in the Roman manner (Nos. 119, 123, 128, 130, 133), and structurally for porticoes, etc. (Nos. 138, 155).
 	
  " I, from no building, gay or
    solemn,
  Can spare the shapely Grecian
    column."
	E. **Columns**, where used, are entirely constructional, or expressive of pressures upon the piers to which, sometimes, they are attached (Nos. 73, 108, 109). The relative proportion of height to diameter does not exist, and the capitals and bases are either heavily moulded or carved with conventional foliage.

F. **Mouldings.**—The principal cornice plays an important part in the style, and in the Florentine palaces is bold and impressive (Nos. 118, 120). Cornices often, however, mark each storey (Nos. 119, 128). The contours of mouldings follow on classic lines, as may be seen in the architrave (No. 117).	F. **Mouldings.**—The parapet, often battlemented, or pierced with open tracery (Nos. 89, 90, 101, 109), takes the place of a cornice, and is less strongly marked than the boldly projecting classical cornice. The contours and mouldings are portions of circles joined by fillets, inclosed in rectangular recesses (No. 116), or in later times based on a diagonal splay (Nos. 82, 92).
Cornices and other features of classic origin (Nos. 121, 129, 130, 146) occur in every building, and are beautifully carved. Refinement is essential.	Tablets and string courses of carved ornament occur, varying in outline and treatment in different centuries. Gothic mouldings depend for effect upon light and shadow.
Cornices, balconies, string bands, and horizontal features generally (Nos. 118, 119, 120, 128) are strongly pronounced, and produce an effect of *horizontality*.	Vertical features, such as buttresses casting a deep shadow, numerous pinnacles, turrets, high roofs, with towers and spires, produce an effect of *verticality*.
G. **Decoration.**—The human figure abandoned as a scale, statuary being often much larger than life-size (Nos. 123, 130, 131, 155).	G. **Decoration.**—The human figure adhered to as a scale, thus helping in giving relative value to parts.
Stained glass is little used, all of the best efforts at colour being by means of opaque decoration, as fresco	Stained glass is extensively used, is the chief glory of internal decoration, and partly the *raison*

RENAISSANCE.	GOTHIC.
or mosaic, which is lavishly applied to interiors. (Ex.: the Sistine Chapel, Rome, by Michael Angelo.)	*d'être* of the immense traceried windows, which acted as a frame for its reception (Nos. 80, 81, 89, 96).
"Sgraffito" decoration, *i.e.*, scratched and coloured plaster, is sometimes applied to exteriors. (Ex.: the *Palazzo del Consiglio*, by Fra Giocondo, at Verona.)	Colour is dependent on the actual material, as in the coloured marbles of central Italy (see No. 110, Florence Cathedral).
Great efficiency in the crafts is noticeable in the work of the early Renaissance architects, who are often painters and sculptors, *e.g.*, Donatello, Ghiberti, and Della Robbia, and students should see their work in the South Kensington Museum.	Carving is often grotesque and rudely executed, but in the best examples possesses a decorative character, in harmony with the architecture. This is effected by the constructive features themselves being enriched.

Note.—It is now necessary to glance briefly through the chief peculiarities of the Renaissance style or manner in each country, noticing the influence of climate and race, and, where possible, the social and political causes which were at work.

As about this period the names of architects begin to be prominently mentioned in connection with their own designs, we shall find it sometimes convenient to group them into schools for that purpose. In this respect the student will derive much benefit from reading "The History of the Lives and Works of the most celebrated Architects," by Quatremère de Quincy, and the biographies of G. Vasari, Milizia, and others, translations of which are published, and will be found in the R.I.B.A. Library. His interest in their works will be much increased by reading of the influences which directed these master-minds, and the various incidents in their lives, which tended to influence their work.

The student should study many excellent examples which have been collected in the architectural courts of the South Kensington Museum; it is only by a close study of the details themselves that the style can be thoroughly grasped.

ITALIAN RENAISSANCE.

"Come, leave your Gothic, worn-out story.
.   .   .   .
They love not fancies just betrayed,
And artful tricks of light and shade,
But pure form nakedly displayed,
And all things absolutely made."—CLOUGH.

THE Renaissance of Italy varies considerably in the chief centres of the great revival, namely, **Florence, Rome,** and **Venice.** This was due to various social and political causes, which we will endeavour to enumerate shortly.

THE FLORENTINE SCHOOL.

" Florence at peace, and the calm, studious heads
Come out again, the penetrating eyes ;
As if a spell broke, all resumed, each art
You boast, more vivid that it slept awhile.
'Gainst the glad heaven, o'er the white palace front
The interrupted scaffold climbs anew ;
The walls are peopled by the painter's brush,
The statue to its niche ascends to dwell."—BROWNING.

1. INFLUENCES.

i. **Geographical.**—It must be remembered that Florence was more than a city, being, in fact, one of the powers of Italy, although its dominions included no large part of Central Italy. The activity and influence of the Florentines caused a Pope to declare that they were the fifth element.

ii. **Geological.**—The quarries of Tuscany supplied large

118.   Palazzo Riccardi, Florence.

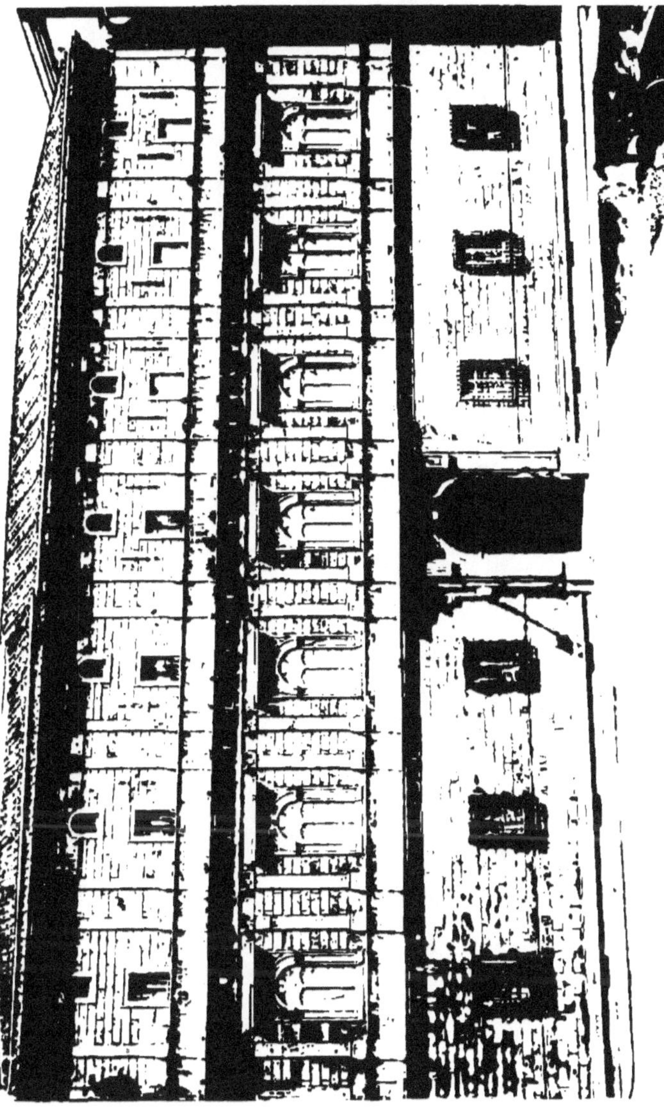

blocks of stone and marble, which, lying near the surface, were easily obtainable for building purposes. The monumental character and massiveness of these materials considerably influence the style of the architecture, as will be at once apparent to every student (No. 118).

iii. Climate.—Among other causes which affected the development of the style, we should note that the bright and sunny climate rendered large openings for light unnecessary. The character of the climate is well indicated by Tennyson :

> " In bright vignettes, and each complete
> Of tower or duomo, *sunny-sweet*,
> Or palace, how the city glittered
> Through cypress avenues, at our feet."

iv. Religion.—At this period Florence produced the great Dominican preacher, Savonarola, whose reforming energy divided the city, and swayed its policy. He looked to the French king to call a general council to reform the church. In art he tended to the Puritan theory. Although suppressed by the Pope, his influence on the minds of his generation was not lost—the Sistine frescoes witness his power over Michael Angelo.

v. Social and Political.—The Medici dynasty, so intimately connected with the rise of Florentine art, was founded by John of Medici, who died 1429. He took the popular side against the nobles, gradually usurping supreme authority over the state. His son Cosimo, who died 1464, employed his wealth liberally in the advancement of art. He founded the Medici Library and Platonic Academy, and was the patron of Brunelleschi, Donatello, Michelozzo, Lippi, Masaccio, and others. Cosimo was succeeded by Pietro and Lorenzo Medici, and Florence became the centre of the Renaissance in art and literature.

The artists of the period were at the same time sculptors, painters, and architects; among these were—Luca della Robbia (1400-1482), famous for his glazed reliefs in terracotta; Lorenzo Ghiberti (1378-1455), the sculptor of the bronze gates to the Baptistery; and Donatello (1386-1466).[1] As showing the commercial prosperity of Florence, we may

---

[1] Famous for his bas-reliefs and statues at Florence and elsewhere.

note that the golden florin was first coined in that city in 1252, and soon became the general standard of value in Europe.

As rival parties in the city were engaged in constant hostilities, safety and defence were primary motives in building. The palaces are in reality semi-fortresses.

vi. Historical.—Florence commenced to grow on the removal of the inhabitants of Fiesole, down to the banks of the Arno in 1125.

The grouping together of the independent commonwealths of Italy is a feature of this period, and, as in ancient Greece, one city bore rule over another. Pisa became subject to Florence in 1406. Florence gradually becomes the chief power in Italy. During this period the nobles were at constant feuds with each other, being divided into the hostile camps of Guelphs and Ghibellines, the former being generally successful. Dante Alighieri (1265-1321) took part in these conflicts. Eventually the wealthy family of the Medici becomes the ruling power in the State (see above). In 1494 Charles VIII. of France occupied Florence, during his brief invasion of Italy, arising from his claims on the kingdom of Naples. The short-lived republic of Savonarola (see above) followed, but the Medici, in spite of successive banishments, were finally reinstated by the Emperor Charles V., who took the town in 1530, acting on behalf of the Ghibellines. During a siege of eleven months, Michael Angelo acted as the engineer of the republic. The suppression of political liberty followed, especially under Cosimo I. (1537-1564), who, however, greatly extended the Florentine dominions, Siena being ceded to him in 1557 by the Emperor. His successors, the Grand Dukes of Florence, followed, until in 1737 the House of Medici became extinct. The Duchy then passed into the hands of Austria till 1801, when, as the Republic, and afterwards as the Kingdom of Etruria, it enjoyed political freedom (with the exception of the years 1807-1814, during which time it was incorporated with France). In 1860 it was united to the Kingdom of Italy.

2. ARCHITECTURAL CHARACTER.

The massive blocks of rusticated masonry in the lower storeys (No. 118) of the Florentine Palaces, give to these buildings that character of solidity and ruggedness for which they are remarkable. The absence of pilasters, as ornamentation, is specially noticeable in the design of the palaces, which are therefore called "astylar." The sparing use of carved detail, and in fact of features of any kind, gives a marked character of simplicity to the style. The grand effect of these palaces is considerably aided by the massive cornice which crowns the structure, being proportioned to the whole height of the building, as in the Riccardi Palace (No. 118).

3. EXAMPLES.

The best-known Florentine palaces are :

The **Riccardi Palace** (No. 118) (1430), by Brunelleschi and Michelozzo.

The **Pitti Palace** (1440), by Brunelleschi and Michelozzo.

The **Strozzi Palace** (1489), by Cronaca.

These are all of the massive type of construction. The Ruccellai Palace (1460), by Alberti, and the Gaudagni Palace, by Cronaca, are lighter and more refined.

The types of doors and windows may be divided into three groups :

(*a*.) **The arcade** type, usual in the heavily rusticated examples, which is employed at the Strozzi, Pitti, and Riccardi Palaces, consists of a round arch, in the centre of which is a circular column supporting a simple piece of tracery (No. 118).

(*b*.) **The architrave** type is that in which mouldings inclose the window, and consoles on either side support a horizontal or pediment cornice, as in the courtyard of the Pandolfini Palace and in the Palazzo Riccardi.

(*c*.) **The order** type is that in which the opening is framed with a pilaster or column on each side supporting an entablature above; this is the final development, as employed in the Pandolfini Palace, ascribed to Raphael, and also shown in No. 120.

Note.—As we have reached the period when the personality of the architect has increased in importance, we will now enumerate very briefly the chief works of Brunelleschi and Alberti, as being the leaders of the Florentine school.

BRUNELLESCHI (1377-1444),

a Florentine by birth, studied the construction of the Pantheon at Rome in order to be able to complete the unfinished dome over the Cathedral of Florence, the carrying out of which he afterwards won in competition. He was thus induced to study the features of Roman architecture, which henceforth exerted a considerable influence over his works.

Brunelleschi's chief works are :

The dome of Florence Cathedral, 1420 (No. 110).
The Church of St. Spirito, Florence. (Built after his death.)
The Chapel of the Pazzi at Florence, 1420.
The Pitti Palace, 1440.

ALBERTI (1404-1472)

was a scholar deeply interested in classical literature. His works exhibit more decorative treatment, and are less massive than Brunelleschi's (compare the Ruccellai and Pitti Palaces). He wrote a work on architecture, " De Re Ædificatoria," which largely influenced men's minds in favour of the Roman style.

His principal works are :

Palazzo Ruccellai (1460).
The Church of St. Francesco at Rimini (1447-1455).
St. Andrea at Mantua (1472).

St. Andrea is important as the type of many modern Renaissance churches, and consists of a single nave with transepts, all barrel-vaulted above a single order on a pedestal. Chapels, alternated with entrance vestibules, take the place of the customary aisles on each side of the nave. Over the intersection of nave with the transept is a dome, in the drum, or lower portion, of which are windows lighting the interior. The chancel is apsidal, lighted by three windows, which cause the entablature to be mitred round the pilasters of the order, which carry the lunetted half dome of the apse.

The perfection of the proportions makes the interior of this church one of the grandest in the style.

> *Note.*—For **Comparative** Table of Florence, Rome, and Venice, see p. 227.

5. REFERENCE BOOKS.

Grandjean and Famin's "Toscane."
"Romola," by George Eliot.   (Historical Novel.)

THE ROMAN SCHOOL.

1. INFLUENCES.

i. **Geographical.**—The unique character of Rome as an influence was its prestige as the seat of an empire that had crumbled away.   The ruins and new buildings are important, on account of their more than local influence.

ii. **Geological.**—The remains of old Rome, such as the Colosseum and the Pantheon, formed the quarry from which much of the material for the Renaissance buildings was extracted.

iii. **Climate.**—Refer to previous sections (pages 51, 182).

iv. **Religion.**—From the time of the Council of Constance, 1415, the popes take a more prominent position as Italian princes.   During the fifteenth century the popes greatly extended their temporal dominions in Italy.   One party hoped that Italian unity would be effected under the papal sway.   Cæsar Borgia, nephew to Alexander VI., proposed to effect this, by absorbing the Italian states as one would eat an artichoke—leaf by leaf. Julius II. besieged Bologna in person, as sacred and secular capacities were often obscured in the same pope. The Jesuits, founded in the later Renaissance period, existed to counter-work the Reformation, by rendering the papal influence universal. See below.

v. Social and Political.—In Rome a central government existed, and in consequence party spirit was checked, thus we do not find the same fortified palaces as at Florence. Rome was the home of the old classic traditions, which would naturally exert great influence in any new development.

During the fifteenth century the popes were temporal princes, and great patrons of art and learning. Splendid new palaces and churches were erected, and the decoration of old ones was carried on. A school of artists and workmen was created who afterwards spread abroad the style of the Renaissance in other parts of Italy and beyond.

vi. Historical.—During the absence of the popes at Avignon, the factions of the barons continued unchecked, except during the brief rule of Rienzi's republican state, 1347. The return of the popes took place in 1376 under Gregory XI. The scandal of rival popes at Rome and Avignon was terminated in 1415 by the Council of Constance, after which Rome rapidly gained in wealth and prestige. Julius II., a warlike and ambitious pope, extended the temporal power, and founded the new S. Peter's and the Vatican.

Spanish influence became powerful, and was not always exerted for good. It was replaced by French influence, which was strong under Louis XIV. Then the growth of the power of Austria was felt throughout the Peninsula, until the rise of national feeling which, though checked in 1848, led in 1870 to Rome becoming the capital of New Italy. This remarkable revolution was effected without Rome ceasing to be the headquarters of the papacy.

2. ARCHITECTURAL CHARACTER.

The classic orders were largely used in the façades and courtyards (Nos. 119, 120), and a general attempt at correctness and conformity to the ideas of ancient Roman architecture prevailed. The size and simplicity of the palaces of Rome produce an effect of dignity (No. 119).

The principle which animated architects in the later school was that of unity, which they endeavoured to attain by making a whole building appear to be of a single storey; for this reason, two or more storeys are included under an order of pilasters, which is sometimes crowned by an attic, but never by another superimposed order. Arcuation is only sparingly introduced, except it be in the form of tiers of arcades, in imitation of the Colosseum.

3. EXAMPLES.

Note.—It will be most convenient and useful to the student if we consider this school under its successive leaders, beginning with Bramante.

BRAMANTE (1444-1514)

was the first Roman architect of note; he was educated as a painter under Andrea Mantegna, and was probably a pupil of Alberti. He was a Florentine by birth, but studied at Rome, first practising in the city of Milan, and in the dominions of its duke. His earlier works, as, for example, the choir of St. Maria della Grazie at Milan, are essentially in a transition style with Gothic tendencies, while his later works exhibit classical " correctness."

Ex. : The Cancellaria Palace, 1508.

The Giraud Palace (No. 119), 1503.

The Belvedere Court of the Vatican, 1506.

The small *tempietto* in the cloister of St. Pietro in Montorio (1502) is a perfect gem of architecture.

Bramante's works of the middle period exhibit especially

delicate mouldings, and great refinement in carving and detail; thus he uses flat pilasters, and circular-headed openings, framed by square lines. His "Ultima Maniera" is seen in the bold and grand designs for the Courts of Law (never finished) near the Tiber, and in his "projects" for St. Peter's.

An article on "The School of Bramante," by Baron von Geymüller, which appeared in the R.I.B.A. Transactions, 1891, is interesting, as tending to show the enormous influence which Bramante, who may be called the "continuator" of the style of Alberti, exerted on the development of the Renaissance in Rome and in every European country. It is well worth careful reading.

BRAMANTE'S PUPILS AND FOLLOWERS.

Baldassare Peruzzi (1481-1536) was the architect of the Villa Farnese at Rome.

Holford House, Park Lane, London, by Vulliamy, is founded on this design.

Also the Massimi Palace, Rome, an example full of refinement and beauty, both in design and detail. The five-domed church at Todi, Perugia, is ascribed to his influence. Few architects of the school were so well trained, and able to execute works so finished in detail, whether of plan, section, or elevation.

Ant. di Sangallo (d. 1546) erected the Farnese Palace at Rome (No. 120). This is the grandest of all the examples of the school. It is executed in brick walling with travertine dressings from the Colosseum.

We may note especially the absence of pilasters to each storey, which appear only as frames to the windows. Each storey is well marked horizontally by projecting string courses. The grand crowning cornice was added later by Michael Angelo, but was a special feature in the design, from the first.

The internal open court ("cortile") is in the style of the Colosseum ; a reduced cast of part of the same may be seen at the Crystal Palace Italian Renaissance Court.

Raphael (1483-1520) was the nephew and pupil of

Farnese Palace, Rome.

120.

121.

THE CAPITOL, ROME.

(Centre.) Palace of the Senators.
(Right.) Palace of the Conservatori
(Left.) Capitoline Museum.

Bramante. Authorities differ as to his exact responsibility for the designs ascribed to him.

His works at Rome: He was engaged on St. Peter's (but did little), and designed the façade of San Lorenzo.

His works at Florence: The Pandolfini Palace, erected in 1530 (ten years after his death).

The excavation of the Baths of Titus gave Raphael an opportunity of studying the interior decoration of ancient Roman buildings. The use of hard stucco, combined with painted work, was one of the things learnt by him from these remains. The surface of the vaulting was found to be painted with studies from the vegetable kingdom, with figures of men and animals; and with such objects as vessels and shields, all blended together in fanciful schemes, rendered pleasing by bright colouring.

The designs for the decoration of the Loggie at the Vatican, which he carried out, were based on these Roman examples.

Giulio Romano (1492-1546) was a pupil of Raphael, and was the architect of the Villa Madama at Rome, and of work at Mantua, including his masterpiece the Palazzo del Té. This latter is a one-storey building, decorated with the Doric order. It is quadrangular in plan, and comprises large saloons round a central court. The recessed arcaded façade to the garden is remarkable, and, as a whole, the design is perhaps the nearest approach made on the part of a Renaissance architect to reproduce the features of a Roman villa.

VIGNOLA (1507-1573)

exercised great influence by his writings. He was the author of "The Five Orders of Architecture," and the architect of

The Villa of Pope Julius at Rome, now the Etruscan Museum.

The Pentagonal Palace at Caprarola (see page 236).

The two small cupolas at St. Peter's.

The municipal palace at Bologna (unfinished).

Being taken back to France by Francis I., he exercised a great influence on the development of French Renaissance architecture.

MICHAEL ANGELO (1474-1564)

a Florentine, famous sculptor, and painter of the roof of the Sistine Chapel in the Vatican in A.D. 1508, also turned his attention, late in life, to architecture. He finished the Farnese Palace, and carried out the dome of St. Peter's (see below). Perhaps his best work is the reconstruction of the Palace of the Capitol (No. 121), a grand example of a one-order building. Reckless detail mars all his architecture.

His principal work at Florence is the Medici Chapel, and the Sacristy and Laurentian Library at S. Lorenzo.

St. Peter's at Rome (1506-1626).

It is thought to be desirable, and probably will be of use to give here a sketch of the **general scheme** *of the construction of this building, with various data.*

In plan (outline plan, No. 125) it is a Greek cross, the later extension of the nave and aisles toward the west, which practically brings the whole scheme to a Latin cross, is excused, solely as inclosing the whole of the area of the previously existing church. The nave consists of four bays of immense size ; the central crossing is covered by the dome, the short transepts are terminated by semicircular apses, the eastern arm being precisely similar. The high altar stands under the dome, within a baldachino, over the alleged tomb of St. Peter. A vestibule at the west end extends the whole width of the church.

The interior (No. 122) has one gigantic order of Corinthian pilasters, crowned with semicircular barrel vaults. The walls are faced with plaster, and coloured to imitate marble, producing a rich though false effect ;—the dome is beautifully decorated in mosaic, and reminds us of Pope's words :

> " No single parts unequally surprise,
> All comes united to th' admiring eyes."

The exterior (No. 123), roughly executed in travertine, has an immense order of Corinthian pilasters, with an attic surrounding the entire building. The view of the dome is entirely cut off, except at a distance, behind the screen wall of the now extended nave. A good idea of the building, in its general distribution, is to be obtained from the model at the Crystal Palace, in which, however, as in most drawings of the church, the detail is rendered less offensive by its smaller scale.

Memoranda:

1506.—Bramante was the original architect, and formulated a design in the form of a Greek cross with entrances at west end. Foundation stone laid.

1514.—Death of Bramante.

1513.—Sangallo (d. 1516), Raphael, Fra Giocondo (d. 1515), are intrusted with superintendence of the work. Division of opinion exists as to altering original plan to a Latin cross.

1520.—Death of Raphael.

1520.—Baldassare Peruzzi appointed architect, but dies 1536. The capture of Rome disorganized all artistic work.

1536.—Sangallo succeeds him as architect. Proposes a picturesque design of many orders, with a central dome and lofty campanili.

1546.—Michael Angelo appointed architect. He rejected the innovations of Sangallo, restored the design to a Greek cross, simplified the form of the aisles, in which process the masterly planning, by Bramante, of the accessories to the dome, which were to give scale to the interior, disappeared, and strengthened the pillars of the dome, which had shown signs of weakness. He planned and commenced the construction of the great dome, the drum of which he completed, and at his death (1564) left drawings and models, for the completion of the work up to the lantern.

1564.—The building of the church was continued by Giacomo della Porta, and Vignola, who added the two smaller domes. These, excellent in themselves, are ineffective in relation to the whole mass.

1606.—Carlo Maderno, instructed by Paul V., lengthened the nave to form a Latin cross, and erected the present contemptible façade.

1661.—Bernini erected the fourfold colonnades inclosing the piazza in front.

> " With arms wide open to embrace
> The entry of the human race."
>
> BROWNING.

In Baron von Geymüller's book, mentioned below, there
is a plan, with the portions of separate dates coloured
differently, which is very interesting, and also a comparison
drawn between the fundamental principles of design which
characterize each scheme.

Comparative plans (No. 124):

	St. Peter's (No. 125).	Milan.	St. Paul's.	Sta. Sophia (No. 48).	Cologne (No. 127).
Area in sq. yds.	18,000	10,000	9,350	8,150	7,400
Length in yards.	205	148	170	118	156
		Pantheon (No. 35).			Florence.
Diam. of dome.	138 ft.	142 ft. 6. in.	100 ft.	106 ft. 9 in.	134 ft. 6 in.

Note.—For **Comparative** Table of Florence, Rome,
and Venice, see p. 227.

REFERENCE BOOKS.

Geymüller, " Les Projets primitifs pour la Basilique de
St. Pierre."

Percier and Fontaine's " Rome."

Letarouilly's " Edifices de Rome Moderne."

" Detail and Ornament of the Italian Renaissance," by
G. J. Oakeshott.

" Rienzi," by Lord Lytton.   (Historical Novel.)

THE VENETIAN SCHOOL.

> " Underneath day's azure eyes,
> Ocean's nursling, Venice lies,
> A peopled labyrinth of walls,
> Amphitrite's destined halls,
> Which her hoary sire now paves
> With his blue and beaming waves.

> Lo ! the sun upsprings behind,
> Broad, red, radiant, half-reclined
> On the level, quivering line
> Of the water's crystalline ;
> And before that dream of light,
> As within a furnace bright,
> Column, tower, and dome, and spire
> Shine like obelisks of fire,
> Panting with inconstant motion
> From the altar of dark ocean
> To the sapphire-tinted sky."—SHELLEY.

1. INFLUENCES.

i. Geographical.—The greatness of Venice was founded in earlier times on her oriental commerce, due to her important geographical position. The effect of this commercial prosperity is visible well into Renaissance times. The history of the Venetian state was always influenced by the proximity of the sea, and the peculiar formation of the coast.

ii. Geological.—The structure of Venice, as a city founded in the sea ; its churches, palaces, and houses being set upon piles, in a shallow lagoon, had an important influence on its art.

iii. Climate. — Favours out-door life. The heat in summer is great, though tempered by sea breezes. The open top storeys, called belvederes, exist in many houses. The northern position renders chimneys more prominent than in other Italian cities.

iv. Religion.—Venice continued to maintain a semi-independence of the Pope, due to her political necessities in those days of the growing temporal power. Strong loyalty to the State even among the clergy was manifested during the attempted interdict of Paul V. The learned theologian Paolo Sarpi (lived 1552-1623) was the adviser of the State during this crisis (1607). The tolerance of Venetian policy is shown by the erection of the Greek church, an interesting example of the local Renaissance.

v. Social and Political.—During the whole of the fifteenth century, Venice was engaged in conquering the surrounding towns, Venetian nobles being appointed their governors.

The government of Venice was a republic, and the rivalry of the leading families led to the erection of fine and lasting monuments, such as the palaces which line the Grand Canal; and these moreover were not fortresses, as at Florence, but the residences of peaceable citizens.

vi. Historical.—In the middle of the fifteenth century (1453) Constantinople was taken by the Turks, and the supremacy of Venice in the East was undermined. By the discovery of the new route to India, at the close of the fifteenth century, its commerce was diverted to the Portuguese. During the sixteenth and seventeenth centuries they were at constant war with the Turks; eventually in 1715 the whole of her possessions, except in North Italy, were taken from her. Yet "the arts which had meanwhile been silently developing shed a glorious sunset over the waning glory of the mighty republic."

2. ARCHITECTURAL CHARACTER.

The Renaissance movement had a very different effect upon the architecture of Venice from that which it produced upon the architecture of Florence, owing to the different circumstances of the two cities. The Venetians had a beautiful type of Gothic architecture of their own, and, being further from Rome, were not so much under the influence of that city as was Florence. Therefore, between the periods of Gothic and fully-developed Renaissance, we find a period of transition, the earlier buildings in the new style having Gothic in conjunction with Renaissance details. We may notice this, for instance, in the pointed arches of the Renaissance façade in the courtyard of the Doge's Palace.

The architecture of Venice is, in general, of a lighter and more graceful kind than that of Florence. Columns and pilasters are used freely in all designs. A special Venetian feature is that the windows are grouped near the centre, leaving comparatively solid boundaries to the façade (No. 128). The façades are comparatively flat, and have no great projections, in consequence of the houses being situated

on the side of canals, and having therefore to keep a straight
frontage with the water.

The rustication of walls, as at Florence, is comparatively
unknown. The façades usually have cornices marking
each floor (No. 128), in contrast with the great crowning
Florentine cornice.

The balconies (No. 128) are a graceful and important
feature, and give light and shade to the façade, having the
same effect as, and taking the place of, recessing.

The regularity of the disposition of a Venetian façade is
described by Browning, who talks of the

> " Window just with window mating,
> Door on door exactly waiting."

In later work, the perfection of the details is the marked
feature of the Venetian Renaissance, as, for instance, in
St. Mark's Library and the palaces by Sansovino. In Longhena's works, and other late examples the detail becomes
large, and projects boldly. Strong effects of light and shade
are produced, and heavy rustication is used to contrast the
basement with the order above (No. 129).

3. EXAMPLES.

PALACES.

The more important buildings are :

The Doge's Palace, commenced 1486, in which we
should remark the Giant's Staircase, erected by Sansovino in
1554, situated in the courtyard of the palace.

    Note.—The Geological Museum in Piccadilly is founded
      on the design of the lower part of the courtyard façade
      of this palace.

The Library of St. Mark, by Sansovino, the design
of which has been followed in the Carlton Club, Pall Mall,
was erected in 1536. (The continuation, one order higher,
round St. Mark's square, is by Scamozzi.)

The Zecca or Mint, erected by Sansovino, 1536.

The Vendramini Palace (1600) (No. 128). Each

storey has an order, the windows are semicircular, with a Renaissance treatment of tracery.

The Cornaro Palace by Sansovino (1532).

The Grimani Palace, by San Micheli (1549), and the **Pesaro Palace**, by Longhena (seventeenth century) (No. 129).

CHURCHES.

In the early period.

St. Maria dei Miracoli (1480), erected by Pietro Lombardo, is noteworthy as having no aisles; the choir is raised twelve steps above the nave, which is covered with a roof of semicircular form, not uncommon in Venice. It is emphasized by a circular pediment on the façade. (This feature also occurs at S. Zaccaria, Venice.) The walls are faced internally and externally, with different coloured marbles, which are delicately carved. The sacristy is beneath the raised choir.

In the later period.

The **Church of St. Francesco della Vigna**, by
  Palladio (1568),
The **Church of the Redentore**, by Palladio (1576),
The **Church of St. Giorgio Maggiore**, by Palladio
  (1560) (No. 130),
are instructive, as exhibiting the difficulties of adopting the classic orders to buildings for modern purposes.

The Church of **S. Maria della Salute** (No. 131), by Longhena, in 1632, is erected on the Grand Canal, and groups most beautifully with the surroundings.

  Plan (No. 132): An octagon with chapels projected one on
    each side, the central space being covered by a circular
    dome. Notice the buttresses (No. 131) to the central
    dome over the aisles, and how their fanciful shapes
    contribute to the effect. A secondary dome covers the
    chancel (projected on the side opposite the entrance),
    and a small tower, also carried up, contributes to the
    picturesque grouping of the exterior.

125.

PALAZZO VENDRAMINI, VENICE.

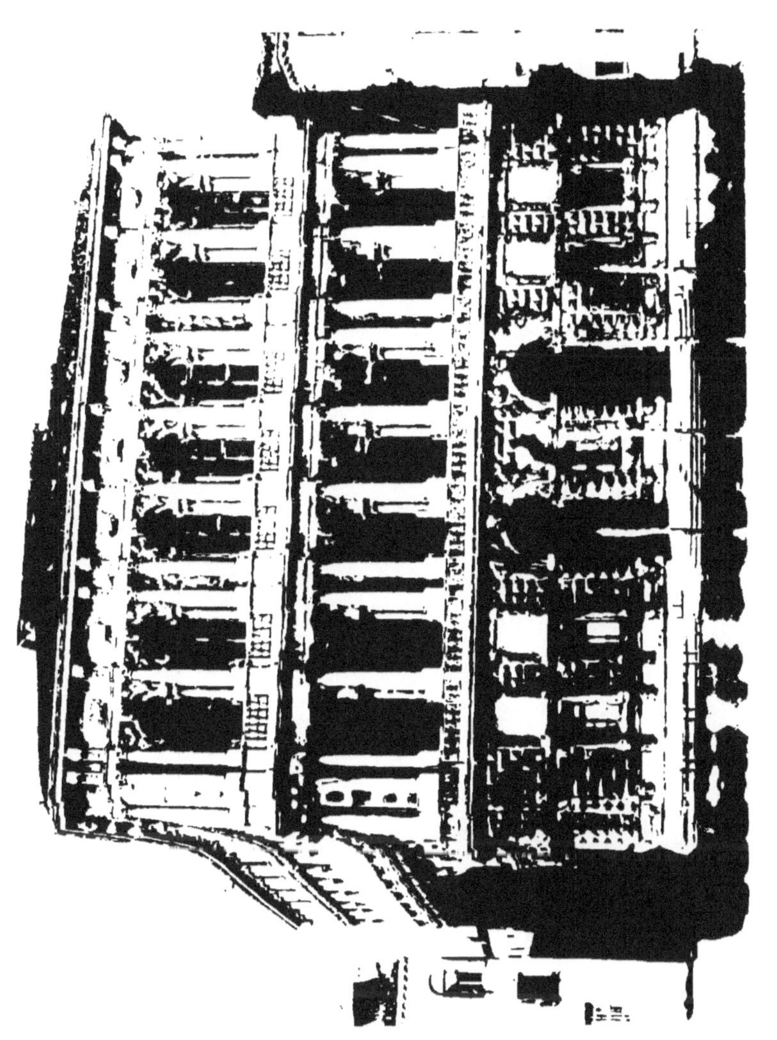

THE PESARO PALACE, VENICE.

129.

130.   S. Giorgio Maggiore, Venice.

131   S. Maria della Salute, Venice.

4. REFERENCE BOOK.

Cicognara's "Venezia."

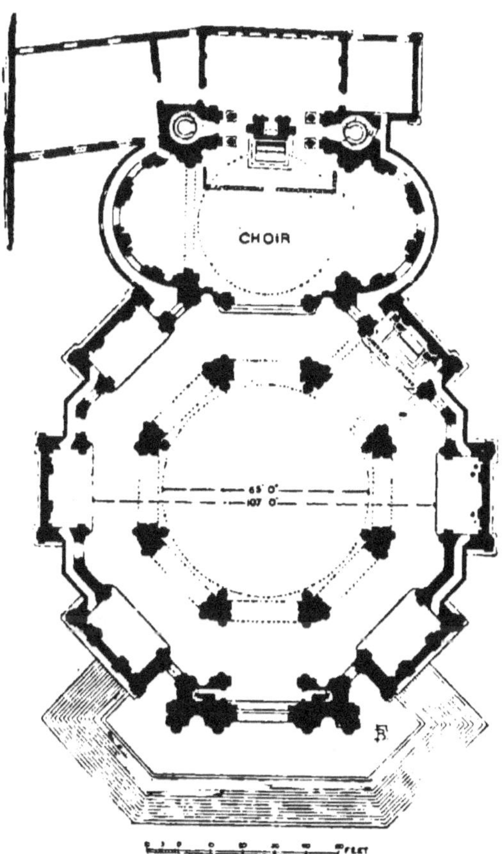

132. STA. MARIA DELLA SALUTE (PLAN).

VICENZA AND VERONA

are also notable cities to the student of Renaissance architecture, they are counted in the Venetian School.

    Vicenza is interesting as the birthplace of **Palladio,**

and as the scene of his labours. Palladio indefatigably studied, and measured, all the Roman antiquities, as may be seen by the drawings in his book on architecture. His designs are mostly erected in brick and stucco, the lower storey being rusticated, and the upper ones having pilasters. A second method of his was to comprise two floors in the height of the order, to obtain scale in that feature, and unity and dignity in the whole composition. There are several examples in Vicenza of this treatment.

The arcade surrounding and casing the mediæval **town hall** at **Vicenza**, is his most famous work (No. 133). It is built in a beautiful stone, and is in two storeys of Doric and Ionic orders.

The **Villa del Capra** (generally known as the Rotunda) near Vicenza is an example of the application of the features of classical architecture carried to an extreme. It is a square building, with a pillared portico on each face leading to a central rotunda, which appears externally as a low dome above the tiled roof which is hipped all ways from the angles of the main building. This building was copied by Inigo Jones at Chiswick, and elsewhere, both in England and on the Continent.

Although Palladio's designs were mainly executed in mean materials, and were often never fully carried out, still their publication in books had a far-reaching influence on European architecture.

At **Verona** the architect **San Micheli**, a man of great ability, erected several palaces, of which the Palazzo Pompeii is the most noticeable.

He was more or less a military architect, being the originator of a new system of fortification. The entrance gateways through the fortifications of Verona, are notable instances of his power of giving character to his works; they are bold and original in treatment. He gave great extension to the use of rustication as a means of effect.

The **Palazzo del Consiglio** at Verona was erected in 1500 by **Fra Giocondo**, and is chiefly remarkable for the coloured "sgraffito work" of the façade.

133. The Basilica at Vicenza, by Palladio.

COMPARATIVE TABLE OF THE FLOREN-TINE, ROMAN, AND VENETIAN SCHOOLS.

A. Plans.

Florence.—The utmost simplicity and compactness, a style of planning adapted to town, rather than country buildings.—Staircases inclosed in *walls* vaulted by ascending barrel vaults.

Rome.—More varied planning on a grander scale. Staircases, circular and elliptical, with columnar supports, are attempted.

Venice.—Where an open site permits, a broken, complex, and picturesque disposition is adopted, otherwise a straight front to the canals has to be adhered to. Staircases, developed in a central area, and with arcades around, belong to this school.

B. Walls.

Florence.—The style of fenestration and rusticated quoins (No. 118); the astylar treatment is adopted, which dispenses with orders and makes each storey complete in itself, while subordinated as a whole by the great top cornice. In pure wall treatment it is akin to Egyptian work.

Rome.—The style of pilasters (No. 121). Storeys are united by an order upon a grand scale (No. 121), several storeys high. Windows become disturbing elements, without which the designs would have the unity of Greek temples.

Venice.—The style of columns (Nos. 128, 129). Storeys are defined by an order to each. Excessive separation by the entablatures is modified, and corrected by breaking them round the columns. In the multiplicity of parts the style allies itself to the Roman, as in the Colosseum.

C. Openings.

Florence.—Openings are small, wide-spaced, and severe in treatment. The typical opening is an archway in rusticated work, divided by a column carrying two minor arches, forming a semi-tracery head (No. 118).

Rome.—Openings seem small in relation to the great

order adopted (No. 121). A square-headed opening is treated with a framework of architrave mouldings, and later on with orders on a small scale, surmounted by pediments (No. 120).

Venice.—Openings are large, numerous, and close set ; the arcade and colonnade, as seen in the Colosseum, are adapted to palace façades. The treatment of a centre and two wings, obtained by window spacing, is continued from previous periods (Nos. 128, 129).

D. **Roofs.**

Florence.—Flat pitch-tiled roofs are sometimes shown (No. 118).

Rome.—Rarely visible (Nos. 119, 120).

Venice.—Balustrades preferred (No. 133).

Florence.— *Vaults*, raking vaults to staircases, and simple cross or tunnelled waggon-vaults in halls, generally frescoed.

Rome.—*Vaults* of a similar kind are more elaborated, treated with coffering or stucco modelling, after the style of the then newly-discovered Baths of Titus. Domes are universal in churches (No. 123).

Venice.—*Vaults.* Pictorial effect is attempted in halls and staircases. Domes are grouped with towers in churches (Nos. 130, 131).

E. **Columns.**

Florence.—Early examples do not have the orders (No. 118), though the columns are used to arcades, the arches springing direct from the capitals.

Rome.—The application of the orders on a great scale is the *motif* of the style. In their use, the scale of openings, and the internal necessities of the building, are not regarded, and even such features as balustrades are not regulated by use, but by the system of proportion to the order employed (No. 121).

Venice.—The problem of successive tiers of orders is worked out (Nos. 128, 129) ; projecting columns are preferred to pilasters, and entablatures are usually broken round these projections.

F. **Mouldings.**

Florence.—Mouldings are few and simple. Those between storeys are reduced to the minimum, to give full effect to the grand crowning cornice, whose details are based on classic examples (No. 118).

Rome.—Close adaptation of the features of the classical orders marks the Roman style (No. 119), until Michael Angelo, and his followers, despising the sound methods of the earlier architects, introduced their arbitrary details.

Venice.—Prominence of detail is characteristic of the late Renaissance works in Venice; entablatures have deep soffits and keystones, etc., and great projection, while spandrels have figures in high relief (No. 129).

G. **Decoration.**

Florence.—Decoration, such as carving and sculpture, is collected in masses, which contrast with the plain wall surfaces. Note the great stone shields at the angle of the palaces (No. 118).

Rome.—Stands midway between Florentine and Venetian work, having more variety than prevails in the sternness of the former, and less exuberance than is found in the latter.

Venice.—Decoration is equally spread throughout the façade. Every spandrel has its figure, and the high relief of sculpture competes with the architectural detail in prominence (No. 129).

SUPPLEMENTARY NOTE ON MILAN AND GENOA.

Although these cities formed no distinct school, as Florence, Rome, and Venice, there were many noteworthy buildings erected in them.

MILAN.

Milan was, as it is now, one of the richest and most populous of Italian towns.

Brick and terra-cotta were the materials chiefly to hand, and were employed in the Church of **S. Maria della Grazie** by Bramante, and in the great courtyard of the **Ospidale Grande** [1] by Filarete, a Florentine. Both these buildings possess a considerable amount of Gothic feeling;

[1] 1457.

the detail is delicately and richly carved, and is very suitable to the material employed.

The powerful family of the Visconti greatly encouraged art, and commenced the Cathedral of Milan, and the western façade,[1] of the **Certosa at Pavia,** near Milan, which is probably the most important of the early Renaissance creations. It is executed in marble. The leading lines are essentially Lombardian Gothic, clothed with Renaissance details. The arcaded galleries, the niches with statues executed by the greatest sculptors of the day, and the wealth of beautifully executed detail, make it one of the richest and most perfect specimens of the architect and sculptor's art. Consult "Architecture Italienne," by Callet and Lesueur.

GENOA.

Alessi (1500-1572) was the principal Genoese architect, and he erected many of the more important buildings in the city. The building materials to hand were brick, which was not used as such, but covered with stucco, to resemble stone work.

The Genoese buildings are remarkable especially for the entrance courts, the arrangement of the vestibules, courtyards, and flights of steps; advantage being taken of the sloping sites, to produce beautiful vistas of terraces and hanging gardens.

The Genoese buildings have their basements generally rusticated; pilasters are freely introduced as a decorative feature; while the façades are crowned by a bold projecting cornice, supported by consoles, the depth of the topmost storey, whose windows occupy the square intervals between these brackets. Many of the palaces are painted wholly in one colour, and receive their name from it, as the Palazzo Bianco (white), Palazzo Rosso (red). This deep rich colouring, with the help of the Italian sun, gives them a very bright appearance. Consult "Modern Palaces of Genoa," by P. P. Rubens; Gauthier's "Genoa."

[1] 1473.

THE ROCOCO STYLE.

The Rococo, or Baroco, style is a debased application to architecture of Renaissance features. Such work is to be distinguished from the mixtures of certain forms of the early Renaissance, when the style was commencing, because the Rococo period, coming after the reign of a highly systematized classical style, represents an anarchical reaction. Sinuous frontages, broken curves in plan and elevation, and a strained originality in detail, are the characteristics of the period. Columns are placed in front of pilasters, and cornices made to break round them. Broken and curved pediments and twisted columns are also features of the style. In the interiors, the ornamentation is carried out to an extra-ordinary degree, without regard to fitness or suitability, and consists of exaggerated and badly-designed detail, often over-emphasized by gilding. These features are specially to be noticed in the **Jesuit churches** throughout Italy and Europe. This style, commencing at the time when the move-ment in religion connected with the Jesuits was in progress, was adopted by them for its essentially modern character, and its almost universal extension is a monument to their activity.

> *Note.*—The attentive student will trace the progress of the Renaissance movement, the application of classical ideas to modern forms, beneath the trappings of bad detail.

Carlo Maderno (1556-1639), **Bernini** (1589-1680) and **Borromini** (1599-1667), are among the more famous who practised this debased form of art.

FRENCH RENAISSANCE.

1. INFLUENCES.

i. **Geographical.**—See previous sections, and note also that France has now become more clearly defined in its boundaries, and hereafter, in spite of the conquests of Louis XIV., the race does not permanently extend its boundaries.

ii. **Geological.**—Refer back to pp. 119 and 164. Note that Paris is built in a quarry, so to speak, of a fine-grained building stone. As London is a brick, so Paris is a stone city.

iii. **Climate.**—Refer back to pp. 119 and 164.

iv. **Religion.**—The Reformation maintained practically no hold in France, the old order remaining until the end of the eighteenth century. As, moreover, the supply of churches erected during the mediæval period proved adequate, it is the domestic work which takes the lead in this period. Thus the Louis XIV., etc., style, which had an universal influence upon interiors, and furniture, had little effect upon churches. The Jesuit style (p. 231) prevailed in those built during this period.

v. **Social and Political.**—Paris at this time was the capital of a compact, and rapidly consolidating kingdom, and from Paris emanated any movement, not only in architecture, but also in science and literature. The invasion of Italy by Charles VIII. in 1494, and by Francis I. in 1527, marks the distribution of Italian artists and workmen over Europe, and more especially France, many returning in the train of the French kings. Among the chief of the artists were Leonardo da Vinci, Cellini, Serlio, Vignola, and Cortana. A band of Italians journeying from place to place was responsible for much of the picturesque early Renaissance, south of the Loire.

vi. Historical.—The English are driven from France in 1453, and the accession of Louis XI. in A.D. 1461 practically leads to the consolidation of France into one kingdom by the reconciliation of the Duke of Burgundy, etc. During the first half of the sixteenth century Italy became the battlefield of Europe. In 1494 Charles VIII. of France, claiming the kingdom of Naples, marches through Italy. In 1508 Louis joins the league of Cambray formed against Venice. Florence is the ally of France during all this period. Francis I. is defeated, and taken prisoner by the Spaniards at the Battle of Pavia, 1525. In these wars the French kings failed, it will be seen, in their actual object, but they were thus brought into contact with the superior civilization of Italy, and drawn into the Renaissance movement. In their own country they were becoming more absolute. From 1558 to the end of the century, the religious wars, between the Huguenots and Catholics, distracted the country. The Massacre of St. Bartholomew took place at Paris, 1572, after which an emigration of Huguenots to England took place. During the reign of Louis XIII., (1610-1643) Cardinal Richelieu strengthens the royal power. Cardinal Mazarin continues his policy, and Louis XIV., ascending the throne in 1643, becomes an absolute monarch. His conquests, in the Netherlands and Germany, lead to a general coalition against him, and to his great defeat at the hands of Marlborough. The Revocation of the Edict of Nantes in 1685 leads to a further emigration of Protestants to England. In the reign of Louis XV. (1715-1774) the evil effects of despotism, and bad government, became more marked, and the writers Voltaire, Rousseau, and others weaken authority by their attacks, and prepare the ground for the great revolution that began in 1792-1793.

2. ARCHITECTURAL CHARACTER.

ITALIAN RENAISSANCE.

A direct return to classic forms occurs.

Principal buildings erected in towns.

Severe classic disposition not only appropriate but necessary in the narrow streets of Florence and Rome, or on straight water-ways of Venice.

Influence of ancient Rome and her buildings apparent in greater purity of detail.

A street front in Florence, Venice, or Rome is only seen from the street, and the architectural features are often in fact *appliqué*, without reference to what was behind (No. 128).

Predominant characteristics are : stateliness and horizontality.

Early buildings are principally churches, in consequence of the comparative fewness of these buildings erected in the Middle Ages. It was essentially a church-building age, although the number of Italian palaces of the epoch was very large.

FRENCH RENAISSANCE.

A period of transition in which Renaissance details were grafted on to Gothic forms. Ex.: Church of St. Eustache (No. 137), Paris, Château of Blois (No. 134).

Principal buildings erected in the country, mostly on the banks of the Loire, being palaces built for royalty and nobility, as Chambord (No. 135).

The picturesque disposition of Gothic origin, more in keeping with the country surroundings, where the chief buildings were erected.

Influence of Rome less apparent, partly because of distance and association.

A country château is seen on all sides, and the importance of a picturesque grouping from every point of view is apparent (No. 135).

Predominant characteristics are picturesqueness, and a tendency to Gothic verticality.

Early buildings are principally châteaux for the nobility. Francis I. was a monarch with literary and artistic tendencies. The enormous number of the churches of the Middle Ages sufficed. It was essentially a palace-building epoch.

134. CHATEAU DE BLOIS, FRANÇOIS Iᵉʳ STAIRCAISE.

<table>
<tr><td>

ITALIAN RENAISSANCE.

The country houses of the nobles in the Venetian territory, in the style of Palladio, are symmetrical and stately, with no traces of Gothic influence.

</td><td>

FRENCH RENAISSANCE.

The châteaux on the Loire are irregular Gothic castles, with a coating of Renaissance detail (No. 135).

</td></tr>
</table>

3. EXAMPLES.

SECULAR ARCHITECTURE.

The style may be divided up into periods, or a chronological review of the principal buildings may be taken. We propose the latter, with just a note on the principal points to be observed in study, and the general direction of the development of the style.

The Château de Blois (No. 134) is one of the more important examples, in which note the pilaster treatment of the façade, the mullioned windows showing the preference for the square section of mullion, the rich crowning cornice and roof dormers, which are elaborately carved. The shell ornament, introduced from Venice, is largely employed. In the view given of the famous staircase, notice the letter F among the carved balusters, and in the bosses to the vaulting; also the repetition of the carving of the salamander, the emblem of Francis I.

The Palace at Fontainebleau was erected for Francis I., and Vignola seems to have been engaged on it. The student should notice the remarkable irregularity of its plan. Contrary to Blois, the chief interest of this example lies in the sumptuous interiors, as in the saloons decorated by Primaticcio. The exterior is remarkably plain.

The Château de Chambord (No. 135) is one of the most famous erected in the Loire district, in central France, and possesses a semi-fortified character. The traditional circular towers of defence, roofed with slate cones, are incorporated in a palace design infused with Italian detail. These conical roofs are broken up, where possible, by rich dormers and tall chimneys, which give to the building its characteristic confusion, yet richness, of sky-line. The central portion, corresponding to the keep of an English castle, is surrounded, and protected on three sides, by buildings inclosing a courtyard; the fourth side is defended by a moat. The central feature, or donjon, is square on plan, with four halls as lofty as the nave of a church, tunnel-vaulted with coffered sinkings; at the junction of these halls is the famous double staircase, built up in a cage of stone, whose lantern crowning is the central object of the external grouping. The smallness of scale in regard to mouldings, the flatness of the projection to the pilasters, the Gothic feeling throughout the design, especially the high-pitched roofs, the ornamented chimneys, and the vertical treatment of the features generally, make this example one of the most characteristic of Early French Renaissance buildings.

It may be compared with advantage to the pentagonal semi-fortress of Caprarola, by Vignola, which is situated on the spur of a mountain looking down into the valley, giving one a recollection of Hadrian's tomb in mass and outline, while internally the circular court is suggestive of the Colosseum façade at Rome.

The Louvre at Paris may be taken as the most important building in the style. Its construction lasted from the time of Francis I. to Louis XIV., and the building exhibits, in consequence, a complete history of the progressive stages of the French Renaissance manner.

The skeleton history of the building is as follows :

Pierre Lescot, the first architect, commenced the work in 1540, under Italian influence. The only courtyard in Italy, to which we can compare that of the Louvre, is the Great Hospital at Milan, commenced in 1456 by the architect Filarete. This is formed of open colonnades in two storeys, due no doubt to climatic influences, whereas the Louvre is throughout of solid walling, broken up only by pilasters and windows, etc.

The general design of the Louvre consists of two storeys and an attic, arranged round a courtyard, 400 feet square. The lower order is of Corinthian, the upper of Composite pilasters, and an order of pilasters of less height is provided for the attic storey.

135.   CHATEAU DE CHAMBORD.

The sculptured work by Jean Goujon is especially noteworthy.

Under Henri IV. the gallery facing the Seine was erected (1595-1603) by Du Cerceau, and shows the debased inclinations of the period. Corinthian columns run through two storeys, the entablature is pierced for admission of windows, and triangular or circular pediments are placed over pilasters, without any reference to construction or fitness. The details are coarsely carved throughout.

Under Louis XIV. Perrault added (1670) the eastern façade, which consists of a solid-looking basement, above which is an open colonnade of Corinthian columns.

Under Napoleon III. the Louvre was finished by Visconti, during 1852-1857, by the addition of the façades north and south of the Place Louis Napoleon, which form one of the most pleasing specimens of modern French art, in which a certain richness and dignity are added to the picturesqueness of the earlier periods.

The building of the **Tuileries** was commenced for Catherine de Medici, from designs by Philibert Delorme, in 1564, and the problem of effecting a proper junction between the two palaces was a crux of long standing because of the want of parallelism between them—this junction was finally effected under Napoleon III. as mentioned above. The destruction of the Tuileries has rendered the connecting galleries architecturally ineffective.

The Luxembourg Palace was erected by De Brosse, in A.D. 1611 for Marie de Medici of Florence, the intention being to imitate the simple and bold treatment of Florentine buildings. In this respect note the similarity of treatment to the courtyard of the Pitti Palace, at Florence.

The Palace at Versailles was commenced by Jules Hardouin Mansard, in 1664, for Louis XIV., and is remarkable only for the uniformity and tameness of its design.

Plan and Arrangement of the typical French Château.

We have already remarked on the number of *châteaux* erected during the early periods of the Renaissance in France, due to social and political causes.

The château at **Bury**, near Blois, is typical (No. 136) of the majority of these buildings, and is shown in comparison with an English typical plan of the same period (No. 149).

By referring to the plan given, it will be noticed that it

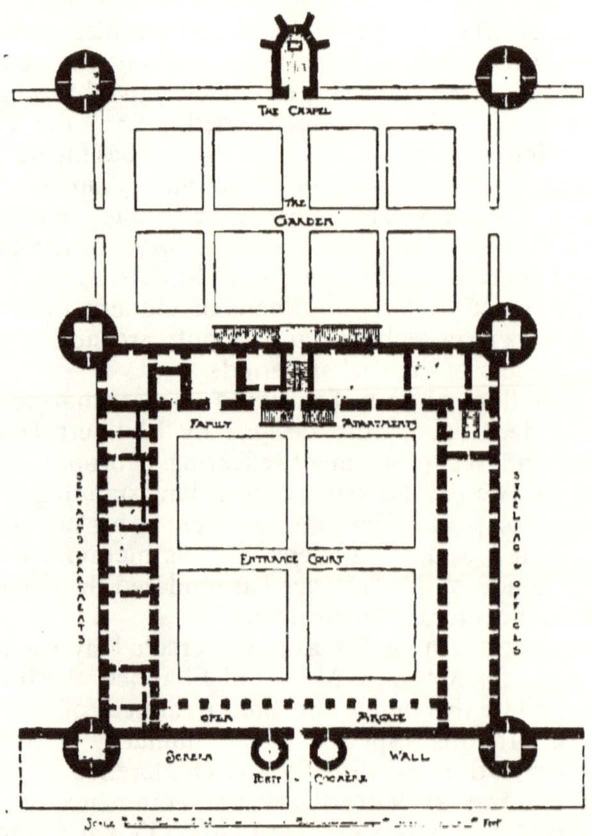

136. Château de Bury (Plan).

consists of a large square court, in front of which is a screen wall, solid externally, but with a colonnade facing the court. The entrance is in the centre of this wall, and is provided with a *porte-cochère*, or carriage entrance. The screen wall is flanked by towers, circular externally, and

St. Eustache, Paris.

square internally, and attached to these, and forming two sides of the court, are long wings containing the servants' apartments and offices on one side, and offices and stabling on the other. These are connected at the further end of the court with the main building, in which the family resided, and which contained the reception rooms. Behind this main building was the garden, and in the centre of one side is placed the chapel. Each of the side wings to the court was generally one storey lower than the main building, which contained the family apartments.

The above description applies equally to French town houses, up to the present day, with slight modifications dependent on site and local necessities.

> *Note.*—In French country houses the windows face internally into a courtyard, as in the ancient Roman atrium (the courtyard responding to the atrium), whereas in English country houses after the time of Henry VII. the windows all face outwards, a courtyard being an exception.

CHURCHES.

St. Eustache, Paris (A.D. 1532) (No. 137). In plan, it is a typical five-aisled Gothic church, with circular apsidal end. As to the exterior, it has high roofs, a kind of Renaissance tracery to the windows, flying buttresses, pinnacles, deeply-recessed portals, and other Gothic features, clothed with Renaissance detail. The church is, in fact, laid out on Gothic lines, but clothed with detail inspired from Italian sources.

St. Etienne du Mont, Paris (A.D. 1537). The same remarks apply as to St. Eustache; to be specially noted is the famous rood-screen, with double staircases and carved balustrading in Renaissance detail, illustrating the highly developed technical ability of the masons of the period.

The Dome of the Invalides at Paris (1680-1706), by Jules Hardouin Mansard, shows no Gothic tendency, and the principles of the Italian Renaissance are paramount.

In plan it is a Greek cross, with the corners filled in so as to make it a square externally. The dome (92 feet in circumference) rests on eight piers. It is provided with windows in the drum, or lower portion, above which is an interior dome, with a central opening; over this comes a second or middle dome, with painted decorations, lighted by windows; lastly, over all is an external dome and lantern of wood, covered with lead.

Notice the difference at St. Paul's, London (No. 154), where an intermediate brick cone supports the external stone lantern.

The Pantheon (1775) at Paris (No. 138) was erected from the designs of Soufflot. In plan (No. 126) it is a Greek cross. Four halls surround a central one, above which rises a dome, 69 feet in diameter. The dome is a triple one (No. 139), *i.e.*, one with three skins, as that of the Invalides, mentioned above, but the outer dome is of stone covered with lead.

The interior has an order of Corinthian columns with an attic over. The vaulting is ingenious, and elegance has been obtained by a tenuity of support, which at one time threatened the stability of the edifice. Frescoes by the foremost French artists of to-day have been placed upon the walls.

The exterior (No. 138) has a Corinthian colonnade, or portico at the west end, the cornice to which is carried round the remainder of the façades, which have a blank wall treatment, the light being obtained for the nave by a clerestory over the aisles.

The Madeleine at Paris was erected by the architect Vignon in 1804. Externally, it shows a direct imitation of ancient Roman architecture, and is a further step towards absolute copyism.

In plan, it is an octastyle peripteral temple, 350 feet by 147 feet. The order has a defect, which often occurs in French work, viz., that the columns are built of small courses of stone, the joints of which confuse the lines of the fluting. The architraves also are formed into flat arches with wide joints.

The interior is fine and original, the *cella*, as it would be called in classic work, being divided into an apse, half-domed, and three bays, covered by flat domes, through the eyes of which is obtained all the light for the church.

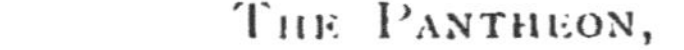

138. THE PANTHEON, PARIS.

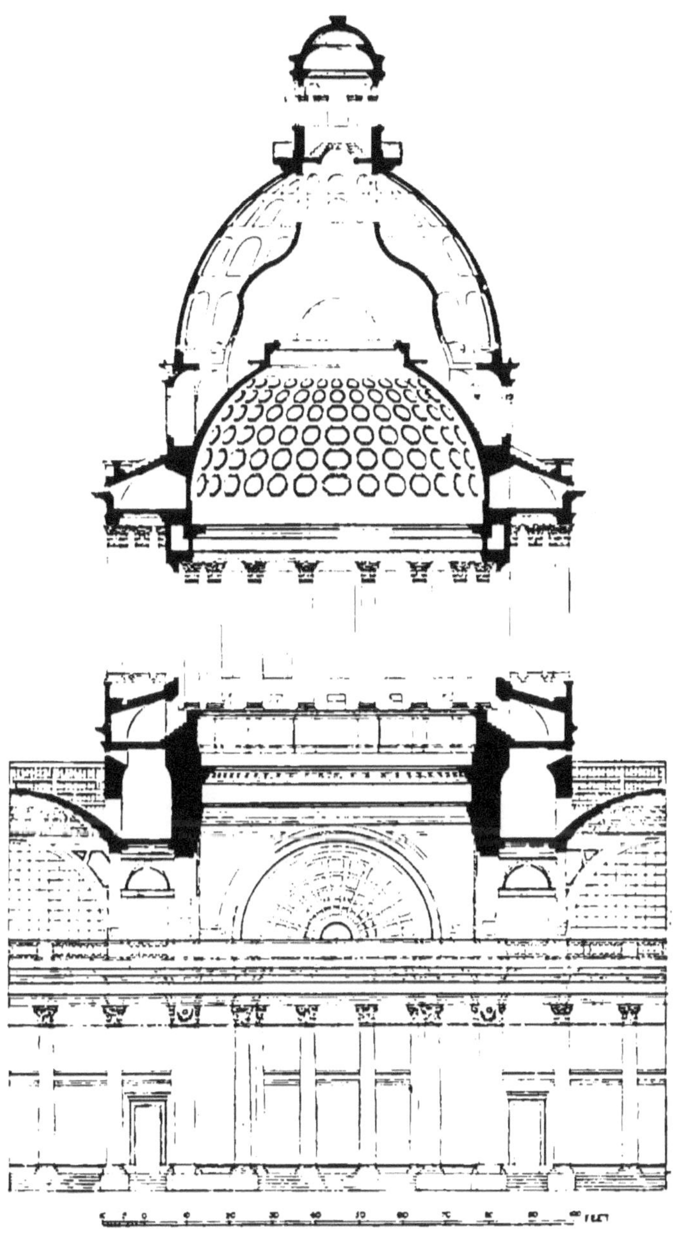

139. THE PANTHEON, PARIS.
Section.

4. COMPARATIVE.

We now treat in a comparative manner the essential differences between Italian and French Renaissance.

It must be borne in mind that the subject is treated generally, and that the comparisons state what usually is the fact, although in many cases features might be found, which do not exactly correspond with the type in every particular.

ITALIAN.

A. **Plans.**—The great feature of Italian houses is the *cortile*, or central open courtyard, which has, in all important examples, a colonnade or arcade round it. It is usual for the main wall, on the first floor, to stand on the piers or columns of this aisle, giving ampler space for the important rooms, which, it must be recalled, are in Italy on the first floor, called the " piano nobile."

B. **Walls.**—Straight façades varied by orders, arcades, or window-dressings (Nos. 119, 128), are crowned by a deep cornice at the top. Attics are rare, but an open top story " Belvedere " is a feature in houses of all classes. —Brickwork is used in large and rough masses with ashlar facing, and attention is concentrated on the window dressings or orders. Later examples, as at Genoa and Vicenza, are in plaster.

C. **Openings.** -- Symmetry regulates the position of

FRENCH.

A. **Plans**—In the châteaux of the early period, the castles of the previous ages influenced both plan and design. Some examples are on the site of, or are additions to such castles. Chambord may be counted as an attempt at an ideal plan of a mansion, half castle, and half palace. The typical house plan (No. 136) in the towns is a main block, and two lower wings inclosing a courtyard cut off from the street by an open or closed screen wall.

B. **Walls.**—The gables, and prominent stone dormers of the early period (Nos. 134, 135) give place gradually to pedimented and balustraded elevations. The mansard roof lends itself to pavilions which mark the angles of the façades, while the centre has often an attic. Chimneys continue to be marked features, though less ornamented. Stone continues the chief material, though red brick is sometimes combined with it.

C. **Openings.**—In early designs the mullions and tran-

ITALIAN.

openings (Nos. 128, 129), and in late examples the use of the classic orders, rather than convenience, determines their position. Early designs are often astylar, the openings are the features upon which all the detail is concentrated. In the later buildings greater plainness prevails to give effect to the orders. It should be noted that in the Rococo period a return was made often to the astylar principle, when excessive prominence and exaggeration of detail marks the window dressings. As the attic is rare in Italian work, on account of the use of the great cornice, the top floor openings are often formed into a deep band, or frieze. In Genoa they are set between great consoles, that give support to the main cornice.

D. **Roofs**—Flat roofs, or nearly so, a special feature, for the reason that in a narrow street high roofs, etc., could not be seen. Chimneys, if used at all, are masked and not made much of (No. 119) except at Venice.

In early examples tile roofs are visible above the great cornice, the latter are nearly always balustraded. Domes are relied upon for sky-line in churches. The Belvedere gives character to villas.

E. **Columns.**—Pilasters were either plain, or carved with

FRENCH.

soms of the Gothic method continue, though changed in detail (No. 134). Vertical coupling of windows is effectively practised, but as the orders, usually one for each storey, come increasingly into use, the horizontal lines of their entablatures prevail. Symmetry in position is carefully attended to in late work. Mezzanine floors are much used in large mansions with bull's-eye openings, the main apartments will then have an upper row of windows, to preserve the range of openings externally. This treatment may be seen at Hampton Court. The attic is a specially French feature, circular windows (œil de bœuf), are often placed there also.

D. **Roofs.**—High roofs are a special feature, also elaborately carved dormer windows and chimneys, to give sky-line and picturesqueness from a distance (Nos. 134, 137).

The French invention of the Mansard form preserves the roof as a feature. As it lends itself to pavilions, square or oblong, such features acquired great prominence, and at the Louvre they are veritable towers.

E. **Columns.**—Pilasters, a decorative adjunct to Gothic

ITALIAN.

delicate foliage. Star-shaped sinkings uncommon. The pilaster in Italy was sooner used for its own sake as an "order" when the panelled decoration naturally ceased (No. 119).

An "order" is often made to include two or more storeys of a building (No. 121). In churches especially a single order prevails.

F. **Mouldings.**—The heavy cornice is provided for protection from the glare of the Italian sun (No. 118). In early examples, strings are of slight projection, to give value to the top cornice. Where the orders are used, the details assigned to each are used in full. Mouldings are usually large but well studied in profile.

G. **Decoration.**—In Italian work we think of fresco and modelled plaster. In the early period, the two were combined as in the arabesques of Raphael. When separated the frescoes were often out of scale with the architecture, and often devoid of decorative value. Compare the Vatican, and the Palazzo del Te at Mantua. Later stucco work suffers in the same way, at Venice are extraordinary examples of its abuse. Interiors, generally in late work, are regulated unduly by the features of

FRENCH.

features, rusticated or panelled in star-shaped patterns, but sometimes treated with foliage. At Chambord, the sinkings are treated with a black inlay, slates being nailed in the sunk faces of the stonework (No. 135).

Each storey has in general its own "order" or column (No. 134). Columns in general do not run through two storeys. The influence of Vignola in this respect is visible.

F. **Mouldings.**—Gothic influence pervades the early work, and combinations of methods, classic and mediæval, in the profilings of mouldings are tried. Some examples, as at Orleans, have extremely small members. French Renaissance has gradually acquired a special character, by its treatment of sections.

G. **Decoration.**—The wood panelling of Gothic times continues in the early period, often splendidly carved with arabesque designs, as at Blois. In later work it continues but gradually loses the character and scale of the material. The Raphael style of decoration is introduced by Italian artists, as at Fontainebleau. The Tapestry, etc., of the early period is superseded by the universal Louis XIV. style of wood and stucco decoration treated in white and gold, a style which is applied completely

ITALIAN.

classic temple architecture, and are often in no relation to their occupants and accessories. Sculpture in later work loses touch with the decorative feeling of architecture, and great extravagances are perpetuated, as in the fountains of Rome.

FRENCH.

to every accessory, and which has the merit of a certain fitness and unity. Sculpture acquires an increasing importance, and few things are better in French modern work, than the constant use of the best available figure sculpture, in conjunction with architecture.

5. REFERENCE BOOKS.

Berty's " La Renaissance Monumentale en France."
Sauvageot's " Palais et Châteaux," etc.
Léon Palustre, " Architecture de la Renaissance."
C. Daly, " Motives Historiques."
" A Gentleman of France," by Stanley Weyman.   (Historical Novel.)

GERMAN RENAISSANCE.

I. INFLUENCES.

i. **Geographical.**—Refer to pp. 126 and 177.

ii. **Geological.**—The absence of stone, in the great alluvial plains of North Germany, influenced largely the architecture of the period; moulded and cut brickwork is used in every variety, the general scale of the detail is small, and surface patterns are formed in raised work. (See remarks on German Gothic, p. 177.)

iii. **Climate.**—See under Romanesque (p. 126) and Gothic (p. 177).

iv. **Religion.**—Martin Luther (1517-1546) attacks the practical abuses of certain doctrines of the Church, and brings about a revolution in the religious life of Germany (see below). Luther's translation of the Bible into High Dutch causes the latter to become the received tongue of Germans.

In architecture little of great interest is produced. Old churches, with all their fittings, continued to be used, but the prominence given to preaching brought in galleries and congregational planning.

v. **Social and Political.**—The country consisted of a number of small kingdoms or principalities, each with its own capital and government. This prevented any national effort as in France, which was under one united head. In the latter part of the sixteenth century, Heidelberg was the centre of "Humanism," and the chief reformed seat of learning in Germany.

We must also take account of the Thirty Years' War, ended by the Peace of Westphalia in 1648.

vi. **Historical.**—Charles V. succeeds to all the possessions of the Houses of Castile, Aragon, Burgundy, and the Low Countries. In 1516 he obtains the two Sicilies, and in 1519 he was elected to the Empire, on the death of Maximilian, becoming the most powerful emperor since Charlemagne.

In 1517 Luther nails up his theses at Wittenberg, marking the commencement of the Reformation, which was aided largely by the revival of learning. In 1520 he defies the Pope, by publicly burning the bull of excommunication, put forth against him by Pope Leo X. The Diet of Spires, 1529, passes a decree against all ecclesiastical changes, against which Luther and the princes who followed him protested, hence the name Protestant. This leads in 1530 to the Confession of Augsburg and the confederation of Protestant princes and cities, for mutual defence, called the Imalcaldic League. The war between the Emperor Charles V. and the Catholics against the Protestant princes, extends from 1546-1555, when the peace of Augsburg is concluded, which puts religion on terms of equality in each German state. The Thirty Years' War commences in 1618, and was carried on in Germany between the Catholic and Protestant princes. Other princes, such as Christian IV. of Denmark and Gustavus Adolphus of Sweden, join in these wars on the Protestant side, under the Elector Palatine Frederick, who had married a daughter of James I. of England. Hence many Englishmen and Scotchmen serve in these wars. France also joins in the war for her own aggrandizement, under Cardinals Richelieu and Mazarin. The Peace of Westphalia, 1648, provided for religious equality in each state. The war had, however, utterly ruined Germany, and caused France to become the leading nation in Europe.

2. ARCHITECTURAL CHARACTER.

The Renaissance style in Germany is chiefly remarkable for picturesqueness of grouping, and grotesqueness of ornament, due in a large measure, no doubt, to the traditions of the preceding style.

140.   HEIDELBERG CASTLE, THE HEINRICHSBAU.

Renaissance architecture was introduced from France, about the middle of the sixteenth century, while the Henri IV. style was in vogue, which may account for a good deal of the coarseness and crudity the style possesses in Germany.

German Renaissance differs from French work in lack of refinement, and in a general heaviness and whimsicality of treatment, while it resembles in some respects our own Elizabethan. It forms, in fact, a connecting link between Elizabethan architecture, and French Renaissance of the time of Henri IV.

It may be noted that examples are mostly found in towns, in contradistinction to French work of the period, which is principally found in the country.

The later period, which commenced at the beginning of the nineteenth century, has been called the "Revival," and consisted in the adoption of classic forms *in toto*, without reference to their applicability, or appropriateness in any way. This movement was chiefly confined to Munich, Berlin, and Dresden.

3. EXAMPLES.

SECULAR ARCHITECTURE.

The façade, by Otto Heinrich (1556), in *Schlosshof*, or internal courtyard of the Castle of **Heidelberg** (No. 140), is one of the most famous examples in the style, and has elaborately-carved string courses, with an order and its entablature to each storey, and classical details surrounding the windows. Symbolical statuary is prominently introduced, and the design suffers from over-ornamentation.

The Cloth Hall at Brunswick is a well-known example, the three-quarter columns marking each floor, with pedestals and entablatures, are a characteristic feature ; also the immense gable in four storeys, each being provided with an order of vase-shaped pilasters, as in Elizabethan work. The scrolls by which the stages of the gable are contracted are also to be noticed.

The porch to the **Rathaus (or Town Hall) at Cologne** (No. 141), erected in 1571, is a purer specimen of the style. It consists of semicircular arcading, with detached Corinthian columns, and a stone vaulted roof. It will be noticed that the arches on the first floor are pointed, and pointed vaulting is also adopted.

The Pellerhaus, Nuremberg (No. 142), is an example of rich domestic architecture, and shows also the richly-treated stepped gables, so characteristic of the period.

The Zwinger Palace at Dresden (1711), the Rathaus at Leipsig (1556), and the Castle at Stuttgart (1553) are amongst other well-known examples.

Of the **Revival** in Munich, **Klenze**, the architect, is responsible for the Glyptotek, the Pinacothek, and the Walhalla. At Berlin, the celebrated architect **Schinkel** (1781-1841) erected the New Theatre, the Museum, and the Polytechnic School. In all of these buildings the great idea has been to copy classical forms and details, applying them to modern buildings.

ECCLESIASTICAL ARCHITECTURE.

The new churches are few and insignificant. There was an abundant supply, for all practical needs, from the mediæval period.

The Frauenkirche of Dresden (1726-1745) and St. Michael's Church, at Munich, are among the best known, and exhibit a desire for wide, open spaces. The former especially is noticeable, being 140 feet square on plan, and covered with a dome 75 feet in diameter, resting on eight piers. It is constructed internally and externally of stone.

4. COMPARATIVE.

A. **Plans.**—The French method of an internal courtyard is adopted. In towns, many-storied houses were erected with great roofs, continuing the practice of the mediæval period. See below.

141. THE RATHHAUS, COLOGNE.

142.　THE PELLERHAUS, NUREMBURG.

B. **Walls.**—Gables assume fantastic shapes; richness is produced, by the application of columnar features as ornament. Brick and stone are used singly and in combination.

C. **Openings.**—Oriel windows of various shapes and design are plentifully used, both in the façade itself, and on the angles of buildings. Such a feature did not appear at Rome, Florence, or Venice, during Renaissance times.

Windows are large, mullioned, and crowned by grotesque, or scrolly pediments. In later work the usual classic features are adopted.

D. **Roofs.**—The large roofs in the town houses, containing many storeys, are a prominent feature in this, as in the Gothic, period. Such roofs served a useful purpose, being used as drying-roofs for the large and frequent wash. There are two methods of treatment: (*a*) by making the ridge parallel to the street front, as we generally find carried out in Nuremberg; (*b*) the other consists in making the ridge run at right angles to the street, as adopted in Landshut, in the south-east of Germany, and many other places.

It will be seen that the first method allows for the display of many tiers of dormer windows, rising one above the other, and the second method permitted the use of fantastically-shaped gables.

E. **Columns.**—The orders are freely employed in a licentious manner, as decorative adjuncts (No. 140), the storeys being marked by rich cornices; the columns and pilasters are richly carved, and are often supported on corbels (No. 142).

F. **Mouldings.**—Boldness and vigour must be set against the lack of refinement and purity in detail. Though Renaissance details are affected by the preceding work, the worst features of the last age of the Gothic style, such as interpenetration, are given up.

G. **Decoration.**—Sculpture is best seen in the native grotesques, wherein much fancy is displayed (Nos. 140, 142). The imitations of Italian carved pilasters are inferior, as at Heidelberg.

The late glasswork is interesting, but the art soon died out.

Fresco work was attempted during the revival at the beginning of the century by the Munich school.

5. REFERENCE BOOK.

"Denkmaeler Deutscher Renaissance," by K. E. O. Fritsch.

BELGIAN AND DUTCH RENAISSANCE.

1. INFLUENCES.

i. Geographical.—See *ante* (p. 173).

ii. Geological.—Also refer back (p. 173). Note that brick is the characteristic material of this phase of the Renaissance.

iii. Climate.—See *ante* (p. 173).

iv. Religion.—The persecutions begun under Charles V., but most severe under the Duke of Alva, viceroy of Philip II. of Spain, lead to a revolt in 1568 which lasted till 1609.

The Belgians, mainly Catholics, however, fall back to Spain, under the able rule of the Duke of Parma, but the Dutch, strongly Protestant, constitute the *United Provinces*, and finally under a republic become a great power. Their architectural expression is limited, the barn-like churches develop no features of great interest. The prominence given to preaching, and the demand for greater comfort regulate planning, but, whether for lack of interest or funds, nothing on a large scale is attempted.

v. Social and Political.—In Holland the character of the Dutch is shown in their buildings, which are in general honest, matter-of-fact, and unimaginative. The gain of trade and riches, in consequence of the discovery of the New World by Columbus, was not, however, mirrored by the erection of monumental structures. Their daring and activity in trade made them one of the chief powers of Europe during the seventeenth century. Their extensive colonies gradually passed over to the English.

vi. Historical.—The Spanish occupation of the Netherlands, the consequent influence of Spanish art in the sixteenth century, together with the loss of liberty under Charles V., and the ultimate expulsion of the Spaniards in 1648, must all be taken into account when dealing with this subject. Belgium, as a Catholic country, remained under the rule of Spain, when Holland freed herself under the House of Orange.

2. ARCHITECTURAL CHARACTER.

Belgian examples are wild, licentious, and picturesque, while sobriety, amounting often to dullness, is the character of Holland. Home comforts were studied, and the details of internal work, including furniture, were perfected. Brick receives its due prominence in this domestic style.

3. EXAMPLES.

The Town Hall at Antwerp,

erected in A.D. 1581 (No 143), is one of the most important buildings. The richness and prosperity of this particular city contributed not a little to the execution of this fine work. We may notice that an order, or row of columns, is given to each storey, that mullioned windows are adopted, that a high-pitched roof with dormer windows occurs, and the whole design is placed on a sturdy rusticated basement.

The Stadthaus at Amsterdam

is certainly not worthy of being mentioned except from its great size.

Domestic Architecture.

If we are disappointed in any large or important works erected during the Renaissance period in north-west Europe, we are amply repaid by studying much of the

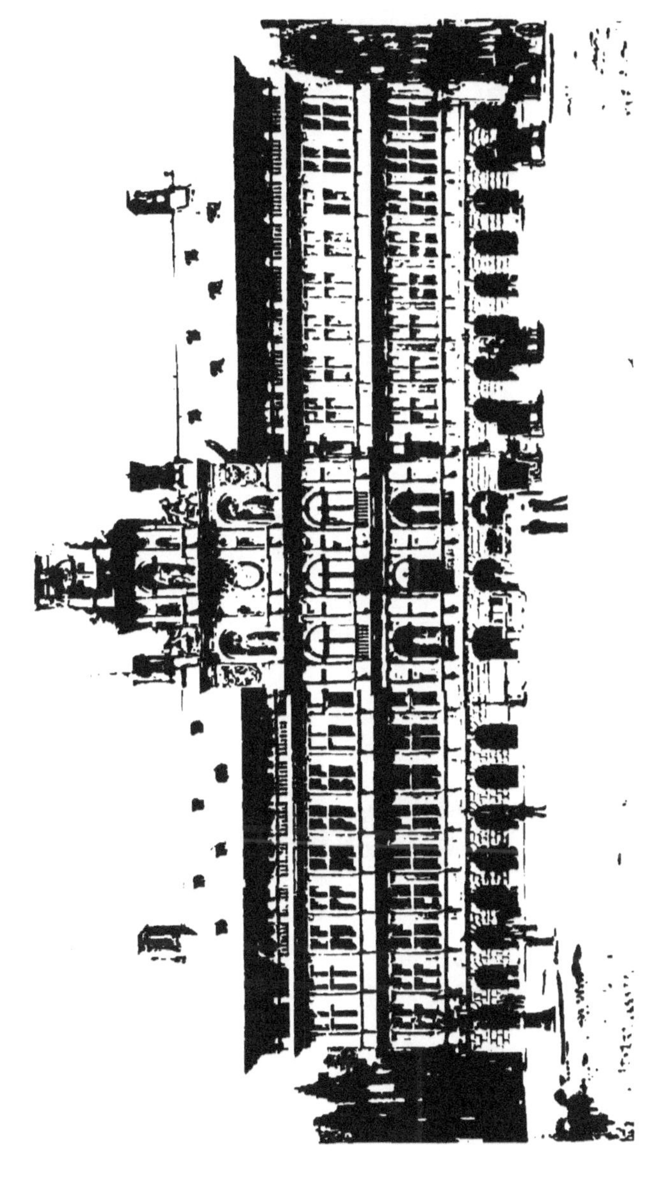

domestic and civic architecture, for while wandering through the streets of these old-world towns, we meet with charming specimens of street architecture, executed in bright red brick, with occasional stone courses and dressings, with the further ornament of gracefully-designed iron ties. In the design of their gables, much originality of treatment is found, leaning rather towards the work found in some of the old German towns, and often verging on the grotesque, but at the same time thoroughly suited to the brick material, and possessing a certain characteristic quaintness of their own.

Many of these street fronts are good examples of the treatment of large window spaces.

In Holland, especially, these quaint buildings, rising very often from the sides of the canals, group most harmoniously, and form fascinating studies for water-colour sketching, full, as they are, of life and colour.

4. COMPARATIVE.

A. **Plans.**—The great development of domestic Gothic is the groundwork of the achievements of the Renaissance, in this country. It was in the modifications of detail that the influence of the latter was felt, Italian forms, generally much corrupted, being gradually adopted.

B. **Walls.**—Gables of curly outline, grotesque, picturesque, and rococo in character, are crowded together in streets and squares, whose general effect and grouping must be enjoyed, without too much inquiry into their *rationale* or detail.

C. **Openings.**—Are numerous and crowded, in continuation of the Gothic practice. The orders take the place of the niches, statuary, and traceried panelling, that surround the windows of the previous period (No. 143).

D. **Roofs.**—The high-pitched forms continue long in favour, as well as the dormers and visible chimney stacks (No. 143).

E. **Columns.**—The orders are used as decorative features, being heavily panelled, rusticated, and otherwise treated in a licentious and grotesque fashion.

F. **Mouldings.**—The same defect, that of coarseness, noted under Gothic, continues in this period. The further divorce of detail from construction and material, rather accentuates the evil.

G. **Decoration.**—Carving of vigorous grotesques occupies any vacant panel or space, the *motifs* being usually Italian, "corrupted" or "original," according to the point of view. The woodwork, and stained glass, of this age is especially worthy of note.

5. REFERENCE BOOKS.

Ernest George, " Etching in Belgium."

" Documents classés de l'art dans les Pays-Bas," by Van Tsendrick.

SPANISH RENAISSANCE.

I. INFLUENCES.

i. Geographical.—The position and power of Spain, arising from the discovery of the new world, combined with the vast hereditary and conquered possessions of the Spanish monarchy, made her the leading nation in Europe.

ii. Geological.—See *ante* (p. 192). The presence of very pure iron ore, in the northern mountains, facilitated the development of decorative ironwork. Granite is much used, and brick only in certain parts.

iii. Climate.—See *ante* (p. 192).

iv. Religion.—The Reformation obtained no hold whatever in Spain. Under the Gothic period, we have pointed out the religious aspect of the great struggle with the Moors, and the national character of the church will be understood. The counter reformation found its motive force in the Jesuit order, founded by a Spaniard, Ignatius Loyola.

v. Social and Political.—The people were a mixed population, in which the Goths of Northern Europe, and the Moors of North Africa, form the most important elements.

From the latter part of the fifteenth century, the power of Spain gradually increased, until she became the chief power of Europe.

Absolute despotism was the policy of Philip II., Jews and heretics being persistently persecuted. Under Philip III. the Moriscos were driven out of the country, which proved a great loss to Southern Spain, which by their hard work had been made to flourish.

vi. Historical.—The accession of Ferdinand and Isabella to the throne, and the fall of Granada in A.D. 1492, marks the consolidation of Spain, the expulsion of the Moors, and the beginning of the Spanish Renaissance.

The great dominions of Spain were due to a succession of marriages, Charles V. reigning over Spain, the Netherlands, Sardinia, Sicily, and Naples, Germany, and Austria. This empire was held together by his skill in government, and by the excellence of the Spanish army, the infantry being the finest at that time in Europe. Philip II. checks the power of the Turks by winning the great naval battle of Lepanto, 1571. His harsh and despotic rule, however, alienates the Netherlands, and the expedition against England ends in the defeat of the Armada in 1588. Provinces are gradually lost, and Spain as a power ceases to exist. Napoleon's invasion, at the commencement of this century, leads to an outburst of national resistance, aided by the English. Many revolutions follow, but progress, as understood by other nations, has been slow.

2. ARCHITECTURAL CHARACTER.

In the early period, Renaissance details, grafted on to Gothic forms, and influenced to some extent by the exuberant fancy of the Moorish work, produced a style as rich and poetic, however careless and incorrect, as any other of the numerous phases of the Renaissance in Europe.

The style of the early period in Spanish Renaissance is called "Plateresco," and lasted to the abdication of Charles V. in 1556. The middle period became more classical, as was usual everywhere in Europe, and the chief expositor was the architect Herrara (d. 1597), a pupil of Michael Angelo. In the late period, the style fell away from true principles, becoming imbued with the Rococo innovations.

3. EXAMPLES.

SECULAR ARCHITECTURE.

Among the most important works, we may mention that the façade of **San Gregorio at Valladolid (No. 144)** well illustrates the peculiar richness of the Plateresco period, and the lace-work character of the detail, derived from Moorish

144.   SAN GREGORIO, VALLADOLID.

145. BURGOS, COURTYARD OF THE
HOUSE OF MIVANDA.
Shewing the Bracket Capital.

influence. The **University of Alcala** has an open-arcaded storey under the roof, a feature specially characteristic of the early period.

The **Archbishop's Palace** at **Alcala** is also noteworthy. Notice the "bracket" capitals, on the first floor in the courtyard, as undoubtedly of wooden origin, their use being to decrease the long bearing of the architrave. This is well shown in the courtyard of the Casa Miranda at Burgos (No. 145).

The **Town Hall at Seville** (No. 146) is generally regarded as the best example of a municipal building in Spain. It has been considerably extended at later periods, when much of the stonework remained uncarved.

The **Alcazar at Toledo**, an ancient square castle of Moorish-Gothic architecture, has one façade in the early Renaissance of Charles V., while the interior has been converted into a two-storied Italian cortile. The arcades rest upon the capitals of the columns of two orders, of one storey each. At the far end is a grand staircase, 100 feet by 50 feet, the flights being of great width. Off the half landing is a grand square two-storied chapel. The whole of this severe and monumental work is executed in granite. The back elevation is an early example of a many-storied building in the classical style.

The **Palace of Charles V.**, erected in 1527, adjoining the "Alhambra" at Granada, is an important specimen of the style. In plan it is a square, 205 feet each way, inclosing an open circular court 100 feet in diameter. The external façade is two storeys in height : the lower, a rusticated basement ; the upper treated with Ionic columns. Both basement and upper order have bull's-eye windows above the lower openings, so that mezzanines could be lighted where required. The circular internal elevation is an open colonnade in two storeys, with Doric order on the lower, and Ionic order, of small height, to the first storey.

It is built in a golden-coloured stone, the central feature of the two visible façades being in coloured marbles ; the sculpture is by Berruguete, and the whole design, which is of the Bramante school, is the purest example of Renaissance in Spain. The palace was never roofed in or occupied.

The **Palace of the Escurial** (No. 147), situated thirty-two miles from Madrid, was commenced by Philip II., and in 1567 Herrara was appointed architect.   It is a group of buildings on a site 640 feet long by 580 feet wide, and consists of a monastery, a college, a palace, and a church, all grouped into one design.   The grand entrance, in the centre of the long façade, leads into an atrium, to the right of which is the college with its four courts, 60 feet square, surrounded with three storeys of arcades ; beyond is the great court of the college.   On the left of the atrium is the monastery, with three courts 60 feet square, and beyond is the great court of the palace.   Immediately in front, at the end of the atrium, is the church, lying between the courts of the palace and the college.   Behind the church are the state apartments of the palace.

The church itself is 320 feet by 200 feet.

The **plan** (No. 147) is Italian in origin, following somewhat the type of the Carignano Church at Genoa.   The detail is classical, and shows that Herrara studied to some purpose in Italy.

The principal Spanish feature is the placing of the choir on a vault, over the lengthened western arm of the cross, beneath which is a domed vestibule—consequently the church interior is, in effect, a Greek cross on plan.

In general grouping nothing could be finer than the dome as a centre, flanked by the two towers and surrounded by the great mass of building, the whole being silhouetted against a background of mountains.   Moreover, the palace proper at the east end is only an annex, and does not conflict with the church, as the Vatican does with St. Peter's.

The entire structure, internally and externally, is built in granite of a gray colour, with a slight yellow tinge, which material may have influenced the design.

It may be said that the taste of Philip II. and Herrara would have produced something equally plain in any material, whether granite or not, but at least the design may be said to be suited to the material.

The masonry is excellent, and in blocks of great size, the architraves of doors being 10 to 12 feet high, in one stone. The exterior façades are everywhere five storeys in height ;

146.

TOWN HALL, SEVILLE.

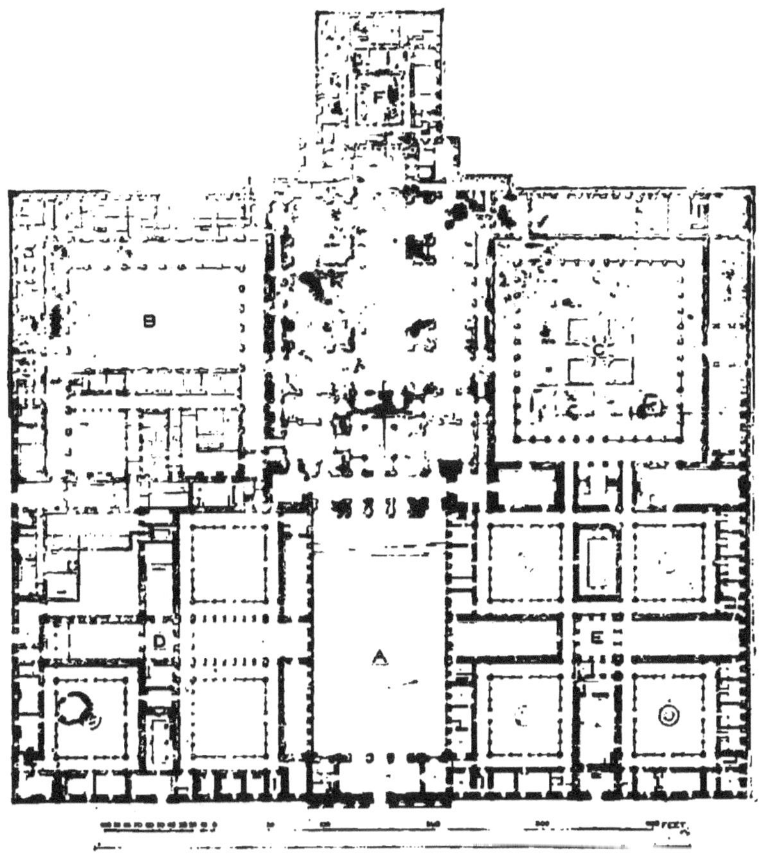

147. THE ESCURIAL, SPAIN.

Plan.

A. Atrium to Church.
B. Great Court of the Palace.
C. Great Court of College.
D. Monastery.
E. College.
F. State Apartments of Palace.

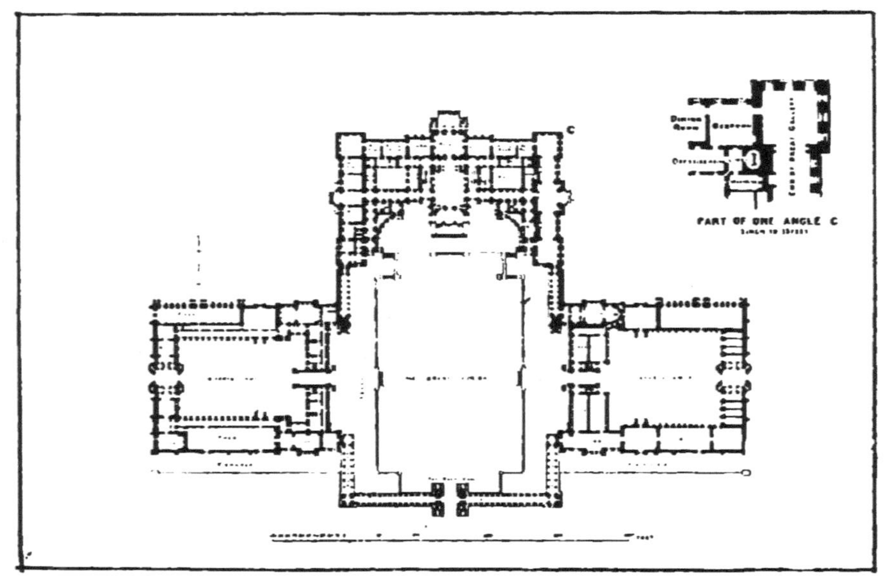

148. BLENHEIM PALACE.
Plan.

the windows square-headed, without dressings of any sort, and without any attempt at grouping, so that they are inferior in effect to the façade by Herrara, at the Alcazar, described above.

As an interior, however, it is most impressive, being of granite with suitable detail, and only the vaults coloured. It has a magnificent reredos in such quietly-toned marbles that one hardly notices how rich it is. The architectural character is so restrained that the structure looks nothing at a mere cursory glance.

THE ROCOCO STYLE IN SPAIN.

In the seventeenth century the Spaniards, revolting from the correct and cold formalities of the school of Herrara, reached the opposite extreme, and erected buildings in which fantastic forms are employed for their own sake, without reference either to good taste or fitness. The style goes by a name as unpronounceable as the result is unfortunate. It is called Churrigueresque, after the name of its chief practitioner.

ECCLESIASTICAL ARCHITECTURE.

The dome at **Burgos Cathedral** (No. 113) belongs to the early period (1567) and is an example of the wealth of detail, so characteristic of the style.

Granada Cathedral (A.D. 1529), by Diego Siloe, is a grand example of the Renaissance churches of Southern Spain. It is a translation of Seville Cathedral into the Renaissance style, the Gothic system being followed, but the orders applied to the piers carrying the vaulting. The lofty circular choir is domed on radiating supports, ingeniously disposed, constituting a fresh and original departure. The general effect of the interior is powerful, but unduly sensational.

Valladolid Cathedral, by Herrara, is more distinctively classic, but remains incomplete. The west façade is imposing, but wholly out of scale, and in the interior the execution and detail are incredibly rude.

The steeples which are placed alongside the cathedrals at Granada, Santiago, Malaga, and Carmona, are examples of a class of structure in which Spain is especially rich, and which are generally treated in a most pleasing manner.

4. COMPARATIVE.

A. **Plans.**—In churches wide naves are usual, sometimes without any aisles. Lanterns or domes are common at the crossing, the transepts being usually shallow, as is also the apsidal chancel, the ritual choir remaining west of the transepts.

In houses the *Patio*, or Spanish form of the Roman atrium, and the Italian cortile, is universal. It has even an added seclusion, which seems due to Moorish influence. The streets of Toledo present walls all but blank, through whose doorways, when open, but a glimpse of the *patio* only can be obtained. Staircases are often large, as in the Burgos transept, and the Casa Infanta at Saragossa, in which last the *patio*, and staircase opening from it, are as picturesque and fanciful as any in Spain. Largeness of scale characterizes palaces as well as churches.

B. **Walls.**—Brickwork is used in large, rough, but effective masses, as at Saragossa. Fine stonework is used in other places, and also granite, as at the Escurial and Madrid. Gables are rarely or never found; a special feature is an eaves arcade, forming an open top storey, and on this feature all the decoration is concentrated, leaving blank walls below, relieved by an elaborate doorway. Arabesque pierced parapets or crestings, are common in the early work, as the *Casa Monterey* at Salamanca. At Saragossa, the great cornices of the brick palaces are of wood, elaborately detailed.

C. **Openings.**—Doorways are emphasized. At Toledo they alone relieve the blank, narrow, walled streets. A special largeness of scale is to be noted, perhaps due to the importance of a gateway in the East.

Windows are treated with well-designed grilles, and their dressings in stonework are frame-like in character. Small orders, resting on corbels, carry a head well ornamented, while the sill is often absent or untreated.

D. **Roofs.**—Not emphasized. Generally flat or of low pitch. Towers, however, have spires of slate or leadwork of fanciful outline, even in designs of the severe classic period. The spire of St. Martin's, Ludgate, may be compared with the angle towers of the Escurial. Internally the great saloons of the early period are remarkable, the walls, for ten or more feet in height, being plain stonework, to be hung with draperies. A light-arcaded gallery of wood rests upon a great projecting wooden cornice, affording a passage in front of the windows in the main wall. This arcade reaches up to the flat wooden ceiling, framed in coffers, and detailed in a style that is suggestive of Arab influence.

E. **Columns.**—In the early style, the orders are used in slight and playful decorative forms (No. 146); the baluster shape, or shafts of an outline suggestive of the forms due to wood turned in a lathe, are used abundantly, being decorated in low relief. In the use of columns with arcades, sometimes very high pedestals are used, and the arches spring at the base line of the column. In the later work, correctness prevails until the outbreak of the Rococo.

F. **Mouldings.**—In early work, much refinement is mingled with forms due to Gothic and Moorish influences. A special feature is the bracket capital (No. 145), by which the long bearings of stone architraves are relieved by corbels on either side, combined in treatment with the cap itself.

In the middle period, the great number of breaks made in the entablatures mitred round columns, is to be noted (No. 145). Especially in church interiors quite a special effect is produced, by the flutter of the many mitres.

G. **Decoration.**—Sculpture varies much in quality (Nos. 144, 145, and 146). Berruguete is the Donatello of the Spanish Renaissance, but his figures often are wanting in decorative treatment. Expression is emphasized unduly and violence of action is not uncommon.

The painting on the sculpture is usually crude and realistic. The great retablos of alabaster, stone, or wood are the finest decorative feature of the churches. The figures are often

life size, and the architectural detail is very elaborate. The
iron *Rejas*, or grilles, are also a source of effect.

Tile work is excellent in Southern Spain. Stained glass
is apt to be loaded in colour and over vivid. The drawing
is frequently clumsy, Flemish influence, not of the best
kind, being apparent. The fresco work of the Escurial is
merely late Italian. The canvases of Murillo at Madrid
and at the church at Seville, though large in scale, have the
character of paintings in oil. In the accessory arts, armour
design was carried to great perfection by the Spaniards.

We shall here bring our remarks to a close, merely men-
tioning that the subject of the Renaissance in Spain has
been well taken up by various travelling students of late
years, and that the following books contain interesting
examples :

5. REFERENCE BOOKS.

Prentice's "Renaissance in Spain."

Verdier and Cattois, "Architecture civile et domes-
tique."

Sir Digby Wyatt, "An Architect's Note Book in Spain."

David Roberts } Views of Spain.
Villa Amil }

Monumentos Espanos, by the Spanish Government.

ENGLISH RENAISSANCE.

1. INFLUENCES.

i. **Geographical.** -See p. 131. It would be hazardous to lay too much stress upon the relations, during the various phases of this period, of England with the Continental powers; but the relative cordiality of our relations with France, or Holland, might be seen by some to be reflected in the architectural fashion of successive periods. The closing of the Continent to travel during the great war at the end of the eighteenth, and beginning of the nineteenth, century certainly coincided with the worst phase of our architecture.

ii. **Geological.**—Refer back to English Gothic, p. 132. In the increase of population and cultivation of the land, forests were reduced, and wood has been gradually disused as an external building material, so that the timber architecture of the mediæval period has died out. In London, the importation of Portland stone by Inigo Jones, a material very similar in weathering and effect, to that used in the Renaissance palaces of Venice, should be noted. The use of brick received a great impetus after the Fire of London, and was again brought into prominence on the introduction of the Dutch fashion. "Flemish" bond, as a technical term, has its significance.

iii. **Climate.**—No change can be alleged here, but at least a great increase of warmth and comfort has been found necessary. The opening out of the great coal industry, by cheapening fuel, has led to each room having a fireplace, and incidentally, to other features that did not complicate the architecture of the earlier periods.

iv. **Religion.**—In the early part of the sixteenth century, a stir in religious matters took place in Western Europe, partly on account of the abuses which had crept into the

Church, which the Popes failed to rectify, and also because the authority of the Pope was increasingly felt to be irksome.

The suppression of the monasteries (1536-1540) caused the diffusion of vast sums of money and land, which Henry VIII. distributed at will among his courtiers.

Monasteries either fell into ruin, or else were converted into the mansions of the new men. Others were cleared away for the erection of houses according to the new taste, the funds for which enterprises proceeded from the newly seized revenues.

The Act of Supremacy, 1559, settles the relation of the English Church to the power of the Crown.

v. **Social and Political.**—The historical and other events which occurred previous to, and paved the way for, the introduction of the Renaissance into England, are many and significant. Some of these have been dealt with under Renaissance (page 200). Of others, we may note:

The end of the Wars of the Roses, which had lasted from 1455 to 1485, during which period architecture was practically at a standstill. Secondly, the terrible destruction to life caused by these wars, for no less than twelve pitched battles were fought, eighty princes of the blood were slain, and the almost entire annihilation of the ancient nobility of England took place. The new men who succeeded, were naturally more susceptible to any new intellectual movement, they desired, moreover, new and important country houses, being in every way anxious to provide themselves with the paraphernalia suited to their rank.

The invention of gunpowder rendered obsolete the ancient castles, and newer fortresses tended to become merely military posts, no longer habitable as palaces by a king, or as seats by the nobility.

The introduction of printing by Caxton (1474) powerfully aided the new movement, by the enlargement of men's ideas, and by the increased spread of knowledge throughout the country.

The death of James IV. of Scotland, at Flodden, 1513. His alliance with France indicates French influence in Scotland.

The court of Henry VIII. was composed of men who

were connected with the new movement, and here, amongst artists, we find Holbein, from Basle; and Torrigiano, from Italy; the latter brought over in 1512 to execute Henry VII.'s tomb in Westminster Abbey. The celebrated John of Padua was also brought over by Henry VIII.

Henry VIII. and Edward VI. employ part of the funds obtained from the suppression of the monasteries (1536-1540) to the erection and endowment of grammar schools and colleges, which play an important part in the development.

The reign of Elizabeth (1558-1603) inaugurates the era of the erection of the great domestic mansions. In literature we have the writings and influence of Spenser, Shakespeare, Burleigh, and Sir Philip Sidney.

Finally, the wars against the Huguenots in France, and the Massacre of St. Bartholomew in 1572, led to the emigration of these skilled craftsmen to England, which influenced, not a little, the efficient execution of the newly-imported classical architecture.

vi. **Historical.**—Henry VIII. had undisputed possession of the English crown. He mixes generally with foreign affairs: the meeting with the French king at the Field of the Cloth of Gold, 1520, is an event of some significance, and bears an important relation to the introduction of Renaissance details into England. Henry declares the Pope to have no jurisdiction in England. Edward VI. continues the Reformation, but Mary's policy was reactionary, and marks the era of Spanish influence in England. Under Elizabeth (1558-1603), the Reformation was finally settled, and the defeat of the Spanish Armada, 1588, marks the decline of Spanish power in Europe. Charles I.'s attempts to develop art are cut short by the outbreak of Puritanism. Under Charles II. French influence was potent, and with Louis XIV. France reaches its greatest glory. The rise of Holland was taking place, and on the expulsion of James II. by William of Orange, Dutch influence made itself felt. With the accession of George I. (the Hanoverian dynasty) commences an era of quiet domestic progress. The growth of London proceeds rapidly. Art slowly deteriorates, until the Exhibition of 1851 marks the commencement of a revival.

ELIZABETHAN ARCHITECTURE.[1]

2. ARCHITECTURAL CHARACTER.

Elizabethan Architecture is a transition style, and immediately follows the Tudor or late Gothic, which carries us to the reign of Henry VIII. (see page 162). It bears the same relation to Anglo-Classic, or fully-developed English Renaissance, as the *Francis I.* period does to fully-developed French Renaissance.

The period of the Elizabethan style resembles that of the Early French and German Renaissance, in that church building is practically at a standstill, practically no church being erected in the Elizabethan style at all, sufficient churches being left from the Middle Ages for the wants of the people. Elizabethan architecture thus differs from the Italian Renaissance, in which church building took the principal place.

Elizabethan resembles French Renaissance, in that the principal examples were erected in the country by powerful statesmen and successful merchants, and differs from Italian Renaissance, in which the principal examples were erected in cities.

The Elizabethan style may be said to be an attempt, on the part of the English, to translate Italian ideas into their own vernacular; it does not confine itself to architecture only, but pervades the whole fitting of buildings, in furniture and decoration. Elizabethan art forms in this respect a style complete in every aspect.

3. EXAMPLES.

ELIZABETHAN MANSIONS.

The principal features are:

i. **The great hall,** a feature handed on from Gothic times (No. 149), lined to a height of 8 or 10 feet with

---

[1] English Renaissance is divided into the following periods: Elizabethan, p. 266; Jacobean, p. 269; Anglo-Classic, p. 273; Eighteenth Century, p. 278; Nineteenth Century (to 1851), p. 284; Nineteenth Century (1851 to the present day), p. 289.

oak panelling, while above are arranged the trophies of the chase, the armour and portraits of ancestors, and family relics and heirlooms.

At one end of the hall, by the entrance, is the carved oak screen, over which is placed the minstrels' gallery, while at the other end is the raised daïs with a tall bay-window, the sill reaching nearly down to the ground. The hall fireplace is much elaborated, and richly carved with the coat-of-arms of the owner, and the timber roof, of hammer-beam construction, is often elaborately treated.

ii. The **broad staircase** of oak is a special feature, with its heavily-carved newels, pierced balustrading, and rich carving. It is generally placed in connection with the hall, and lends to the interior an air of spaciousness and dignity.

iii. The **great gallery** on the first floor, extending the whole length of the house. The proportions of this apartment vary considerably from the hall, in being comparatively low and narrow in proportion to the length. The length is relieved by room-like projecting bays—those at Haddon Hall being as large as an ordinary room (15 feet by 12 feet), with stone-mullioned windows, glazed with leaded panes. The walls are panelled in oak the full height, and the ceiling is richly modelled in plaster. There is no feature of an old English mansion more characteristic than these galleries.

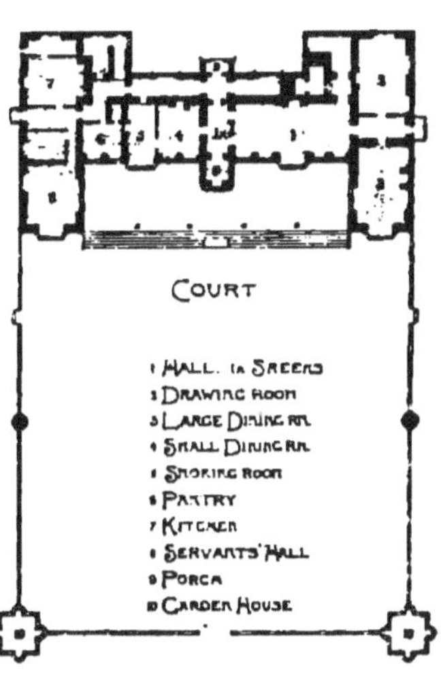

149. MONTACUTE HOUSE (PLAN).

The term "picture gallery" is supposed to be derived from these apartments.

The gallery at Aston Hall is 136 feet long by 18 feet wide and 16 feet high.

iv. Other rooms, besides the above, are the withdrawing room, or solar of Gothic times, very often a chapel, and the bedrooms, which increased considerably in number and importance, after the close of the Gothic epoch.

LIST OF SOME FAMOUS ELIZABETHAN MANSIONS.

Name.	*Date.*	*Architect.*
Knole (Kent).	1570.	
Penshurst (Kent).	1570-85.	
Burleigh (Lincs.).	1575-89.	John Thorpe.
Longleat (Wilts.).	1579.	John of Padua.
Westwood (Worcest.).	1590.	
Wollaton (Notts.).	1580.	John Thorpe and R. Smithson.

Moreton Hall (Cheshire) (No. 150), 1550-1559, is an example of many of the timbered houses, erected in the period, for which Lancashire is specially famous.

ELIZABETHAN COLLEGES.

Many of the colleges at Oxford and Cambridge were erected during this period, and these buildings, being situated within the seats of revived learning, naturally gave a great impetus to the new style, as object lessons to the rising generation.

CAMBRIDGE.

Name.	*Date.*	*Architect.*
The Gate of Honour, Caius College.	1565-74.	Theodore Havenius of Cleves.
The Quadrangle, Clare College.	1638.	
Neville's Court, Trinity College.	1615.	

150.   LITTLE MORETON HALL. CHESHIRE.

151. THE TOWER OF THE OLD SCHOOLS, OXFORD.

Oxford.

Gateway of the Schools.   1612 (No. 151).   Thomas Holt.
(Note the superimposed
  orders.)
Quad. of Merton Coll.
Quad. of Wadham Coll.
  and others.

ELIZABETHAN TOWN HOUSES.

Many interesting specimens have come down to us, and among them are several houses of half-timber construction. as, for example, in London, Staple Inn, Holborn, Sir Paul Pindar's House in Bishopsgate (now in the South Kensington Museum), and many other examples in Chester. and other of the country towns throughout England.

4. COMPARATIVE,

taken with Jacobean, p. 270.

THE JACOBEAN STYLE (1603-1625.

1. INFLUENCES

are taken with Elizabethan, page 263.

2. ARCHITECTURAL CHARACTER.

During the reign of James I. the Renaissance style, although a continuation of the Elizabethan in many respects, was further developed, losing more and more of Gothic tendency and picturesqueness, as classic literature and models became better known, and the use of the classic columns with their entablatures was more and more general. The celebrated architect, John Thorpe, erected several of the mansions of this epoch, and his book of " compositions," preserved in Sir John Soane's Museum, should be studied by the student.

In examining the buildings of this style, we shall be struck with their suitability to the wants of the people, in whose era they were erected. Some of the detail and ornamentation may be considered questionable, but they were at least the outcome of the social conditions of the age in which they occur, and we can only say that an examination of the mansions, erected during the Elizabethan and Jacobean periods, most of which are easily accessible to the student, will bring as much if not more pleasure than the study of the buildings of any other period of Architecture in England. Jacobean furniture design continues on the same lines as the architecture.

3. EXAMPLES.

List of some Famous Jacobean Mansions.

Name.	*Date.*	*Architect.*
Holland House, Kensington.	1607.	John Thorpe.
Bramshill, Hants.	1607-1612.	
Hatfield House, Herts (No. 152).	1611.	
Longford Castle, Wilts.	1612.	John Thorpe.
Audley End, Essex.	1616.	Bernard Jansen.
Kirby Hall, North Hants (No. 153).		John Thorpe.
Losely Park, near Guildford.		

4. COMPARATIVE.

ELIZABETHAN AND JACOBEAN.

A. **Plans** are often E or H-shaped on plan, the entrance being in the middle of the letter, and the two ends forming wings, as at Bramshill, Hardwick, Longford, Hatfield, Longleat, Burleigh, Loseley, and Audley End, while many are irregular in plan, as Knole, Penshurst, and Haddon (ball-room wing), such grouping being often brought about through the work being an addition to a previous Gothic house.

Broad terraces raised above the garden level, and leading thereto with wide flights of steps and balustrades, are a

152.

Hatfield House.
South Front.

153. COURTYARD OF KIRBY HALL, NORTHANTS.

charming feature in the style. These are often laid out in a formal manner, with yews and other trees cut in fantastic patterns.

B. **Walls.**—Elevations have the character of picturesqueness, and the classic orders are used in a free and easy manner, often placed one above the other in the façades, as at Hatfield House (No. 152), the Gateway of the Schools at Oxford (No. 151), and Kirby Hall (No. 153).

The gables are often of scroll-work, following in a general way the slope of the roof (No. 153).

The chimney stacks (No. 153) are a special and prominent feature, they are often treated in a classical manner, with orders, but generally are of cut brickwork, the shafts being carried up boldly, so that they play an important part in the composition and outline of the house.

Parapets are pierced with various designs with characteristic detail (No. 152).

C. **Openings.**—Bay windows are largely used, as at Longleat, and Kirby Hall (No. 153), and form an important element of the style.

Large heavily-mullioned windows (No. 153), filled in with leaded glass, and crossed by horizontal transoms, are a special feature adapted from the late Gothic period.

Arcades are often introduced, as at Hatfield (No. 152).

Dormers are largely used, and turrets (No. 152) are in common use.

D. **Roofs.**—The use of high roofs, and also of flat or low roofs with balustrades, occurs both separately and in the same design. Lead and tiles are both used, and also stone slates in certain districts. The balustrade, arcaded, pierced, or battlemented, is a constant feature (No. 152).

E. **Columns.**—The orders are employed rarely with purity; at Longleat, the most Italian-like example, the topmost are the smallest, corresponding to the local use of the best rooms on the ground floor. Bramshill has a centre which is perhaps the most licentious specimen of the style. A characteristic treatment is the reduction downwards, more especially in pilasters, accompanied by bulbous swellings. Square columns are used, banded with strap ornamentation; pilasters are similarly treated or panelled.

Arcades are much employed, especially in the form of recessed *loggie*.   Ex. : Bramshill and Hatfield (No. 152).

F. **Mouldings.**—Local and coarse in many instances. Two characteristics are the corona of a cornice, as a huge cyma above a small ogee ; and the use of convex cornices, often banded or carved at intervals.   Plaster work seems to have influenced in many ways the sections employed.

G. **Decoration.**—Strap ornamentation is formed by bands of raised plaster, of about the width and thickness of a leather strap, interlaced in grotesque patterns, as in the ceilings of the period.   It is considered by some as derived from the East, through France and Italy, in imitation of the damascened work which was at that period so common. This type of detail is also found in pilasters, as at Hatfield (No. 152).

Grotesquely carved figures as terminals occur, and are a remnant from Gothic times (Nos. 152 and 153).

Prismatic rustication, or the projection of blocks of stone of prismatic form (No. 153), occurs in pilasters and pedestals, and in later times coloured stones are inserted in their stead.

Plaster work is used with great skill in design, and adaptability to the material for ceilings.   Broad friezes in the same material are sometimes modelled with much quaintness and grotesque feeling, as at Hardwick.   Tapestries continued to be used for walls.   Colour decoration made little or no progress.

5. REFERENCE BOOKS.

John Thorpe's original drawings in the Soane Museum.
C. J. Richardson's "Old English Mansions."
Gotch and Talbot Brown's "Architecture of the Renaissance in England."
Shaw's "Elizabethan Architecture."
Nash's "Mansions of the Olden Time."
"Kenilworth," by Sir W. Scott.   (Historical Novel.)
John Inglesant," by Shorthouse.   (Historical Novel.)

ENGLISH RENAISSANCE.

(THE SEVENTEENTH CENTURY, OR ANGLO-CLASSIC.)

INIGO JONES (1572-1652).

SIR CHRISTOPHER WREN (1632-1723).

1. INFLUENCES (see page 263).

2. ARCHITECTURAL CHARACTER.

Elizabethan and Jacobean, which are transitional styles, between late Gothic and the purer classicism of the period we are about to discuss, at length gave way before the influence of Inigo Jones and Wren. These architects are to be considered as the founders of the Anglo-Classic, or fully-developed Renaissance, in England.

3. EXAMPLES.

INIGO JONES (1572-1652).

His work was influenced by long study in Italy, at Venice, and especially at Vicenza, Palladio's native town. He was invited to Copenhagen by the King of Denmark, but returned to England in the train of the wife of James I. He revisited Italy, in 1612, for further study, and on his return introduced a purer Renaissance style, founded on Italian models and ornamentation. Palladio was Inigo Jones's master in design, and has since always had a great influence on English architecture.

The Commonwealth intervened, and checked the execution of many of Inigo Jones's designs.

His principal Buildings and designs are :

The Quadrangle of **St. John's College, Oxford,** in the early transition style.

Chilham Castle, Kent, also transitional ; E-shaped façade, with radiating side wings, forming a horseshoe court at the back. *Materials :*—Brick and stone dressings.

The Banqueting House, Whitehall (A.D. 1619-1621), which is a part only of a Royal Palace, one of the grandest architectural conceptions of the Renaissance. The greater part of the building was to be three storeys in height, each storey 30 feet, and the height to the top of parapet was to be 100 feet. The remainder, being curtain wings to the main blocks, in design like the Banqueting House, was to be 75 feet high, divided into two storeys. The plan was arranged round courtyards, one of which was to be circular (compare Spain, p. 257). The great court would have vied with that of the Louvre. In this design, proportion, elegance, and purity of detail, are more happily combined than in any other Renaissance scheme of the kind.

St. Paul's, Covent Garden, was erected in A.D. 1631, and the main characteristics are that it is severe and imposing, by reason of its simplicity and good proportions.

The Duke of Devonshire's **villa at Chiswick** was founded on Palladio's villa at Vicenza (see p. 226). It is important because it marks the earliest introduction of the "pillar and portico" style, which in the next century leads to the neglect of those fundamental principles of architecture, namely, suitability of purpose, utility, and appropriateness.

The river façade of **Greenwich Hospital**, in which the two lower storeys are included under one huge Corinthian order, and

Wilton House, Wiltshire, Houses in Lincoln's Inn Fields, Great Queen Street, and Ashburnham House, Dean's Yard (notable staircase), are other examples of his works.

SIR CHRISTOPHER WREN (1632-1723)

was a scholar and a mathematician. His brilliant success at Cambridge as a scientist, and as an astronomical professor at Oxford, prepared him for many important constructive feats, in after life. Wren's great opportunity was

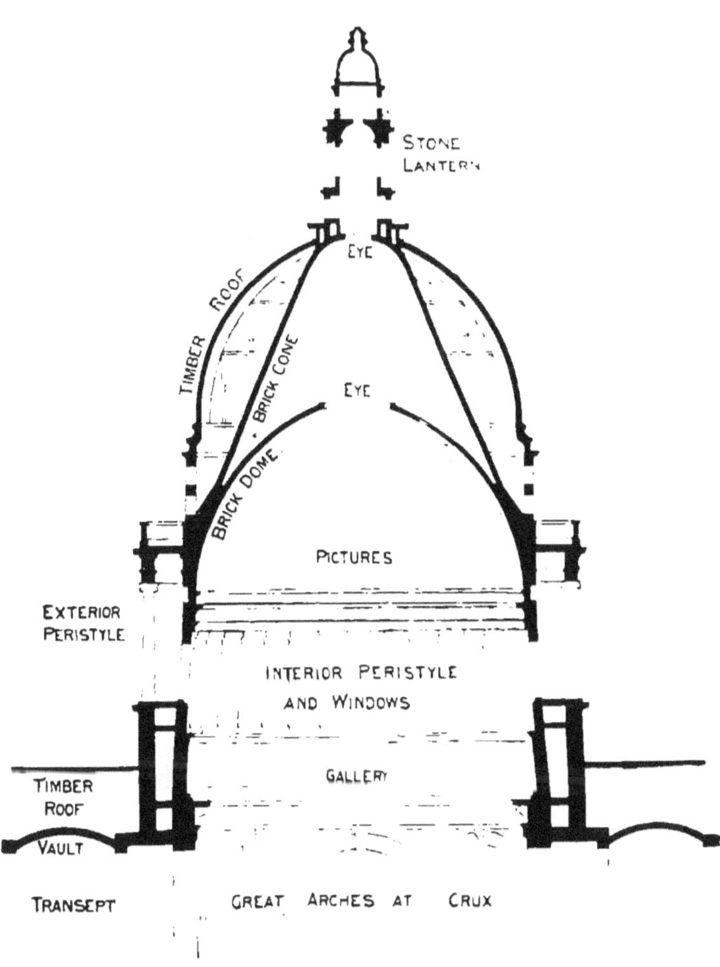

154. ST. PAUL'S CATHEDRAL, LONDON.
Section through Dome.

the destruction of London by the Great Fire in 1666, after which he devised a grand plan for the reconstruction, which was, however, abandoned for pecuniary and other reasons. As an architect, he lacked the more thorough technical education of Inigo Jones, and was not always able to clothe his constructive forms in equally appropriate detail.

Wren's study of French work at Paris, and elsewhere in France was, however, an important part of his education as an architect. The works on the Louvre were then in progress, and constituted a great school of art; in consequence, his work shows more French influence than that of Inigo Jones, which is pure Italian.

Palladio continued to be the inspirer of English work, as compared with Vignola, whom the French followed, but Wren gave often a semi-French turn to his designs, more especially in the decorative detail, as the attentive student will discover, on comparing his work with that of Inigo Jones.

His work is of course all tinged with classical colouring, the classical column and details are always paramount. In many of his designs, in which he was obliged to study cheapness, he made up for it, as has been said, by spending thought, and all his designs, as Opie said, are mixed " with brains." A careful study of proportion of part to part is exhibited in his works.

Many of these, as St. Paul's and the City churches, are executed in a material, Portland stone, which by its good weathering properties adds to the dignity and importance of monumental work : while in domestic work, he used red brick, with stone dressings, as at Hampton Court, Marlborough House, etc.

The **principal works** of Sir Christopher Wren are :

i. The **Sheldonian Theatre, Oxford,** 1664.

    The constructive carpentry in the roof is an evidence of his scientific skill, as is also the splendid acoustic properties of the hall.

ii. **St. Paul's, London,** 1675-1710.

    The first design prepared by Sir Christopher Wren was in plan a Greek cross ; as can be seen by the model in the north triforium at St. Paul's Cathedral. He was, however, compelled by the influence of the clergy to adopt the Latin cross, and mediæval type of plan (No. 124), which he clothed with the forms of classic architecture.

By the comparative set of plans (No. 124) given, it can be compared with St. Peter's, the Pantheon, Paris, and Cologne Cathedral.

St. Paul's is essentially an English type of plan, it is long, and has the dome in the middle of its length.

The section (No. 154) clearly shows the triple construction of the dome, which is carried on eight piers. It is, externally, perhaps the most beautiful dome in existence. Notice particularly the unbroken exterior colonnade, and the blocking up of every fourth intercolumniation (No. 155), which produces an effect of strength and solidity. The supports of the dome are seen externally carried down to the ground, which is æsthetically satisfactory.

The façade is two orders in height (No. 155), the lower being Corinthian, and the upper Composite. The upper storey of the façade is, in reality, only a screen wall (No. 156), with nothing behind it, because the aisles are only one storey high; it is added simply to give dignity and expression to the composition. It is interesting to compare the construction with that of St. Peter's, Rome.

The poetess Joanna Baillie has well described the majestic appearance of St. Paul's, on a foggy day :

        " Rear'd in the sky,
'Tis then St. Paul's arrests the wandering eye :
The lower parts in swathing mists conceal'd,
The higher through some half-spent shower reveal'd.
So far from earth removed, that well I trow,
Did not its form man's artful structure show,
It might some lofty Alpine peak be deem'd,
The eagle's haunt, with cave and crevice seam'd.
Stretch'd wide on either hand, a rugged screen,
In lurid dimness nearer streets are seen,
Like shoreward billows of a troubled sea
Arrested in their rage."

	Time Building.	*Architect.*	*Master Mason.*	*Bishops.*
St. Paul's.	35 years.	One.	One	One.
St. Peter's.	100 years.	Six.	—	Twenty.

thus referred to by Pope in one of his epistles to the Earl of
Burlington.

> " You show us, Rome was glorious, not profuse,
> And pompous buildings once were things of use.
> Yet shall, my lord, your just, your noble rules,
> Fill half the land with imitating fools ;
> Who random drawings from your sheets shall take,
> And of one beauty many blunders make ;
> Load some vain church with old theatric state,
> Turn arcs of triumph to a garden gate ;
>
>   *   *   *   *   *   *
>
> Shall call the winds through long arcades to roar,
> Proud to catch cold at a Venetian door."

This passage suggests what really did happen, and characterizes the style of architecture so truly, that it is well worth
quoting.

Note.—At the end of the century are found architects
dividing into the two opposite camps of Classic and
Gothic styles, which were henceforth to battle for the
pre-eminence. In this section we shall enumerate the
more important architects, and, as they were practising
concurrently, it has been thought better to put their
works into two columns.

In this century we shall notice that the design of the
buildings, not excepting the domestic class, is influenced by
a passion for symmetry and grandeur at all costs, which
almost entirely puts aside, as unworthy of consideration, the
comfort and convenience of the people who had to occupy
these buildings.

We might in this respect agree with Pope that

> " 'tis very fine,
> But where d'ye sleep, or where d'ye dine ?
> I find by all you have been telling
> That 'tis a house, but not a dwelling."

Or we may quote Lord Chesterfield, who said that General
Wade had better take a lodging opposite his Palladian
mansion (by Lord Burlington), if he liked nothing of it but
the front.

We must not, however, overlook the fact that, at this time,
there grew up a vernacular style, most of the less important
houses being erected in the useful and modest Queen Anne

and Georgian type of square house.   Moreover, corridor planning and the now fast developing trade of the joiner, did much to further convenience and comfort in domestic architecture.

3. EXAMPLES.

Hawksmoor (1666-1736) was a pupil of Wren and followed him in his practice.   Principal works : St. George's, Blooms-bury ; Church of St. Mary Woolnoth, in Lombard Street, London ; St. George's in the East, London.

In Hawksmoor's work, ideas, of some originality and grandeur, are too often marred by eccentricities of treatment.

Badly-designed detail is a weak point with the pupils of Wren.

James Gibbs (1683-1754). Principal works were : St. Martin's in the Fields ; St. Mary-le-Strand (notice that the tower of this church, on plan, is an oblong, not a square) ; the Radcliffe Library, Oxford ; the Senate House, Cambridge ; Bartholomew's Hospital, London.   He published a book of his own designs, in which the above works, with others, may be found.

Sir John Vanbrugh (1666-1726).   Principal   works : Blenheim Palace (No. 148), the most important mansion of the period erected in England, is both picturesque and stately. It is the commencement of the Palladian type of house, in which a striving after symmetry and monumental grandeur, at the expense of usefulness, led to the debasement of architecture.   In the plan of Blenheim, we should observe the extensive use of corridors as communicating passages, which is a great development in planning, and a step towards the privacy which is now insisted upon.   Castle Howard, Yorkshire, is another example of a ponderous yet magnificent character.

Thomas Archer (d. 1743) was a pupil of Sir John Vanbrugh. He erected St. John's, Westminster, in the Rococo style, and St. Philip's, Birmingham, in the somewhat heavy style of his master.

Colin Campbell (d. 1734) was the compiler of the " Vitruvius Britannicus," which contains plans and elevations of all the country houses of any importance erected during the century, and which should be consulted by the student.

SOMERSET HOUSE, LONDON.

From the Embankment

Kent (1684-1748), in collaboration with the Earl of Burlington, erected the Horse Guards, London, in which note the skilful grouping of the parts; the Treasury Buildings, Horse Guards Parade; Devonshire House, Piccadilly; Holkham Hall, Norfolk.

The Brothers Adam.

Robert Adam (1728-1792) published " Diocletian's Palace at Spalatro," in the year 1760, a book which influenced architectural design. He erected two sides of Fitzroy Square; the Adelphi Terrace (named after the four brothers); the screen in front of the Admiralty, Whitehall; Caen Wood, Hampstead ; Keddlestone Hall, Derbyshire ; and the College at Edinburgh.

The brothers Adam were the authors of a sufficiently marked style of interior decoration that is known by their name. Furniture and decoration were treated together with the design of the rooms themselves.

Henry Holland (1740-1806) erected Claremont House, Esher; Carlton House (since destroyed, the Corinthian columns being employed at the

Sir Robert Taylor 1714-1788) erected the Pelican Fire Office, Lombard Street; Ely House, Dover Street.

George Dance, senior (died 1768), City architect of London, erected the Mansion House, London.

His better known son was the designer of Newgate, the most appropriate of prison designs, also of St. Luke's Hospital.

John Wood (1704-1754) of Bath, in conjunction with Dawkins, published the " Illustrations of Baalbec and Palmyra " in 1750, creating a taste for Roman magnificence. His best known work is Prior Park, Bath.

Sir William Chambers (1726-1796), first Treasurer of the Royal Academy, wrote the " Treatise on the Decorative Part of Civil Architecture." He carried on the traditions of the Anglo-Palladian school, objecting strongly to the Greek revival then commencing. He travelled largely in Europe and the East. His great work is Somerset House (No. 157), which is grand, dignified, and simple in its parts. A single order runs through two storeys, and rustication is largely employed. The character of his work in general is correct and refined, but lacking somewhat in originality and strength.

James Gandon (1742-1823), a pupil of Sir W. Chambers, erected the Custom House and the Law Courts at Dublin.

Sir John Soane (1750-1837),

National Gallery); Brooks's Club, London ; the vestibule to Dover House, Whitehall, which is a charming and refined piece of work.

James Wyatt (1748-1813) studied in Rome. His works in London are: the Pantheon (1772) in Oxford Street, and White's Club ; Lee Priory, Kent; Castle Coote, Ireland; Bowden Park, Wiltshire ; and Fonthill Abbey. He undertook the restoration of many of the cathedrals in England and Wales, and the small knowledge of the true spirit of Gothic architecture then existing is responsible for his inability to effect these with any degree of success. Pugin has starred him with the affix "the destroyer."

a pupil of the architect of Newgate, on his return from Italy was, in 1788, appointed architect to the Bank of England. This important building occupied many years of his life, and constitutes his masterpiece. Comparing this design with Newgate, it fails in the quality of apparent suitability of purpose. His designs are those of an original mind, but he was unable to clothe them with suitable details. There is a consequent taint of eccentricity. The Dulwich picture gallery is by him. The student should visit Sir John Soane's Museum, in Lincoln's Inn Fields, which was formerly his private house.

4. COMPARATIVE OF ENGLISH ARCHITECTURE IN THE SEVENTEENTH AND EIGHTEENTH CENTURIES.

A. **Plans.**—Are marked by regularity and symmetry in many instances, showing signs of being dictated by a preconceived elevation. The Italian use of a *piano nobile* above a storage basement, ruinously affected many country houses. Excessive cellarage, or bad offices, occupy the ground floor, and the best rooms are reached by a great external staircase and portico, or by a mean approach from a side door through the basement. Note the use of octagonal, circular, and elliptical-shaped apartments, often cubical in proportion. Suites are arranged of such saloons in various combinations. Staircases receive much attention, ingenious domical, or other top lights, being introduced. Corridors gradually supersede the hall and *en suite* systems of planning.

B. **Walls.**--Are usually thick, and filled in solid between the varied shapes of the rooms, on plan. Brick is used most commonly for the walling. and often for the facing, but in later work it is usually stuccoed. Stone is used as an ashlar facing and for dressings. Unbroken surfaces set off the porticoes,. pilasters, or window dressings of the composition. Blank walls, to mask undesirable necessities, are not uncommon. Chimneys are often concealed. Pediments are the only form of gable, and are used with and without balustrades.

C. **Openings.**—Windows are reduced as much as possible, but infrequency of openings is compensated for by large and unobstructed window areas. Porticoes and arcades are regulated by the proportions of the classical orders, and the minimum condition of having to pass through them; the maximum scale was a question of material and expense. Vertical grouping of windows is effectively developed (Ex.: houses in Hanover Square). Large compositions of the windows of more than one room or storey are not affected by party or floor divisions. Ex.: Adams' works in Fitzroy Square, etc.

D. **Roofs.**—"No roof but a spherical one being sufficiently dignified," for this style, balustrades or attics conceal whatever is left of the lowest pitch of slates or tiles possible. In the smaller works tiles, and a wooden eaves cornice, are often effectively used. Domes, cupolas, and turrets are well designed. Those on a large scale are lead covered, small examples are sometimes entirely of wood. The splendid steeples of the period, in stone and leaded wood, rival mediæval spires in fanciful and skilful outlines.

E. **Columns.**—The orders are used everywhere that funds permitted. The small size of stone obtainable in England prevented single order porticoes on a large scale, until stucco and iron came in. Pilasters, however, are most often of two or more storeys in height. In interiors, columns, often purely decorative in function, are employed with considerable effect.

F. **Mouldings.**—The standard mouldings of the classic orders become the stock in trade of every workman, being applied in every material with small modification.

Work is thus often found of equal standard in very varied classes of building. The great use of wood, even in main external cornices, gives, by its possible smallness of scale and ease of working, some elaboration and refinement, to very simple buildings.

G. **Decoration.**—Fresco artists are sometimes employed, as in the case of Verrio and Sir James Thornhill, but white-wash is usual. Besides the orders, executed with facility in wood or composition, or both combined, decoration, founded on Roman, or in the later period, on Greek examples, is modelled in stucco with great skill and effect. French work of the style of Louis XIV. and his successors, was also followed, while the Brothers Adam and others imported Italian workmen, who carried the art to a high pitch of technical excellence.

5. REFERENCE BOOKS.

The "Vitruvius Britannicus," published in successive editions, contains the designs of the more important buildings erected during the seventeenth and eighteenth centuries.

"Palladio," by Isaac Ware.
Chambers, "Civil Architecture."
Adams, "Spalatro and Works of the Brothers Adam."
Gibbs, "Books of Designs."
Burlington, "Designs of Inigo Jones."
"Esmond," by Thackeray. }
"The Virginians," by Thackeray. } Historical Novels.

THE NINETEENTH CENTURY.

(1800 TO 1851.)

(THE AGE OF REVIVALS RUNNING CONCURRENTLY.)

ARCHITECTURAL CHARACTER.

The notes on this period are only to be taken as, in some slight degree, explanatory of the general course which architecture has taken during this century. The beginning of this century saw Palladianism on the decline, and eclecticism was henceforth to be the governing feature of our architecture. Our isolation from the Continent, due to the Napoleonic wars, practically shut off all new ideas in art. On the other hand, the works by Stuart and Revett, and Adams, etc., published in the last century, were producing that movement in architecture which we know by the name of the Greek revival. Somewhat later we feel the full force of the romantic Gothic revival, started in the latter part of the last century by Horace Walpole at Twickenham, in the erection of Strawberry Hill, a pseudo-gothic abbey in lath and plaster.

EXAMPLES.

Note.—The Classic and Gothic schools of architecture, which now, for the first time, run concurrently, are placed side by side.

⁎ The mention of architects still living has been decided upon, not without a certain amount of hesitation, but the authors will be glad to receive any corrections.

CLASSIC SCHOOL.

In this section we must notice the influence of classical writings on architecture, such as Stuart and Revett's "Athens" (A.D. 1762), Robert Adam's "Spalatro," Inwood's "Erechtheion," and the publications of the Dilettante Society, etc.

The Elgin marbles were brought to England in 1801-1803 by Lord Elgin, and considerably influenced the public taste in favour of classic work. (For the work of this generation, see Shepherd's "London," with text by the elder Elmes.)

GOTHIC SCHOOL.

The influence of literature, such as Battey Langley's "Gothic Architecture Improved," etc.; John Britton's "Architectural Antiquities" (1807-1826); Rickman's "Attempt to Discriminate the Gothic Styles" in 1819; and the writings of the elder Pugin, from 1821 and onwards, help on the Gothic movement.

Strawberry Hill, completed in 1770, an absurd lath and plaster abbey, by its notoriety is important.

Fonthill Abbey, by James Wyatt, completed in 1822, also

CLASSIC SCHOOL.

H. W. Inwood (1794-1843):
New Church of St. Pancras in
1819, an attempt to copy absolutely the purest of Greek
detail.

Nash (1752-1835) of the Re-
gency, introduces the age of
stucco: Haymarket Theatre;
Buckingham Palace; Regent
Street, with Quadrant (for
colonnades, since taken down,
see old prints). The laying out
of Regent's Park in palatial
blocks of theatrical architecture.

William Wilkins (1778-
1839): University College,
London; the National Gal-
lery (fettered with conditions);
St. George's Hospital, London;
Museum at York; Downing
College, Cambs.; The Grange
House, Hants (1820).

Sir Robert Smirke (1780-
1867), a pupil of Sir John
Soane: The British Museum
(1823-1847), (in which remark
the application of the useless
but grandeur-giving porticoes
to public buildings); General
Post Office; King's College,
London (1831); Carlton Club,
after the library of St. Mark's,
Venice.

George Basevi (1795-1845),

GOTHIC SCHOOL.
represents the idea of repro-
ducing the monastic buildings
of the mediæval period, the
internal arrangements being
those of everyday houses.

St. Luke's, Chelsea (1820), an
early attempt at revived Gothic,
the barn-like and galleried
church of the period, being
clothed with details, directly
copied from old cathedrals and
churches, may be compared
with St. Pancras Church (1819),
a copy in many respects of the
Erechtheion at Athens.

Sir Jeffrey Wyatville (1766-
1840) transforms Windsor
Castle in 1826. This started
a fashion for castellated mansions, internally of the vernacular architecture, and externally
battlemented and turreted in
imitation of the Edwardian
castles. Ex.: Belvoir Castle,
Penrhyn, etc.

William Wilkins: New
Court, Trinity College, Cambs.,
and the New Buildings, King's
College, Cambs.

*Augustus Welby Northmore
Pugin* (1812-1852), from being
employed upon his father's
books of mediæval architecture, acquired an extraordinary
knowledge of the style. He
published a rousing pamphlet
contrasting the "degraded"
architecture of the day with
what he called the "Christian" style. A new spirit of
church building was awakened,

CLASSIC SCHOOL.

a pupil of Sir John Soane, erects Fitzwilliam Museum, Cambs.

Decimus Burton (1800-1881): Screen at Hyde Park Corner in 1824; Athenæum Club, Pall Mall; United Service Club, Pall Mall.

H. L. Elmes (1815-1847): St. George's Hall, Liverpool, the most perfect design of the Classical School. The main hall is after the manner of the Roman Thermæ. Externally a colonnade and portico design is handled with great effect. On the early death of Elmes, who, at the age of twenty-three, had successfully competed for the building, Prof. Cockerell completed the decoration of the interior. The vault was executed in hollow tiles by Sir Robert Rawlinson.

Sir W. Tite (1798-1873): Royal Exchange, London.

Professor C. R. Cockerell, R.A. (1788-1863), travelled much in Greece and Italy, and published an important folio of the Greek temples of Ægina and Bassæ. He erected the Taylor and Randolph Institute, Oxford; the Sun Fire Office, Threadneedle Street, London; branches of the Bank of England at Manchester, Bristol, and Liverpool; and Hanover Chapel, Regent Street (lately condemned to destruction).

Sir Charles Barry (1795-1860) travelled extensively in Egypt, Greece, and Italy. He abandoned the fashion of useless porticoes, and brought in

GOTHIC SCHOOL.

and, by the earnest study of old work, a new era in the Gothic revival began. Pugin erects Roman Catholic churches at Nottingham, Derby, etc.; St. George's Cathedral, Southwark; St. Augustine's, Ramsgate, 1855. He works under Sir Charles Barry on the stained glass, metal work, fittings, etc., of the Houses of Parliament.

Sir Charles Barry: Birmingham Grammar School, 1833; Houses of Parliament, 1840 (No. 158), in which note the symmetry of leading lines on

CLASSIC SCHOOL.

the "astylar" treatment of design. The Travellers' Club House, Pall Mall, shows the influence of the Pandolfini Palace, Florence. It was followed by the Reform Club, Pall Mall, a design inspired by the Farnese Palace at Rome. In Bridgewater House, the third of the series (1849), the influence of the Gothic revival is evidently felt, greater richness is sought after, and the Italian feeling is less strong. His final work, the Town Hall at Halifax, is a still more ornate example of the Renaissance, the intention being to combine picturesqueness with symmetrical stateliness. Other important works in the country are : Trentham Hall (where landscape gardening of the Italian School is admirably carried out), Shrublands, Highclere, Cliefden, etc.

Sir James Pennethorne (1801-1871), at one time assistant to Nash, and influenced by Sir Charles Barry, also discarded porticoes as unnecessary and useless, and commenced a treatment more after Renaissance than Classic lines : Geological Museum, Piccadilly (after portion of the internal courtyard of the Doge's Palace, Venice); London University, Burlington Gardens; Somerset House, western façade. In his works the orders are sparingly used, but the detail is refined.

GOTHIC SCHOOL.

plan, the simplicity of idea, and the character of richness pervading the whole design, which is Classic in inspiration, and Gothic in clothing, carried out with scrupulous adherence to the spirit and detail of the Perpendicular period.

Pugin, under Sir Charles Barry, directed the execution of the fittings, agreeing with the style of the building and in marked contrast to the previous buildings of the Revival.

The immediate effect of the design of this great building was slight. It was the climax of the first idea of the movement—that of carrying on the Tudor style—so that, at the time of its completion, in 1860, the attention of all was riveted on the earlier phases of mediæval architecture which everyone was engaged in imitating.

Barry marks the close of the Classic Revival. The influence of the Gothicists is now paramount, and the final touch to this influence is given by the 1851 Exhibition, which in the end has done so much to raise the arts and crafts to a higher state of perfection.

158.   THE HOUSES OF PARLIAMENT, LONDON.

THE NINETEENTH CENTURY.

(1851 TO THE PRESENT TIME.)

The Great Exhibition of 1851 causes the raising into prominence of the minor arts, such as metal work, glass painting, mosaics, decoration, sculptured works. etc., etc. The popularization of architecture by the architectural courts and models of buildings in the various styles, aroused an interest in the subject. The publication of "The Stones of Venice," by Ruskin, in 1851, and the works of Beresford-Hope, Parker, Prof. Willis, Sharpe, Rev. J. L. Petit, and others, helped on the Gothic movement, while Prof. Cockerell and Prof. Donaldson were writing on the Classic side.

CLASSIC.

E. M. Barry (1831-1880): Covent Garden Theatre ; The Art Union Building, Strand ; Charing Cross Station.

Nelson: Junior United Service Club.

F. P. Cockerell: The Freemasons' Tavern.

Sir Gilbert Scott (1810-1877): The Foreign Office.

Sir Digby Wyatt (1820-1877): Courtyard to India Office.

Messrs. Banks and Barry: Burlington House; the Courtyard and façade to Piccadilly.

Sidney Smirke: The storey added to Burlington House; British Museum reading-room, etc.

Vulliamy : Dorchester House, London, a Venetian Renaissance palace has unique decorative work inside by Alfred Stevens.

GOTHIC.

Sir Gilbert Scott (1810-1877): St. Mary, Stoke Newington ; the Martyrs' Memorial, Oxford ; church at Haley Hill, Halifax (1855); church at Hamburg ; St. George's, Doncaster (1853); St. Mary's Cathedral, Edinburgh ; St. Mary Abbots, Kensington ; the Albert Memorial ; St. Pancras Station ; many other new churches, houses, and restorations.

Benjamin Ferrey: St. Stephen's, Westminster.

William Butterfield: Keble College, Oxford ; All Saints, Margaret Street, London: and St. Alban's, Holborn, all of which show the increasing desire for and study of colour.

G. E. Street (1824-1881) erects St. Mary Magdalene, Paddington; St. James the Less, Westminster, and the Law Courts, London. House in

<table>
<tr><td>

CLASSIC.

John Gibson : National Provincial Banks in London and the provinces ; the Society for the Promotion of Christian Knowledge, in Northumberland Avenue, London ; Todmorden Town Hall.

</td><td>

GOTHIC.

Cadogan Square ; the Convent, East Grinstead ; House and Church at Holmwood, etc., etc.

W. Burges (1828-1881) erects Cork Cathedral ; restores Cardiff Castle, and builds his own house in Melbury Road, etc.

E. W. Godwin : Congleton Town Hall and Bristol Assize Courts.

A. Waterhouse : Manchester Town Hall and Assize Courts.

Deane and Woodward : The Oxford Museum, directly the outcome of Ruskin's teaching in architecture.

</td></tr>
</table>

Note.—The work of the last four on the Gothic side, with that of Street in the Law Courts, may be taken as fully exemplifying the results of the revival in the sphere of domestic architecture.

The restoration of a large number of cathedrals and churches, and the erection of an immense number of new churches, had powerfully aided the Gothic revival, which it was attempted to extend to buildings for every purpose ; until the movement met with a severe check in the decision, acquiesced in by Sir Gilbert Scott, to erect the Home and Foreign Offices in the classical, or as it was called, the modern style. The design thus dictated to Scott was not likely to be a masterpiece, and it is in fact but a poor compromise between modern French and the traditional Italian ideas of the Renaissance. After this crisis a new movement, due to Norman Shaw, Nesfield, and Philip Webb, then arose in favour of the Queen Anne style, or Free Classic, for domestic buildings, while churches and kindred buildings continue to be erected in a developed style of Gothic architecture.

The works of Mr. Norman Shaw at this period were : The New Zealand Chambers in Leadenhall Street, London ; many country houses such as "Whispers ;" and Lowther Lodge, Kensington, while his influence on the design of the smaller buildings in suburbs and country, by the erection of houses, etc., at Bedford Park, Chiswick, was immediate and fruitful.

CLASSIC SCHOOL PRACTICALLY RESERVED FOR SECULAR WORK.

The Science College, South Kensington, and the Albert Hall, by General Scott (assisted).

E. M. Barry endeavours to introduce the Early French Renaissance, as in Temple Chambers, Victoria Embankment, London.

Crossland: Holloway College, Egham (after Chambord).

Whichcord: S. Stephen's Club.

Davis and Emmanuel: City of London Schools.

Burns: Duke of Buccleugh's House, Whitehall.

Bodley and Garner: London School Board Offices, Thames Embankment. The student confined to London may obtain an idea of the early French Renaissance style, by an inspection of the above.

H. Gribble: The Oratory at Brompton. (The Italian style a condition of the competition.)

W. Young: Glasgow Municipal Buildings, in the Palladian manner.

GOTHIC SCHOOL PRACTICALLY RESERVED FOR CHURCH WORK.

J. L. Pearson, R.A.: Truro Cathedral. His eight London churches:

(1) Holy Trinity, Bessborough Gardens.
(2) St. Anne's, Lower Kennington Lane.
(3) St. Augustine's, Kilburn.
(4) St. John's, Red Lion Sq.
(5) St. Michael, West Croydon.
(6) St. John's, Lower Norwood.
(7) Catholic Apostolic Church, Maida Hill.
(8) Chiswick Parish Church, additions.

James Brooks: churches in Holland Road, Kensington, Gospel Oak, and many others round London.

G. G. Scott: St. Agnes, Kennington; churches at Southwark and Norwich; the Greek Church, Moscow Road, London; additions to Pembroke College, Cambridge.

Bodley and Garner: church at Hoar Cross, Staffordshire; Clumber Church; churches at Folkestone, etc.

John Bentley: Roman Catholic church of St. Mary, Watford; the Convent in the Hammersmith Road, etc.

Sir Arthur Blomfield: St. Mary, Portsea, and many other churches; Sion College, Thames Embankment; the Church House, Westminster.

Note.—In the Admiralty and War Office competition, only one Gothic design was selected for the second competition. This practically publishes the death of the Gothic style for public buildings. The foundation of the South Kensington Museum carried further the influence of the 1851 Exhibition, by its illustration of ancient decorative art, and by the atelier which was there maintained for some years.

CLASSIC SCHOOL PRACTICALLY RESERVED FOR SECULAR WORK.

R. Norman Shaw (later buildings): Alliance Assurance Office, Pall Mall; houses at Queen's Gate, London; house near Salisbury, in the Wren style; New Scotland Yard (Anglo-Classic).

T. G. Jackson: Work at Oxford. The examination schools, and additions to colleges in revived Elizabethan.

Ernest George and Peto. Influence of Flemish Renaissance: works at Collingham Gardens and Cadogan Square, London; houses at Streatham Common; Buchan Hill, Sussex, etc.

E. R. Robson and J. J. Stevenson. Work for London School Board: London vernacular style in red dressings and yellow stock bricks.

Revival of terra-cotta as a building material.

Charles Barry: Dulwich College.

Alfred Waterhouse: The Natural History Museum.

R. W. Edis: Constitutional Club, London.

GOTHIC SCHOOL PRACTICALLY RESERVED FOR CHURCH WORK.

Paley and Austin: churches in Lancashire.

Douglas and Fordham: churches and half timber-work domestic in Chester, etc.

J. D. Sedding (1837-1892): Holy Trinity Church, Chelsea, marks the raising of the arts and crafts into their proper importance; the church of the Holy Redeemer, Clerkenwell (a new version of the Wren style); St. Clement, Bournemouth, and domestic work adjacent.

The latest works of various tendencies.

T. E. Collcutt: Imperial Institute.

E. W. Mountford: Sheffield Town Hall; Battersea Town Hall; Battersea Polytechnic.

J. M. Brydon: Chelsea

Aston Webb and Ingress Bell:
Birmingham Assize Courts.

T. E. Collcutt: English Opera
House, London ; City Bank,
London.

Town Hall and Polytechnic ;
Bath Municipal Buildings.

J. Belcher: Institute of
Chartered Accountants, London.

ADDENDA.

During the last fifty years, the pages of the professional
journals have contained most of the noteworthy buildings
erected, and it is a source of much pleasure and instruction,
to go carefully through these records of the developments
which have taken place ; and which seem to show that a style
or manner in architecture is being slowly worked out, which
may, it is to be hoped, resist all revivals and fashions, and
become the free expression of our own civilization, and the
outward symbol of our nineteenth century progression.

GLOSSARY OF ARCHITECTURAL TERMS, WITH REFERENCES TO THE ILLUSTRATIONS.

Abacus (Gk. *abax* = a board). —A square or rectangular table forming the crowning member of a capital. In Grecian Doric, square without chamfer or moulding (No. 15). In Grecian Ionic, thinner with ovolo moulding only (No. 23). In the Roman Ionic and the Corinthian, the sides are hollowed on plan and have their angles cut off (Nos. 24 and 26). In the Romanesque period, the abacus is deeper but projects less and is moulded with rounds and hollows, or merely chamfered on the lower edge. In Gothic architecture we find that the circular or octagonal abacus is mostly favoured in England, while the square abacus is a French feature (No. 79).

A b u t m e n t. — The solid masonry which resists the lateral pressure of an arch.

Acanthus.—A plant, whose leaves conventionally treated, form the lower portions of the Corinthian capital (No. 31, D, F).

Acroteria (Gk. the extremity of anything). Bases or blocks of stone resting on the vertex and lower extremities of the pediment and intended for the support of statuary or ornaments.

Aisle (Lat. *ala* = a wing). —The lateral divisions which run parallel with the nave in a Gothic Cathedral (Nos. 69, 70, 71).

Amphi-prostyle (Gk. both with columns before). —A Temple having a portico at both extremities (No. 18, v.).

Annulet (Lat. *annulus* = a ring). - A small flat fillet encircling a column. It is used several times repeated under the ovolo or echinus of the Doric Capital (Nos. 20 and 21).

Anta (plural *antæ*). —Pilasters terminating the side wall of a temple.

An·efixæ (Lat. *ante*, before, *figo*, I fix).—Ornamental blocks, vertically fixed at regular intervals along the lower portion of a roof, to cover the joints of the tiles (Nos. 15, 31).

Apse (Gk. signifying an arch). The circular or multangular termination of a cathedral choir; the term being firstly applied to a Roman basilica. The apse is a continental feature, contrasts with the square termination of English Gothic work (Nos. 42, 43, 44, 62).

Arches are of various forms, and can be best understood by referring to No. 159.

Architrave (Gk. = chief beam).

--The beam or lowest division of the entablature which extends from column to column (No. 15). The term is also applied to the moulded frame which bounds the sides and head of a door or window opening.

Archivolt.--The mouldings on the face of an arch resting on the impost (No. 58).

Ashlar --Squared stonework in regular courses, in comparison with rubble work.

Astragal (Gk. = a knuckle-bone). A small semicircular moulding.

Astylar.--A treatment of façade without columns (No. 118).

Attic.--A term generally applied to the upper story of a building above the main cornice; also applied to low rooms in a roof (Nos. 101, 141, 143).

Ball-flower.--The characteristic ornament of decorated Gothic architecture (No. 84).

Baluster.--A small pillar or column supporting a handrail (No. 134).

Base.--The lower portion of any construction.

Basilica (Gk. *basileus*, a king). A term which came to be applied to a large hall for the administration of justice (page 59), Nos. 45 and 46.

Bay.--The divisions into which the nave of a mediæval church is divided.

Belfry.--A term generally applied to the upper room in a tower in which the bells are hung (No. 104).

Boss (Fr. *bosse* = lump or knob). A projecting ornament, placed at the intersection of the ribs of ceilings, whether vaulted or flat. The term is also applied to the curved termination to the weather-mouldings of doors and windows. Bosses are often carved with great delicacy, with heads of angels or flowers and foliage (No. 91).

Broach-spire.--A spire rising above a tower without a parapet, as in Early English works.

Buttress (Fr. *aboutir* = to lie out).--A mass of masonry projecting beyond the face of the wall to resist the pressure of an arch or vault. The development in each century will be noted under each style (Nos. 97, 98, 99, 100).

Byzantine architecture. --The style evolved at Constantinople or Byzantium in the fifth century (page 89), and which is essentially the style of the Eastern or Greek church to the present day.

Canopy.--A covering over niches, tombs, etc.

Capital (Lat. *caput* = a head). The upper portion of a column or pilaster (Nos. 20, 21, 23, 24, 25, 26, 54).

Chancel (Lat. *cancellus* = a screen).--The portion set apart for the clergy and choir and separated by a screen from the body of the church.

Chapels. Places of worship, attached to churches, in honour of particular saints, sometimes erected as separate buildings (Nos. 69, 70, 71, 94, 95).

Chapter-house (Lat. *capitulum*) usually opened out of the cloisters on the easternmost side, as at Westminster. It was the place of assembly for the dean and canons of a cathedral for the transaction of business. It was usually polygonal on plan, with a vault resting on a central pillar. Ex. Lincoln, York, etc. (Nos. 69, 73); sometimes oblong as at Canterbury.

Chevet.--The circular or polygonal termination of a cathedral, the apse being surrounded by chapels (No. 95).

Choir (*see* Chancel).

Choragus.—A term given in Greece to those who superintended a musical entertainment, and provided a chorus at their own expense.

Clerestory.—The upper division in the nave of a church above the triforium (Nos. 97, 98, 99, 100). Probably derived from the French *clair* = light, being obtained at this stage.

Cloisters. — A square open space, surrounded by covered passages of communication, connecting the cathedral to the chapterhouse, refectory, etc., of the monastery to which they were attached. They were generally placed on the south of the nave, and west of the transept, as at Westminster (Nos. 69, 73). The desire for sunlight and warmth probably suggested this position.

Coffers.—Panels formed in ceilings, vaults, or domes (Nos. 35, 46, 139).

Column (Lat. *columna*).—A vertical support, generally consisting of a base, shaft, and capital (Nos. 20, 21, 23, 24, 25, 26).

Corbels (Lat. *corbis* = a basket) are blocks of stone projecting from a wall, and supporting the beams of a roof or any weight ; they are often elaborately carved and moulded (No. 75).

Corinthian.—The third order of Grecian architecture (Nos. 25, 26).

Cornice (Fr. *corniche*)—In Greek architecture the crowning or upper portion of the entablature (Nos. 15, 20, 21, 23, 24, 25, 26), used as the term for any crowning projection (No. 118).

Cortile.—The Italian name adopted in English for the internal area, or courtyard, surrounded by an arcade of a palace, or other edifice (No. 145).

Corona.—The square projection of the upper part of the cornice, having a broad vertical face generally plain, and with its soffit or under portion recessed so as to form a drip, which (as its name implies) prevents water from running down the building (Nos. 15, 20, 21).

Crocket (Fr. *croc* = a hook). Projecting leaves or bunches of foliage used in Gothic architecture to decorate the angles of spires, canopies, etc. (Nos. 84, 86), as in the spires of Ratisbon (No. 106).

Crypts (Gk. *krúptē* = a vault), are vaults, either entirely or partly beneath a building. In churches they generally occur beneath the chancel. In early times they were used as places of burial.

Cupola (L. *cupa* = cup). — A spherical roof, rising like an inverted cup over a circular or multangular building (Nos. 35, 49, 50, 52, 53, 60, 122, 123, 131, 138, 139, 154, 155).

Cusps (Lat. *cuspis* = a point).— The trefoil, quatrefoil etc., terminations of Gothic tracery (Nos. 81, 82, 83, 86).

Cymatium. — The crowning member of a cornice, so called from its contour resembling that of wave (Nos. 15, 30).

Decastyle.—A portico of ten columns (No. 18, x.).

Dentils (Lat. *dentes* = teeth).— Tooth-like ornaments occurring originally in the Ionic and Corinthian cornices (Nos. 25, 26).

Diaper.—Any small pattern of flowers etc., repeated continuously over the wall as at the nave, Westminster Abbey.

Dipteral (Gk. = double-winged). —A temple having a double range of columns on each of its sides (No. 18, x.).

Dog-tooth.—An ornament resembling its name, specially occurring in Early English work (Nos. 82, 84).

Dome. — (It. *duomo* = cathedral). — The custom in Italy being to erect cupolas over churches, the word *dome* in English and French has passed from the building to this form of roof (*see* cupola).

Doric. — The earliest "order" of architecture (Nos. 15, 20, 21, 22).

Dormer. — A window in a sloping roof. It was usually the window of the sleeping apartments, hence the name (Nos. 101, 141, 143).

Dripstone, also label, and hood-mould, is a projecting moulding in Gothic architecture placed over the heads of doorways, windows, archways, etc., generally for the purpose of throwing off the rain (Nos. 82, 86, 92).

Early English. — The first of the three divisions of Gothic architecture, which was being evolved during the thirteenth century.

Eaves. — The lower portion of a roof projecting beyond the face of the wall (No. 150).

Echinus. — Properly the egg-and-dart ornament originally used in the Ionic capital; often used for the bold projecting ovolo of the Doric cap (Nos. 15, 20, 21, 29).

Entablature. — The portion of a structure supported by a colonnade, in Greek architecture comprising the architrave, frieze and cornice (Nos. 15, 20, 21, 23, 24, 25, 26).

Exhedra (Gk. = out of a chair). — A recess occurring in a larger room. In Greek buildings, the disputations of the learned were held in such recesses, so called from containing a number of seats.

Façade. — The front view or elevation of a building (as No. 119).

Fan-vault. — A system of vaulting peculiar to English perpendicular work, all the ribs having the same curve, resembling the frame-work of a fan (No. 85, F, No. 91).

Fascia (Lat. *facies* = a face). — A flat vertical face in the entablature. The architrave of the Ionic and Corinthian orders is divided into two or more *fasciæ* (Nos. 23, 24, 25, 26).

Finial (Lat. *finis* = the end). — The top or finishing portion of a pinnacle, bench end, or other architectural feature (Nos. 75, 86, 101).

Flèche. — A term generally applied to a wooden spire surmounting a roof.

Fluting. — The vertical channelling on the shaft of a column (Nos. 15, 20, 21, 23, 24, 25, 26).

Flying-buttress. — A buttress springing by means of an arch over the aisle of a church, and counteracting the thrust of the nave vault (Nos. 89, 90, 97, 98, 99, 100).

Frieze (It. *fregio* = adorn). — The middle division of the entablature (Nos. 15, 20, 21, 23, 24, 25, 26).

Gable. — The triangular portion of a wall, marked by the inclosing line of the roof (Nos. 75, 80). (In classic architecture it is called the pediment, No. 15.)

Gargoyle. — A projecting water-spout in Gothic architecture to throw off the water from the roof, often grotesquely carved (No. 100).

Groin. — The angle formed by the intersection of vaults (No. 85).

Guttæ or **Drops.** — Small pyramids or cones occurring under the triglyphs and mutules of the Doric entablature (Nos. 15, 20, 21).

Half-timbered construction. — A structure formed of wooden posts, and the interstices filled with brick or plaster (No. 150).

Hammer-beam roof.—A Gothic form of roof for diminishing the thrust on the walls, the finest example being Westminster Hall.

Hexastyle.—A row of six columns (No. 18, vi., vii.).

Hypæthral (Gk. = under the air). A building or temple without a roof or possessing a central space open to the sky.

Hypostyle —A pillared hall.

Impost (Lat. *impono* = I lay on). The member usually formed of mouldings, on which the arch immediately rests (Nos. 38, 58, 82, 86).

Intercolumniation.—The space between the columns (No. 19).

Ionic.—(*See* p. 42, Nos. 23, 24.)

Jambs.—The sides of the openings of doors and windows (Nos. 116, 117).

Keystone.—The central stone of an arch (Nos 38, 159).

King-post.—A beam extending from the ridge, supporting the tie-beam in the centre (No. 156).

Lancet arch.—A sharp pointed arch, resembling a lancet, chiefly in use during the Early English thirteenth century period (Nos. 83, 159).

Lierne.—A short intermediate rib in vaulting (No. 91).

Lintel.—The piece of timber or stone that covers an opening, and supports a weight above it (Nos. 4, 8, 28).

Loggia.—A gallery open to the air, and forming a shelter.

Metope (Gk. = a hole between). —The space between the Doric triglyphs. In ancient examples it was left quite open, hence the name (Nos. 15, 20, 21).

Modillions.— The projecting brackets in the Corinthian cornice (Nos. 24, 26).

Module.— A measure of proportion, by which the parts of a classic order or building are regulated, being usually the semi-diameter of a column, which is divided into thirty parts or minutes (Nos. 15, 20, 21).

Mosaic.—A method of forming decorative surfaces by small cubes of stone, glass and marble ; much used in Roman and later times for floors and wall decoration (*see* Nos. 44, 49, 52, 61).

Mouldings. — The contours given to projecting members (*see* page 48, etc., Nos. 29, 30).

Mullions are used in Gothic architecture, to divide the windows into different numbers of lights, these being usually glazed in leaded panes (Nos. 81, 83, 89, 90).

Mutule.—The projecting inclined blocks in the Greek Doric cornice, supposed to be derived from the ends of wooden rafters (Nos. 15, 20, 21).

Naos.—The cell or principal chamber in a temple, see sheet of plans (No. 18). The English *nave* is derived from the Gk. *naos*, and signifies the central or main division of the plan (Nos 69, 70, 71, 94, 95).

Nave (*see* Naos). The central division of a church, west of the choir (Nos. 69, 70, 71, 94, 95).

Necking.—The space between the astragal of the shaft and the commencement of the cap proper (Nos. 15, 20, 21, 23, 24, 25, 26).

Newel.—(1) The central shaft, round which the steps of a circular staircase wind, (2) also applied to the post in which the handrail is framed.

Niche.—A recess in a wall for the reception of a statue or ornament (No. 93).

Norman.—The style which preceded the Early English in this country, also termed English Romanesque.

Octastyle.—A range of eight columns (No. 18, viii., xi., xiii.).

Ogee.—A term applied to a form of moulding (No. 30).

Opisthodomus.—The space or chamber behind the cella in a Greek Temple, *see* plans (No. 18).

Order.—In architecture, signifies a column, with its base, shaft and capital, and the entablature which it supports (Nos. 15, 20, 21, 23, 24, 25, 26).

Oriel.—A window, semi-hexagonal or octagonal on plan, corbelled out from the face of the wall by means of projecting stones (No. 105).

Ovolo.—(*See* No. 30).

Panel.—The compartments formed by the framing of timbers.

The parapet (Ital. *parapetto*= breast high), is the upper portion of the wall above the roof; it is sometimes battlemented, a method derived from purposes of defence (Nos. 75, 80, 84, 89).

Pediment.—In classic architecture the triangular termination of the roof of a temple (*see* frontispiece and Nos. 15, 22). In Gothic architecture, it is called the Gable.

Peripteral.—An edifice surrounded by a range of columns (No. 18, iii., viii., etc.).

Peristyle.—A range of columns surrounding a court or temple (*see* sheet of plans, No. 18).

Perpendicular.—A phase of English Gothic evolved from the Decorated style, and in use during the fifteenth and sixteenth centuries in England (*see* page 158), so called from the lines of the tracery in use.

Pier.—The mass of masonry supporting an arch or beam, etc.,

in contradistinction to a circular column (Nos. 66, 87, 88).

Pilaster.—An anta or square pillar, projecting about one-sixth of its breadth from the wall, and of the same proportion as the order with which it is used (No. 26).

Pinnacle.—A small turret-like termination, placed on the top of buttresses or elsewhere, often ornamented upon its angles by bunches of foliage called crockets (Nos. 80, 90, 107).

Piscina (Lat. = a reservoir of water) is a small niche near the altar, with a hole in the bottom to carry off the water in which the priest washed his hands, and also that in which the chalice was rinsed.

Plinth.—A low square step on which a column is placed (Nos. 21, 23, 24, 25, 26).

Plan.—The representation of a building showing the general distribution of its parts in horizontal section (*see* Nos. 18, 39, 40, 42, 48, 51, 55, 69, 70, 71, 94, 95, 111, 112, 124, 125, 126, 127, 132, 136, 147, 148).

Podium.—A low pedestal wall; also the inclosing wall of the arena of an amphitheatre (Nos. 27 and 37).

Portico.—The space inclosed within columns and forming a covered ambulatory (Nos. 34, 138, 155).

Pronaos.—The part of the temple in front of the naos (often a similar meaning with Portico).

Propylæum (Gk. = a portal in front of).—An entrance gate or vestibule, in front of a building or set of buildings.

Prostyle (Gk. = a column in front).—An open portico, standing in front of the building to which it belongs (No. 18, iv.).

Pseudo-dipteral (Gk. false double-winged), *i.e.*, in which the inner range of columns is omitted in a colonnade, which is apparently two columns in depth (No. 18, xi.).

Pulvinated (Lat. = a pillow). A frieze, whose face is convex in profile, is said to be pulvinated.

Pycnostyle.—(*See* No. 19.)

Quatrefoil (Fr. *quatre-feuilles* = four leaves).—In tracery a circular panel divided into four leaves (No. 159).

Renaissance (Fr. rebirth).— The re-introduction of classic forms in architecture, all over Europe, in the fifteenth and sixteenth centuries. (For the causes which led up to this movement, *see* page 200.)

Rib.—A term used in Gothic vaulting (*see* Nos. 59, 85).

Ridge.—The highest point of a roof, running from end to end.

Rococo style.—A debased application of Renaissance feature (*see* page 230).

Rose - window, *see* wheel-window (Nos. 63, 65, 75, 93).

Rustication.—A method of forming stonework with a roughened face, principally employed in Renaissance buildings as at Florence etc. (No. 118).

Screen. — A partition or inclosure of wood, often elaborately carved, and separating the choir from the nave. The Latin *cancellus* = screen, corrupted to "chancel," primarily used for the inclosing object, was afterwards applied to that which it inclosed (No. 52).

Scotia (Gk. *scotia* = darkness). —The concave moulding in the base of a column, throwing a deep shadow (No. 30).

Section.—A term used by architects to express the representation of a building, divided into two parts by a vertical plane, so as to show the construction. The term is also applied to any solid in the same way. (Nos. 3, 6, 16, 17,

43, 56, 97, 98, 99, 100, 139, 154, 156).

Sedilia (Lat. = seat) are the seats for the priests, generally of masonry, placed in the wall on the south side of the chancel.

Shaft.—The portion of the column between the base and capital (No. 15).

Soffit. The ceiling; the underside of any architectural member.

Spandrel. — The triangular space between the curve of an arch and the square inclosing it (Nos. 38, 62).

Spire.—The pointed termination to the tower of a church in Gothic architecture; usually octagonal on plan (Nos. 78, 96, 106, 113).

Stalls are divisions or fixed seats for the clergy and choir, and are often elaborately carved. They have large projecting elbows and carved "misereres," and are often surmounted by overhanging canopies. The bishop's seat is called the "throne." The student should visit Henry VII.'s Chapel at Westminster, and the Abbey Choir.

Steeple.—The term applied to the tower of a church, including the spire.

Stilted arch (*see* Nos. 74, 159).

Stoa.—A portico (Nos. 34, 138, 155).

Storey.—The vertical divisions of a building, by the means of floors.

Stylobate.—The base or substructure on which a colonnade is placed (Nos. 15, 16, 17, 22).

Systyle.—(*See* No. 19.)

Tenia.—The band or fillet forming the upper member of the Doric architrave (Nos. 15, 20, 21).

Terra cotta.—Earth baked or burnt and formed into moulds, and used ornamentally. A fine example, used constructionally, is Layer Marney Towers, Essex.

Tetrastyle.—A portico of four columns (No. 18, iv., v., xii.).

Torus. — A large convex moulding, used principally in the bases of columns (Nos. 29, 30).

Trabeated (L. *trabs* = a beam). —A style of architecture, such as the Greek, in which the beam forms the constructive type.

Tracery is the ornamental pattern-work in stone, filling the upper part of a Gothic window; it may be either "plate" or "bar" tracery. The term is also applied to work of the same character in wood panelling, etc. (Nos. 81, 83, 89, 90, 93, 96, 101).

Transept — The part of a church, projecting at right angles to the main building (*see* Nos. 69, 70, 74, 94, 95).

Transoms are the horizontal divisions or cross-bars to the windows (Nos. 83, 89, 90).

Trefoil (*trois-feuilles* = three leaves).—A term applied to this distribution in Gothic tracery (No. 159).

Triforium.—The space formed between the sloping roof over the aisle and the aisle vaulting. It occurs in large churches only, and, from having no windows to the open air, is often called a blind storey (Nos. 72, 97, 98, 99, 100).

Triglyphs (Gk. = three channels) occur in the frieze of a Doric entablature (Nos. 15, 20, 21).

Turrets are small towers, often containing staircases (No. 89).

Tympanum.—The triangular space within the raking cornices of a pediment (*see* frontispiece, and No. 15).

Vault.—An arched covering in stone or brick over any space (Nos. 35 and 85).

Vestibule.—An ante-room to a larger apartment, or to a house.

Volute (Lat. *voluta* = a scroll). The scroll or spiral occurring in the Ionic and Corinthian capitals (Nos. 23, 24, 25, 26).

Wheel-window.—A circular window, whose mullions converge like the spokes of a wheel, hence the name (Nos. 63, 65, 75, 93).

NOTE.—Buildings and architects of England of the 18th and 19th centuries are not placed in this Index, but will be found in a tabulated form on pages 280-293.

CHISWICK PRESS :—CHARLES WHITTINGHAM AND CO.
TOOKS COURT, CHANCERY LANE, LONDON.